P9-CLO-672

WRAPPED IN THE FLAG

WRAPPED IN THE FLAG

A PERSONAL HISTORY OF AMERICA'S RADICAL RIGHT

Claire Conner

BEACON PRESS, BOSTON

Beacon Press
25 Beacon Street
Boston, Massachusetts 02108-2892
www.beacon.org

Beacon Press books
are published under the auspices of
the Unitarian Universalist Association of Congregations.

16 15 14 13   8 7 6 5 4 3 2 1

This book is printed on acid-free paper that meets the uncoated paper
ANSI/NISO specifications for permanence as revised in 1992.

Text design and composition by Wilsted & Taylor Publishing Services

Library of Congress Cataloging-in-Publication Data
Conner, Claire.
Wrapped in the flag : a personal history of America's radical right / Claire Conner.
pages cm
Includes bibliographical references and index.
ISBN 978-0-8070-7750-4 (alk. paper)
eISBN 978-0-8070-7751-1
1. John Birch Society. 2. Right-wing extremists—United States—History—
20th century. 3. Right and left (Political science) —United States—
History—20th century. 4. United States—Politics and government—1945–1989.
5. Conner, Claire, 1945—Political and social views. I. Title.
E740.J6C66 2013
322.4'4—dc23   2012049353

For my children and my brothers and sisters

For B^2, always

Contents

I Know What Extremism Looks Like

Five years ago, I was sure I'd heard the last of conspiracies, secret Communists, and America's imminent collapse. After all, the Cold War had been over for twenty years, my parents and most of their fanatic friends were dead, and the Bush administration was killing America's appetite for right-wing Republicans. "There's no one left to hoist the extremist flag," I told myself.

I was wrong. By 2008, political discourse sounded eerily similar to that of 1958, when a brand-new right-wing, populist movement—the John Birch Society—burst onto the American scene. All across the country, newly awakened Birchers rallied to "take our county back." Two dedicated Birch leaders mobilized the Midwest: Stillwell and Laurene Conner—my parents.

Dad and Mother had been primed for their lurch to the right for many years. They loved Joseph McCarthy and hated the Communists. They'd decided that government assistance made people weak and lazy, and that the New Deal was really a bad deal. They loathed Franklin Roosevelt and blamed Democrats for destroying our free-enterprise system.

So in 1955, when Mother and Dad were introduced to Robert Welch, a candy-company executive turned conspiracy hunter, they immediately recognized a kindred soul. My father said Welch was "a brilliant mind and the finest patriot I've ever had the privilege to know." Three years later, when Welch founded his John Birch Society, Mother and Dad didn't hesitate— they signed up and immediately handed over $2,000 for lifetime memberships, the equivalent of about $15,000 today.

The John Birch Society became my parents' lifelong obsession; nothing was allowed to interfere with the next meeting, the next project, the next mailing. At fourteen and thirteen, respectively, my older brother and I were deemed old enough to take up the cause as full-fledged adult members. During Birch activities, the other Conner children were banished upstairs, where my ten-year-old sister was put in charge of the baby (eighteen months) and my six-year-old brother fended for himself. In only a few months, the entire Conner family lived and breathed Birch.

Night after night, Birch activists and new recruits filled our living room.

They received hours of instruction about the secret conspiracy, the New World Order, hidden codes on the dollar bill, and Communist spies inside our government. Birchers were schooled in the evils of creeping socialism, Communism, and Marxism. Good Birchers understood the sins of welfare and Social Security. It was time to rise up against the unholy alliance of the Left—Communists, socialists, liberals, union bosses, and the liberal press.

Robert Welch identified Communists as one enemy in this epic struggle to save the country. Of course, in the 1950s the march of the Communists across Eastern Europe and Asia was scary to Americans, but Welch was more worried about the Communists lurking inside our country, often holding positions of influence. These home-grown American Communists were ready to spring into action to take down our Constitution and replace it with a socialist manifesto.

Birchers believed that those American Communists were all over the place. They served on school boards, advocated putting fluoride in drinking water, and taught subversive university classes. Others organized labor unions, led the civil rights movement and served in the Congress.

The Birch message resonated. Membership exploded and revenue spiked. My father was rewarded for his dedication with a promotion to the Birch National Council, where he served for thirty-two years.

————

From the outset, the GOP applauded the Birchers for their patriotic zeal and embraced them as good Republicans. But after a scandal rocked the society in 1961, the GOP worried that its closeness to the Birchers would taint the Republican brand. It could not afford to be painted by the Democrats as the political arm of the radical right. Republican leaders decided to label the Birchers as crackpots and push them out of the party. Problem solved.

The effort worked. Before long, the Birchers had joined the Ku Klux Klan, Aryan Nations, and other kooks as the most extreme reactionaries in American politics. The Republican Party took credit for saving the United States from fringe-of-the-fringe crusaders who imagined that even the president was a Commie.

In the late 1960s and early 1970s, while the politicians and pundits declared the Birchers dead and buried, the moneyed Birch leadership went to plan B, redirecting their cash and their influence into think tanks and foundations. My parents joined in that diversifying effort. They founded a right-wing Catholic organization, the Wanderer Foundation, in St. Paul, Minnesota, and donated to every right-wing organization and political-action committee they could.

My parents never had big money, but other Birch families spent huge sums to bankroll Birch ideas. Fred Koch, one of the original Birch founding members and a National Council member with my father, invested a small fortune on his pet projects, including the so-called right-to-work laws, designed to hamper union organizing.

His sons, David and Charles Koch, inherited their father's multimillions, turned them into multibillions, and invested liberally in their favorite political causes: the Cato Institute, the Heritage Foundation, Americans for Prosperity, and others. Those organizations incorporated many John Birch Society ideas and effectively increased both their reach and their impact on American politics. Since *Citizens United*, the 2011 Supreme Court decision that opened the floodgates to unlimited and unregulated corporate political donations, the Kochs have contributed hundreds of millions of dollars to individual candidates and political-action committees.

The Kochs and their allies envision the same framework for American government that I heard from my father and his John Birch Society allies: the New Deal dismantled, the federal government reduced to a quarter of its current size, and most federal programs gutted. In this right-wing, libertarian utopia, businesses and individuals would be free to do anything, unrestrained by rules or taxes.

In 2008, when the economy tanked and Barack Obama emerged as the Democratic nominee for president, the radical right went on the offense. The Democrat was labeled a Marxist, a Socialist, and a friend of terrorists. Folks unfurled the yellow "Don't Tread on Me" flag and shouted about trees of liberty being watered with the blood of tyrants.

When I heard frenzied voters at a Republican rally shouting, "Treason," and "Kill him," in response to one of Sarah Palin's anti-Obama rants, I worried. "My parents are back," I told anyone who'd listen.

People looked at me like I'd lost my mind. I realized that the Birch Society had faded out of America's memory. It had been confined to a footnote on a footnote for political wonks.

Six months after President Obama was inaugurated, a new right-wing, populist movement arose. The Tea Party—bankrolled by the Koch brothers and Americans for Prosperity—staged rallies and protests across the country. Self-appointed zealots suggested "Second Amendment remedies" if they didn't achieve their goals at the ballot box. I shuddered when I heard my father's favorite rally cry: "We've come to take our country back."

These newly minted right-wingers were rattling off old Birch slogans:

- Immigrants are the enemy. Protect our borders and deport all illegal aliens.
- Gays are ungodly. Pray the gay away from children and teens.
- Unemployed people don't want to work, and poor people keep themselves poor, on purpose. If we cut the minimum wage and eliminate unemployment compensation, everyone will have a job.
- Unions caused the economic collapse by shielding lazy, incompetent public employees.
- Rich folks are "job creators," and we need to protect their wealth.
- Social Security is unsustainable, and Medicare and Medicaid have to be restricted so that corporations and "job creators" have lower tax rates.
- Abortion is murder and must be outlawed even in cases of rape and incest. No exception means no exceptions; even in cases where the mother's life is in danger.
- The economic meltdown of 2008 came from high taxes on corporations, too many regulations, and poor people taking out mortgages they couldn't afford.
- The government can't create jobs, so stimulus programs don't work. Cutting taxes creates jobs.
- The government can't limit the right to own or carry guns. If guns are outlawed, only outlaws will have guns.
- America is God's chosen nation, but our president can't understand our exceptionalism. After all, he's not a "real" American; he's a Marxist, Socialist, Muslim racist who hates America.

I know that this new radical Right is a rewrite of the old John Birch Society. This time, however, the movement has enormous political muscle, unlimited dollars, and right-wing media support. This reality hit me after studying my parents' files and personal writing, combing historical archives, and reading contemporary accounts and documents produced by the Birch Society itself.

My notes credit published works and archival documents, but much of this narrative comes from my experience. This book chronicles the history of the John Birch Society and its impact on America, past and present.

But above all, *Wrapped in the Flag* is my story.

November 1963

At 11 a.m. on Friday, November 22, I stood in the crowd on Main Street. The early morning rain had stopped and it was nearly seventy degrees. For a Chicago girl used to bundling up in November, that morning in Dallas was glorious. I stripped off my light jacket and lifted my face to the sun.

Above me, red-white-and-blue banners hung in rows. As far as I could see, those pennants marched toward Dealey Plaza. People lining the street waved miniature American flags along with the occasional Confederate and lone star of Texas flags.

Around me, people chatted. Some talked politics; others talked weather. Everyone seemed perfectly polite. Given the anti-Kennedy drumbeat that characterized this right-wing city, I was surprised. It looked like the efforts of the Dallas officials, the chief of police, and the newspapers to tamp down the vitriol had worked.[1]

"So this is 'Texas-nice,'" I thought.

Sometime later, people surged to the curb. To my right, I saw a line of motorcycles and a white convertible. I didn't recognize any of the passengers.

A long, black, open-top limousine followed. John Connally, governor of Texas, and his wife, Nellie, were in the first seat, but I barely noticed. My eyes were on Jackie Kennedy, sitting in the back seat and wearing a bright-pink pillbox hat. The president sat to her right. For the briefest second, he turned in my direction, smiled, and waved. I waved back.

"We're with you all the way!" some people cried.

"Help Kennedy stamp out democracy!" others answered.

In less than a minute, the motorcade had passed. A few Dallas cops on motorcycles brought up the rear.[2] Folks pushed to cross the street and head for their cars. I heard comments about "beating the worst of it" and "the traffic will be deadly."

As I stepped off the curb, I noticed a rumpled paper on the ground. Staring up at me were two photographs of John Kennedy, a front and side image. "It's a mug shot," I thought. The banner below screamed "Wanted for Treason" in bold black letters.[3] I picked up the sheet and scanned the list of grievances.

THIS MAN is wanted for treasonous activities against the United States:

1. Betraying the Constitution (which he swore to uphold): He is turning the sovereignty of the U.S. over to the communist controlled United Nations. He is betraying our friends (Cuba, Katanga, Portugal) and befriending our enemies (Russia, Yugoslavia, Poland).
2. He has been WRONG on innumerable issues affecting the security of the U.S. (United Nations—Berlin wall—Missile removal—Cuba—Wheat deals—Test Ban Treaty, etc.)
3. He has been lax in enforcing Communist Registration laws.
4. He has given support and encouragement to the Communist inspired racial riots.
5. He has illegally invaded a sovereign State with federal troops.
6. He has consistently appointed Anti-Christians to Federal office; Upholds the Supreme Court in Anti-Christian rulings. Aliens and known Communists abound in Federal offices.
7. He has been caught in fantastic LIES to the American people (including personal ones like his previous marriage and divorce).

These indictments of the president were not news to me. Over the last three years, I'd heard my father and other John Birch Society leaders attack Kennedy repeatedly for these same "crimes." No doubt, the society hated this president. It wouldn't have surprised me if Birchers in Dallas had printed the flyer.

Hours later, I fell onto my bed in the University of Dallas dorm. The president of the United States was dead and I was in shock. My neck hurt. I had a headache behind my eyes. My stomach growled, reminding me that I hadn't eaten since breakfast, but I knew I couldn't keep anything in my stomach. I needed to call my parents at home in Chicago.

My father picked up on the second ring. He immediately launched into a litany of the facts as he knew them.

"Don't talk to anyone about this," he warned me. "You may need a lawyer."

"Me? Why?" I asked.

"They might think we did it," Dad said.

"Did the Birch Society have anything to do with this?" I asked my father. He hung up without answering.

I walked back to my room, pasted a "Sleeping" sign on my door, and curled up on my bed. I needed time to think about my father, what he'd said—and what he hadn't said. If the John Birch Society had anything to do with the murder of the president of the United States, he'd become an accessory to the crime of the century. I knew there would be lawyers, investigations, testimony, trials, and . . . prison for the guilty. I could only imagine what would happen to me.

I finally fell asleep despite a raging headache. Several hours later, I awakened with my first full-blown migraine. The campus nurse gave me a pat on the shoulder and a pill to kill the pain. "Get some rest," she said. "You'll feel better in no time."

Soon, the crashing pain and the lights pulsing behind my eyes vanished. The side effects from that magic pill kept me in a fog for most of the weekend, but I didn't care. Unfortunately, however, all the drugs on campus could do nothing to ease my heartache. Until that day, I'd never, ever imagined that my father and his friends might—and this is still hard to write so many years later—be part of killing the president.

All day Saturday, the university buzzed over the assassination. Oswald had been arrested and identified as a Communist, but it was a stretch to believe that he'd hatched and executed the plot all alone.[4] Some folks insisted that the radical Right had to have played a part. Cuban freedom fighters had plenty of reasons to want revenge, and local anti-Kennedy groups, including the John Birch Society, had created a toxic atmosphere in Dallas. Others thought that Kennedy had run afoul of the Communists during the Cuban Missile Crisis and that they'd decided to avenge their humiliation.

I was still too fragile to talk much. As soon as I finished my breakfast, I walked back to the dorm and climbed into bed.

On Sunday morning, my friends and I jammed the TV room. In front of me, a dozen kids sat on the floor. Behind the last row of chairs, a dozen more stood. Scattered around the room were remnants of the weekend: partially eaten sandwiches, empty Dr. Pepper bottles, and overflowing ashtrays.

We watched the formal procession of the president's flag-draped casket down Pennsylvania Avenue to the Capitol. We heard the clack of the horses' hooves and the methodical drum beat of the military escorts. At the Rotunda, the honor guard carried the body of their commander in chief up the thirty-six stone steps to lie in state.

Around 11 a.m., KRLD-TV switched to its live, local feed for the transfer of Lee Harvey Oswald to the Dallas County Jail. Just as Oswald appeared on the screen between two police guards, we saw a hat move toward the prisoner. A second later, Oswald crumpled into the arms of the deputies. The reporter screamed: "He's been shot! He's been shot! Lee Oswald has been shot. There's a man with a gun. It's absolute panic!"[5]

Behind me, someone whispered, "Shit. What the hell?"

When the shooter was identified as Jack Ruby, one of my friends said, "He's the Mob's man in Dallas." At 1:07 p.m., Oswald died in Parkland Hospital, the same hospital where Kennedy had died two days earlier.

It was my turn to ask, "What the hell?"

By Monday, shock, chaos, and confusion had given way to raw grief. Whatever I'd thought before, whatever my politics, on Monday, November 25, I was an American burying my president.

I watched as the white horses pulled Kennedy's coffin toward St. Matthew's Cathedral. Behind the caisson, Jackie, draped in a black veil, walked to her husband's funeral followed by family, friends, and world leaders. Units of the armed services came next, with the Black Watch piping a haunting dirge.[6] My roommate put her arm around my shoulder and pulled me close. Tears streamed down our cheeks. It was hard to see how we'd ever be the same again.

A few days later, I talked to my father. "Don't get emotional," he reminded me. "Kennedy was a traitor. The Commies killed one of their own."

Chapter One
Rally Cry

Today we are engaged in a final, all-out battle between Communistic atheism and Christianity. The modern champions of Communism have selected this as the time. And, ladies and gentlemen, the chips are down — they really are down.
— SENATOR JOSEPH MCCARTHY[1]

The first time I met my father, I was eight months old. I was an easy conquest for the handsome, kind fellow just home from World War II. "You knew your father right away," my mother told me. "The minute he picked you up, all you did was laugh and coo."

As a child, I believed everything my father said, and I trusted everything my father did. When he worried about the Communists and the end of the United States, I worried too. When he agonized about the destruction of freedom, I agonized with him. As he fretted over the future, so did I.

As he careened toward extremism, I still believed him. A little, nagging voice inside me didn't grasp his ideas about African Americans or Jews, but I was my daddy's girl. If he said it, it had to be so.

I knew how much my father hated John Kennedy, and Kennedy was not the first or the last Communist my father hated. With the help of his arch-right-wing friends, in and out of the John Birch Society, Dad could recite a list of "dirty Reds," as he called them, who had gotten themselves elected president of the United States. From Franklin Roosevelt to Dwight Eisenhower and John Kennedy to Jimmy Carter, the Oval Office had seen its share of Commie dupes, Commie sympathizers, and out-and-out Commies.

According to Dad, those presidential traitors were just the tip of an enormous iceberg of bad guys who planned to bring down our country. These men may have looked like Americans and talked like Americans, but they actually were players in a two-hundred-year-old conspiracy to take over the world. His secret bogeyman, the Illuminati—with its New World Order scheme—would conquer the United States under the Red hammer and sickle.[2]

Even after the Soviet Union collapsed and China turned more toward business than conquest, my father kept sounding the alarm. He knew the Communists—and their real bosses—were still coming, whether the rest of us did or not.

"As long as there is breath in my body, I'll keep on fighting," Dad said. "I swore my life and my sacred honor to save freedom. I won't quit now."

"No, you won't," I said.

And we were both right. He'd go to his grave rigid, uncompromising, and—in his mind—justified. In 1992, as pancreatic cancer ate his body and he slipped in and out of consciousness, I knew he remained true to the cause. "You are still ferocious," I whispered to him one afternoon. "You always were."

In the family stories I heard about my father, he was always the hero. He was "Jay dear" to his mother, Mabelle, a divorcee and self-made entrepreneur. He was "my dear brother" to his only sister, Ever Louise, who adored him as her protector and mentor. He was "a prince of a man" to his wife, Laurene, the beautiful, shy girl he'd met on a blind date in 1934 and married four years later.

He was Major Stillwell J. Conner to the Army of the United States, serving with honor during World War II. When he was sent to India in late November 1944, he saw human misery and bureaucratic nightmares on a scale that shocked him and changed him.

"In India, you could see the heat," my father had told me. It shimmered around half-naked men pulling rickshaws, cows wandering in the square, and the starving people outside his bedroom door. Every day, skeletons lifted hands toward him, hoping for a small charity. Babies lay motionless in their mothers' arms while black flies sucked at their eyes.[3]

Dad was so shocked by the horror that he gave half of his daily rations to children who were still able to chew. Often the gift was refused; it wasn't rice.

His valet, an Indian fellow who had lived in Calcutta forever, told him, "You can't go hungry to save them. This is India. People starve all the time."

Before long, my father listened to his valet and stepped over the bodies in his path. He turned away from the raised hands. "I had orders," he explained. "Winning the war trumped everything."

Dad had arrived in India with one task: get the war supplies out of Calcutta and into the hands of the Allied troops on the China-Burma front. He quickly realized that his job forced him to deal with the British and their irksome bureaucracy. One day, Dad arrived at his office and discovered that the railroad yard was at a complete standstill. Not one crate of supplies moved an inch while the Brits consulted maps, read manuals, and convened meetings. Finally, my father grabbed a pair of binoculars, scrambled up a narrow ladder on the side of a boxcar, and perched himself on the roof where he could survey the situation.

A British officer, decked out in his jodhpurs with a riding crop in hand, watched. "I say, old boy," he said. "You ought not be up there. It's inappropriate for an officer of your rank, really."

"I'm here to win this war!" my father shouted back. "If that means climbing every railroad car in India, I will . . . sir."

That day, Dad discovered the problem: several cows had wandered on the tracks and been run over. He didn't bother to ask who had the authority to move the dead animals; he just ordered the tracks cleared. Before long, Major Conner had the main supply depot back in operation.

He also had his proof that bureaucracy made small problems into big problems. India convinced Dad that Britain, which he called socialist England, had delayed the Allied victory in World War II by an entire year.

On August 15, 1945, not long after the United States dropped atomic bombs on Hiroshima and Nagasaki, the Japanese surrendered. World War II was over. My father, however, didn't get home for months. He was part of the clean-up crew that moved thousands of GIs back to the States and sorted mountains of supplies into military warehouses. When Dad was finally discharged on April 14, 1946, Lieutenant Colonel Stillwell J. Conner came home to his wife, my two-year-old brother, and me.

My father needed a job. He polished his resume and took any interview he could wrangle. In a matter of weeks, he understood that he was late; the help-wanted signs had come down six months earlier. Undaunted, Dad convinced two brothers he'd known since college to join him in a great adventure: their own business.

"Owning the joint is the quickest way to get rich," he told them.

The three men merged their cash and their last names—Conner and Rothbauer—and set out to make some money. Each partner contributed, but when it came to closing deals, my father was the star. Modestly, he described himself as an "old-fashioned peddler."

His partners thought otherwise. "Your dad could sell ice to Eskimos," they said.

As I got a bit older, I realized that the Rothbauer brothers knew of what they spoke. My dad had paid for college by giving speeches. At one point, he crisscrossed the Midwest speaking for the Women's Christian Temperance League—yes, the queens of prohibition. When I got older, I thought it was both curious and hilarious: my dad had been making and selling bathtub gin at the same time.

The grown-ups saw my dad as a master salesman; I didn't. To me, he was my Daddy and my pal. Many evenings he barely got his suit coat hung up and his tie loosened before Mother plopped me into his arms. "You can have her," Mother said. "She has been difficult all day, and I'm exhausted."

"Look at her eyes. Maybe she can't see," Dad said.

"Nonsense," Mother said. "She's just naughty."

Dad ignored my mother and took me himself to an eye doctor downtown. A few hours later, I had tiny glasses and a patched eye. According to Mother, I fussed and fought every time she tried to change the patch. "Jay, you handle this," she said. He did.

When I was little, I had the strongest, smartest, handsomest, bravest Daddy in the whole wide world. I hugged him so tight he could never, ever get away. That's how it would be forever—cross my heart and hope to die.

———

Years later, I realized there was no postwar peace for my father. He quickly became immersed in new battles, battles about our country, its emerging enemies, and an increasingly uncertain future. Every morning before the sun came up, the paperboy tossed the *Chicago Tribune* on our porch. Around seven, Dad retrieved the paper, poured himself a cup of coffee, strong and black, and settled down for a read. Every few minutes, he lit another cigarette, took a deep puff, and sighed. I heard him mumble about "storm clouds" and "cold wars." As Mother bustled around, feeding and dressing babies, she paused occasionally to commiserate with Dad's worries.

By the time I was four, the Communists had accelerated their march across Eastern Europe. It was 1949 and millions of souls had fallen under Red control, subdued by torture, hunger, and a vicious secret police. By the middle of the 1950s, the Soviet Union's empire stretched from Poland to China, from East Germany to the border of Greece.

The Red Menace was sucking up everything in its path.

Mao took China and my father began to believe that the Communists could take over the entire world. "The Reds are coming for us," he told my mother. "We need a savior, now."

When I was five, the United States and the United Nations went to war in Korea. I knew little about the whole mess, but I remember Dad saying, "North to the Yalu." The undeclared war in Korea under the guise of a "police action" confirmed Dad's hatred of both the United Nations and Harry Truman.[4] Dad's arguments against the UN always included quotes from General MacArthur. One of his favorites was: "In war there is no substitute for victory."[5] My father never retreated from that position.

When I was six, I could name three great Americans: George Washington, the father of the country; Benjamin Franklin, the man with a kite and a key; and Joseph McCarthy. I wasn't sure who the last fellow was or what he'd done, but my father raved so much about him, I knew he had to be really, really important. "McCarthy is our only hope," Dad often said.

This fellow McCarthy had become a hero when he announced that he could and would name over two hundred people inside our State Department who were secret Communists.[6]

Soon, the senator was investigating Communists everywhere: in the Truman administration, in the Eisenhower administration, in the Voice of America, in the Army. My parents were thrilled with the senator and his defense of all things anti-Communist.

"God willing, McCarthy will be our next president," Dad told me.

When I was seven, I'd graduated from listening to my parents talk about the news to actually trying to read the paper myself. I didn't understand a lot of the stories, but I was able to decipher most of the words. When I ran across a word that puzzled me, I'd ask for help. "Sound it out," my mother always said.

As I pored over the *Chicago Tribune* on June 19, 1953, I came across an article about two people named Rosenberg. From what I could gather, they had been in jail at a place called Sing Sing because they had given secrets to the Russians. One word made no sense to me. I could sound it out, but I didn't know what it meant. "What is *e-lec-tro-cut-ed?*" I asked.

Dad put down his paper and looked at me. "Claire, those goddamn Commie traitors were strapped in chairs and fried until they died. Now they're in hell, where they belong."

I didn't understand what frying people meant, but I did understand that the Rosenbergs had done something very, very bad. Based on my dad's reaction, I figured that those two people deserved whatever they got.

When I was eight, Senator McCarthy ramped up his investigations. To hear McCarthy tell it, the entire government, from top to bottom, was packed full of Communists. He promised to take all of them down.

McCarthy was unstoppable until he accused General Ralph W. Zwicker, a decorated war hero, of being "unfit to wear the uniform."[7] That nasty comment got the full attention of the Eisenhower administration. Public hearings were scheduled, but this time, the firebrand senator would be under scrutiny. Television networks were invited to broadcast everything.

For over a month, Americans tuned in to see Joseph McCarthy in action—live and unfiltered. But the man they saw was not the guy they'd come to love. Day after day after day, more and more folks soured on their hero as he revealed himself to be a bully and a thug. Even his Senate colleagues got disgusted and censured McCarthy.[8]

The great Joseph McCarthy, the king of the anti-Communists, ended his career in disgrace.

Most of the country abandoned everything McCarthy, but my parents remained staunch supporters. "The Senator was smeared," my father claimed. "The Commies won."

When I was eleven, Joseph McCarthy died, reportedly from cirrhosis of the liver. My parents were outraged. "That's a lie!" my father shouted to my mother. "Senator McCarthy did not drink himself to death. He was murdered."[9]

"They had to kill him because he knew too much," my mother replied.

I couldn't count the number of times I heard my father insist, "It will take a lot more Joes to save this country."

When I was thirteen, my father took his place in a new anti-Communist army led by a new anti-Communist McCarthy. My mother joined him. Like it or not, I tagged along.

Chapter Two

The Captain's Law

Although American political life has rarely been touched by the most acute varieties of class conflict, it has served again and again as an arena for uncommonly angry minds. Today this fact is most evident on the extreme right wing, which has shown . . . how much political leverage can be got out of the animosities and passions of a small minority.

—RICHARD HOFSTADTER[1]

M‍y father didn't become a fire-breathing, anti-Communist zealot without help. A healthy dose of it came from one man: Harry Curtis of Gloucester, Massachusetts, a retired sea captain who was married to my father's only sister, Ever (yes, that is her name). My uncle Harry shoved my father to the far, far right. I can't say he lit the final fuse, but Harry did hand my father the match.

My uncle was gruff, opinionated, and, sometimes, downright mean. Even at the age of eleven, I knew this, so I tried to love him from a safe distance. My parents had picked Uncle Harry as my godfather and that gave me special standing as his favorite niece, but that didn't change anything.

Every so often, Uncle Harry gifted me with a few dollars and a pat on the head. "Take this," he said. "From me, for your birthday." I knew he had no idea when my birthday was, but I took the money, thanked him politely, and made my getaway as soon as possible. Any conversation with my uncle was a minefield. Harry knew, or believed he knew, everything about everything. From meteorology to religion, brain surgery to politics, the Captain had an opinion. I heard Harry criticize anyone who disagreed with him; I avoided him as much as possible.

Most days, Harry held court in the kitchen, hunched over the long plank table, with a cup of coffee at his elbow. On the wall above his head was a plaque, hand-lettered in bold script.

It read: *The Captain's Word Is Law.*

Harry took a simple approach to selling his point of view. He just got louder and louder. This method worked so well, he kept it up. Before long, folks either agreed with the Captain or pretended they did.

Most summers, my family spent the month of August in Gloucester. We piled into the house on Eastern Point with our cantankerous uncle, his wife, who escaped most days to her medical practice in town, four Curtis kids, and Ollie, the live-in housekeeper.

The cocktail party was a regular event at the Curtis home. Several times a week, guests began trickling in around six. By seven, the evening was in full swing. Usually, my brother, my oldest cousin, and I were summoned to the living room to greet the adults. The room was a hum of conversation, much of it political.

I was not invited into the chats, but I picked up on words and phrases that I later understood as right-wing buzzwords. It seemed to me, at the time, that everyone was talking about tyranny, brainwashing in schools, Communists and socialists, Jews and money, Negro problems, gun rights, and taxes. Sometimes I wanted to put my hands over my ears, but I was a Conner girl and I'd never be rude in front of adults.

Around nine, the grown-ups staggered out for dinner at the Gloucester House, leaving behind dirty glasses and smelly cigarette butts. It took the kids, under Ollie's direction, a couple of hours to set the place to rights. Cleanup was our favorite part of the whole operation. When Ollie wasn't looking, we ate the leftover crackers and cheese while sipping dregs from the cocktails. Once, my brother lit one of the half-smoked cigarettes and handed it to me. One puff was enough—I swore off Lucky Strikes.

The next morning, Harry and my parents dissected the evening. Before long, the same words were flying around the breakfast table. My mother jumped on the brainwashing in schools while my father embraced the Communist, socialist lines. Uncle Harry made a bouillabaisse of Negroes, guns, and Jews with a dash of taxes on top.

For whatever reason, these conversations usually degenerated into arguments. The minute voices were raised, I ducked out the back door to the yard where a big, wet, lovable red flash greeted me with licks and drool. While I scratched the Irish setter's ears, I mulled the ruckus in the kitchen. "They're yelling, again," I told the dog. Pal looked at me and tilted his head. "Good boy," I said as I hugged him. "Let's play catch."

———

In August of 1956, rainy weather trapped us kids in the house for a string of long days. We were all getting restless.

One afternoon, I heard Aunt Nellie, Uncle Harry's sister, on the steps. "Hello," she called. She poked her head in. "How about a movie?"

Nellie volunteered to take us to town, as long as our parents agreed. Before I knew it, I was the spokesperson. "No one will say no to you," my brother said.

I asked my father. "If it's okay with your mother, it's fine with me," he said.

I asked my mother. She agreed it was fine, as long as the Captain agreed. "It's your uncle's house and you're taking his children. You have to ask him."

I found my uncle in the kitchen, under the Captain's Word notice. Without any preliminaries, I asked if we could ride into town with Aunt Nellie to see the afternoon matinee. Harry put his coffee cup down and asked, "What's the movie?"

"It's *Black Beauty*," I said. "I loved the book so much. Black Beauty is a horse who tells his life story."

Harry jumped out of his chair. His face turned red, and he raised his hand, to me, his favorite niece. I stepped back. "I know about the goddamn story and its goddamn horse," he screamed. "You are not taking my children to a Commie movie made by a Commie kike director. Get out of my sight."[2] Uncle Harry's bellowing followed me up the stairs. I fell down on my bed and pulled the pillow over my ears. When I stopped shaking, I imagined Black Beauty kicking Uncle Harry's backside. That was before I knew the word ass.

When I came downstairs for dinner, my father said nothing. My mother said nothing. My Aunt Ever said nothing. Nellie, who had floated the movie plan in the first place, said nothing. I knew they'd heard the uproar; everyone in the house had. Heck, anyone on Eastern Point could have heard it.

Just before I fell asleep, Aunt Ever leaned over and kissed my check. "He can be gruff, but he's a good man," she told me.

"It was about a horse," I said. "What's wrong with that?"

"Honey," she answered, "you have to trust your uncle. He knows the Reds have taken over Hollywood. They use movies like *Black Beauty* to brainwash little children."

"I hate it when he yells," I said.

"I know, but he's trying to protect you from bad men."

My aunt did not explain that uncovering and naming Reds in the entertainment industry had become a right-wing obsession. One popular pamphlet, *Red Channels: The Report of Communist Influences in Radio and Television*, contained a list of 151 persons linked with a variety of "Communist causes." Called "the Bible of Madison Avenue," *Red Channels* held sway in hiring and firing decisions. Political screening and loyalty oaths became the norm in movies and theatre, and the blacklisting of actors, screenwriters, and directors continued until the late 1960s.[3]

I never found proof that the director of *Black Beauty*, Max Nossek, was named in any of the investigations, but he did leave the country in 1950 and return to his native Germany. Uncle Harry was correct about one fact: Max Nossek was Jewish.

It would be many years before I understood what Pulitzer Prize–winning author David Halberstam said of the '50s: "It was a mean time. The nation was ready for witch-hunts."[4]

———

Shortly after the *Black Beauty* uproar, my aunt and uncle hosted the last soiree of the season—a farewell event for my parents. Among the guests was a man new to the Curtis parties, a retired candy manufacturer from the Boston suburb of Belmont who was summering just down the road. My parents were so drawn to this man that they spent the entire evening talking with him. The next morning, Dad announced that our trip home would be delayed a few days so that he and my mother could spend time with their new friend at his Belmont home.

That was the very first time I heard the name: Robert Welch.

Welch had made his fortune in the candy business and, since his retirement, had become a fierce anti-Communist. From their first meeting, my father was devoted to Welch. "Bob is the most brilliant man I've ever met," he said.

Mother was equally enthralled. "Bob understands everything that's happening."

In a short time, it became apparent that my parents were willing to go wherever Bob Welch led. More than once, my father said, "I'd follow Bob to the depths of hell."

For years, my father's unbreakable bond with Robert Welch puzzled me. Dad was a loyal man, for sure, but this intensity had a mysterious quality to it. Five years after my father met him, the first pieces of the puzzle fell into place for me. I learned, quite by accident, that Welch had entrusted to my father a copy of a book Welch had written in which he named Dwight Eisenhower, the president of the United States, as a Communist. This secret book, which my father hid somewhere in our home or his office, ultimately cost my dad his reputation, most of his friends, and a large part of his business.[5]

Uncle Harry did not share my parents' enthusiasm for Welch. Over the years, Harry became downright hostile about the man my parents so admired. More than once, I heard my uncle shout, "Robert Welch, ha! That man is too goddamn *liberal* for my taste."

Chapter Three

Sacrifices

Franco is undeniably one of the great villains of Spanish history. His fascist forces not only plunged Spain into Civil War from 1936–39, but resulted in a harsh and violent dictatorship that lasted until his death in 1975. When he died, it was allegedly impossible to buy a bottle of champagne in Spain: They were all sold out.
— HELENE ZUBER[1]

Early in January of 1957, I awakened in the middle of the night. After a few minutes of staring at the ceiling, I crawled out of bed. I crossed the hall and heard something in the kitchen. I turned and saw my mother, silhouetted against the pale wallpaper. She braced one hand on the back of a chair; the other she held to her mouth. A pale stream of light touched her face. She was crying. I knew this was none of my business, but I couldn't look away.

Slowly, she turned her head toward me. Neither one of us spoke.

The next day, Mother called me into her room. "I have something to tell you, Claire," she said. "Our family is growing. As the eldest girl, I expect your help."

I tried to hug her, but she pushed me away. "Go do your chores and check on your little brother."

At the door, I turned. "I saw you crying last night. I'm sorry."

"What are you talking about, young lady?" she said. "I was not crying, not at all." Her eyes looked tired. She clenched a tissue in her hand. "Off with you. I'm going to take a short nap."

Mother stretched out on the bed still wearing her brown leather pumps. Without a word, I walked to her, slipped off her shoes, and covered her with a corner of the bedspread. I bent over and kissed her cheek. "It'll be all right," I whispered. She turned away.

———

As tough as the next months had to be for her, no one could tell. From all appearances, my forty-four-year-old mother breezed through her fifth pregnancy. She went so far as to deny even a twinge of a labor pain. "I slept through the whole thing," she said. Many years later, I learned that Mother had also suffered three miscarriages, making this her eighth pregnancy.

The baby was over a week old when Mother came home from the hospital. Jay R., Janet, Larry, and I got a brief glance at our new sister, Mary Elizabeth, before Mother dashed off to the bedroom. "We have to rest now," she explained.

Several days later, I interrupted my mother rocking the baby. Mother quickly covered herself but not before I realized Mary was sucking on a breast. "I'm feeding her," Mother explained. "It's better for the baby."

I didn't understand, but I was too embarrassed to ask what she meant. I closed the door and went back to my book.

I know how crazy this must sound now, but in 1957, when I was eleven, I'd never seen a woman nursing a baby. I was only seven when my brother Larry was born, and though I loved him to pieces, I never thought about how he got his food. The idea that his milk came from inside Mother's body was beyond my imagination. And, believe it or not, as little as I knew about feeding babies, I knew even less about how babies came to be. In the next few years, some of those blanks were filled in, not always accurately, by my girlfriends.

When I'm tempted to castigate my mother for leaving me in the dark about babies and sex, I remind myself that she was born in 1913, only twelve years after the death of England's Queen Victoria. Mother, a cradle Catholic, embraced all the teachings of "Holy Mother Church," including a strong emphasis on purity. I remember her teaching me that the greatest gift I could give my husband on my wedding day was my chastity.[2]

Talking about sex or, horrors, about birth control was an "occasion of sin," an "external circumstance that enticed or encouraged immoral action."[3] My mother would never put my soul or hers at risk talking about sexual matters.

Mother bore that unplanned pregnancy as she bore every trial she faced in her life. "I offer it all up," she always said, "for the forgiveness of sins and the redemption of souls." Laurene Conner was first and always a staunch daughter of the Holy Roman Catholic Church. No emotion, no fear, no sorrow would deter her from her responsibility to Jesus Christ and his Church.

———

A few weeks later, my brother shocked me with an absurd story about Mother, Dad, and some European vacation. "You're crazy," I said. "They would never go now. Mary is only a month old."

"Just wait," he said. "They're going with Uncle Harry and Aunt Ever."

"I don't believe you," I said.

"You will."

That evening, Dad proved Jay R. right. Over dinner, he announced their big trip: a cruise across the Atlantic with side visits to Portugal, Spain, and Italy. "Your mother and I planned this last summer while we were in Gloucester," Dad explained. "Your grandmother [Dad's mother, Mabelle] will take care of the five of you. Your mother has been looking forward to this vacation for a very long time; she finally will get to see Fatima, Madrid, and Rome."

"It will be glorious," Mother added. "You children are to be obedient and helpful. It won't be easy for your grandmother with so many of you."

"Your grandmother will give a full accounting when we get home," my father said. "Don't cause any problems for her, or you'll deal with me."

I looked across the table at Jay R. I could read his lips as he mouthed, "Told you."

The day our parents left, the four of us—Jay R. (thirteen), Janet (nine), Larry (five), and me (twelve)—stood in the hall while my parents and our grandmother finished their conversation. Mother kissed the baby and handed her to me. Five minutes later, Mother and Dad were away, and our grandmother, who insisted we call her "Vanny," started complaining. She kept it up, almost nonstop, for the next six weeks.

Anyone listening would figure that the poor woman was being worked to death at her son's house. The reality was quite different.

Alberta and Maddie, our African American maids, came every day for those six weeks. They usually arrived at eight if the street cars ran on time and worked seven hours cleaning, washing, and ironing. Both of them loved our little sister and took turns caring for her during the day.

Vanny was careless with these women, forgetting to set out their lunches or put out their pay. Sometimes she added a last-minute chore that kept them past quitting time. Of course, she didn't apologize or pay them for that extra hour. Alberta and Maddie never complained. All I ever heard was one comment: "Best to put up."

These women needed their jobs; being fired, even by a crabby old lady, would make it hard for them to find another position.

For those weeks, I felt like I had to "put up" too. Vanny missed no opportunity to criticize me or my brothers and sisters. Clearly, the last place she wanted to be was in Chicago babysitting. "You are very difficult children," she often said. "I'll need a long vacation when I finally get home to Gloucester."

"How much longer?" . . . "Is it time?" . . . "When are they coming?" Every ten minutes, five-year-old Larry poked me and asked another question. Finally, I drew a clock for him on a sheet of paper. "When our real clock looks like this one, they'll be here," I said.

At suppertime, we stood in the living room watching out the front windows. When a cab stopped and Mother and Dad got out, we all lined up in the hall. The door opened, and there they were. Mother lifted Mary out of Janet's arms. "She's so big. I hardly recognize her!" Dad greeted each one of us. When he reached me, I threw my arms around his middle and hugged him tight.

When the adults wandered to the living room for cocktails, Jay R. and I hung around in the hall eavesdropping. We wanted to know what Vanny was reporting. "Maybe we'll get lucky," my brother whispered in my ear.

I put my finger to my lips and shook my head. We inched a bit closer to the doorway. "Fatima was glorious," Mother was saying.[4] "All across the plaza, women crawled on the stones, praying the Rosary."

"She skipped the 'down-on-the-knees' part," Jay R. whispered. I agreed. Mother loved the Rosary, but she hated getting her clothes mussed. Snagged or torn stockings from crawling on stones, absolutely not. Finally, Mother said, "Enough now. Let's go in to dinner."

Jay R. pushed me down the hall.

———

Mother blotted her mouth and set the napkin aside. She pushed her chair out from the table, crossed her right leg, tapped a Viceroy from the pack, and lit it. She inhaled deeply and exhaled smoke from both nose and mouth.

"Children, I have a story to tell you about Spain and patriotism," she started. "It was marvelous to see our holy faith flourishing. In every village, the church is the center of life. Children flock to daily Mass with their parents. The Rosary is prayed, and devotion to Our Lady is strong.

"This grand Catholicism flows from Spain's leader, General Francisco Franco. Because of him, Spain shines as a monument to faith and freedom," Mother explained. "Twenty years ago, the Spanish were fighting a great civil war against the Communists, who wanted to make Spain into Russia. Franco led the fight to save his country."

My father explained who was who in 1930s Spain. "The good men, under Franco, were the Nationalists," Dad told us. "The bad guys, the Communists, were the Republicans. Commies and left-wingers from all over the world flocked to Spain to help the Republicans. Even Commies from the U.S.

got in on the act. Ultimately, Franco won, but at the time of your Mother's story, no one knew who would win."[5]

Mother continued, "In Toledo, a town south of Madrid, there were terrible battles. The Republicans attacked over and over; they committed atrocities too terrible to mention. In the face of this, however, the Nationalist general refused to surrender. Instead, he used skill and prayer to best the enemy. Then, during one ferocious battle, the Communists captured the general's thirteen-year-old son and imprisoned him in a secret location.

"'Release your prisoners by nightfall or you'll never see your son alive,' the Communists said. The brave general refused.

"In a last, desperate attempt to get what they wanted, the boy was put on the phone to talk to his father. The general had a message for his son: 'Say your prayers, my son, and die like a true Spaniard.' The general hung up the phone. A Communist put his gun to the boy's head and pulled the trigger."[6]

Mother raised her napkin to wipe her wet eyes and looked at me. "That's real sacrifice," she said. "True devotion to duty."

"Did the boy die?" I asked.

"Yes, Claire, the boy died. I don't know the other details, but I do know the young man was an obedient son and he died for his country."

Mother and Dad were blind to the fascist leanings of the Franco regime because the general was a staunch anti-Communist and a strict Roman Catholic. They paid no attention to his ruthless suppression of dissent and his destruction of the Spanish economy.[7] For my parents, a Roman Catholic anti-Communist dictator, no matter how brutal, was always one of the good guys.

———

Later that night, I couldn't fall asleep. I stared at the ceiling above my bed and I thought about that poor boy, all alone in a cold prison cell. He must have cried for his mother. He must have prayed for his father to rescue him. I could "see" a snarling man push a pistol to the boy's head. I heard the trigger cock just before . . . blackness.

I finally fell into a restless sleep swirling with guns, shots, and screams. Suddenly, I heard my father's voice: "Claire, say your prayers and die like a true American."

I sat up in bed, shaking and crying, "Please come for me, please."

Something happened to me after that night. I had frequent headaches and stomachaches. A rash appeared on my neck, arms, and legs. It itched so much that I scratched until my arms bled. The doctor prescribed creams and ointments, but nothing seemed to stop the onslaught.

Bad dreams disrupted my sleep. Sometimes it was the Spanish nightmare. Sometimes it was some other ghoulish imagining. When I woke up frightened and shaking, it was hard to get back to sleep.

I didn't connect all of this with my parents. But I did realize that Mother and Dad had returned from Europe with a heightened fear of the Communists. It was easy to assume that the culprit in all of this was Uncle Harry, but as I became more aware of my parents' connections with Robert Welch, I was less willing to heap all the blame on the Captain.

I do know this: Before I'd turned thirteen, I was terrified of the Reds. I was positive that they had already identified my parents and singled them out for execution. After Mother and Dad were dead, I knew that one of the Commies would put a pistol to my head and pull the trigger.

Chapter Four

Textbook Wars

In the mornings, still groggy from too little sleep and too many bad dreams, I had to face my own waking nightmare: seventh grade.

In the classroom, footsteps tapped on the wood floor. The click-clack of rosary beads and the rhythmic clap of the ruler on skin told me she was close. "Where?" I mouthed to a classmate.

John pushed his book to the edge of his desk and pointed to the page number, but I couldn't make out the small print. Realizing my problem, he placed three fingers followed by two on the book in front of him. "One second," I prayed while flipping pages as fast as I could.

Behind me, I heard the first slap. Followed by a second.

She'd found a target; I was safe . . . for now.

My headache—the one that simmered behind my right eye—exploded. I reached into my pocket and found the tissue where I'd stashed half a dozen Bayer. As I spread the tissue on my desk, I saw white and black swing toward me. "What are *you* doing," the nun hissed.

"Taking aspirin, Sister. I don't feel well."

"Get a drink and come right back. Do not dally in the hall."

I did exactly as I was told.

Before that year, I had loved my school and my teachers. My friends used to tease me for being teacher's pet, but I didn't care. I worked hard, finished all of my homework, and handed in reams of extra credit. When other kids got in trouble for misbehaving, I thanked God that I'd never be in that situation.

Then seventh grade happened.

Our teacher needed only the tiniest reason to drag some poor kid into the cloakroom and slap him—or her—around. Anyone who made a low score on a test or struggled to read a passage aloud or wiggled at his desk became a target. The kid who missed an arithmetic problem or mispronounced the Latin words of the Mass got slapped. Sister took out her ruler for forgotten homework or talking back. Sometimes she hit, pinched, pulled hair, and twisted ears . . . just because.

As her smacks and the cries of her victim echoed around the room, the rest of us stared at our desks and waited. We knew we'd be in that place eventually; we just didn't know when.

In good Catholic families, like mine, kids who "had" to be punished at school "had" to be punished again at home, for good measure. We had been taught that the nuns were the "Brides of Christ"; any disrespect toward them was a direct affront to our Savior.

Child abuse didn't exist in the Catholic schools of the 1950s and '60s. No matter how much damage was done to children, the adults—from the bishop to the parents—covered their ears and their eyes. They heard no smacks and saw no ruler marks. Any whiff of scandal was vigorously denied, while the offending priests and nuns were quietly shuffled from parish to parish and school to school. I prayed that seventh grade would improve as soon as my parents got home from Europe. Despite the fact that Mother and Dad had never disagreed with a teacher—as far as I knew—I was sure they'd realize that this nun was not strict. This woman was downright sadistic.

To my surprise, my parents had barely unpacked when they announced a new house rule: my brother and I were instructed to bring our schoolbooks home every day.

"We want to know what you're being taught," Mother explained.

"What do I tell Sister?" I asked. "We are only allowed to take workbooks out of the room."

"Just bring home the books," Dad said.

The next day, when the final bell rang, I grabbed all the books from my desk and dashed to the door. Luckily, Sister was preoccupied; she didn't even look up as I left the room.

After dinner, Mother sat at her end of the table, hunched over a book. Her eyes moved while she tapped a pencil on the pad next to her. Something stopped her, and she made a note and scratched a line under it.

"Jay, listen to this," she said.

Dad leaned forward while Mother read to him. "It's everywhere," he said. "Nothing is sacred."

"Just like Bob Welch told us," Mother said. "He really is aware of the depth of the problem."

I kicked the leg of my chair and rested my chin in my hand. My hope for a quick exit from the table had evaporated thirty minutes before.

"Take your elbows off the table and sit up straight," Mother snapped. "We're doing this for you."

"What did Sister talk about today?" Dad asked.

I hesitated. "Nothing much," I said.

"Answer your father, young lady," Mother said.

"It wasn't anything, really. I did learn that farms in Sweden had electricity in their barns before most farms in the U.S., that's all."

Traffic whooshed by on Maplewood followed by a sharp honk and a quick screech of brakes. Outside our window, a small crowd of sparrows chirped away in the elm tree. The cuckoo in our clock marked eight o'clock. I yawned.

Mother sighed deeply, took a gulp of her scotch, and lit a cigarette. At the other end of the table, Dad mirrored her perfectly.

The boom of my father's voice surprised me.

"What in God's name are you talking about? Sweden? Sweden is a socialist country. One of the worst in the world."

I sat there. My heart beat in my throat.

"Say something!" he shouted.

"I didn't know," I said, very softly.

"Now you do. Tomorrow you'll tell your teacher."

For the next hour, I sat while Mother and Dad reeducated me with the "correct" information about socialist Sweden. I was sent to school with the notes my parents had written and clear instruction to tell my teacher exactly what they had told me.

My teacher was not amused when I read my parents' notes to the class.

"You dare talk back to me," Sister screamed as she slapped my face. "Go home now and don't return until you can be polite."

That day, I was sure I'd get sympathy from my parents. Instead, Mother and Dad insisted I continue to speak up in class.

"Please, don't make me," I begged.

"You'll obey your parents or answer to me," my father said. "It's time you learned to stand up for the truth."

My parents loved to describe this incident to their right-wing associates. Dad usually introduced me and then explained how their "brainwashed" twelve-year-old daughter had awakened them to the dangers lurking in schools, even Catholic ones. It was not unusual for Dad's friends to pat me on the back and congratulate me for having parents who cared enough to teach me the truth.

When I was in college, I did discover that my seventh-grade textbook had been correct about the electrification of Swedish farms: over 50 percent had electricity in 1930 compared to 13 percent in the Midwest and 3 percent in the South.[1] I gradually came to understand that facts never changed my parents' minds; they believed that socialist Europe was too bureaucratic and too anti–free enterprise to best the United States in anything. Their reasoning demanded that those socialist farms could never have had electricity before American farms did. That was that. Facts be damned.

After the Sweden debacle, my brother coached me on ways to avoid parental booby traps. "You're telling me to lie," I complained. "I'm not good at lying."

"You're not exactly lying," he explained. "You're telling them what they want to hear."

"I want this to stop," I told Jay R. "When will they stop?"

"They're just getting going."

I was catching it on both fronts—home and school—until a miracle happened. After Easter vacation, Sister Mary Austin was gone. "Sister was ill and needed rest," we were told. No adult ever said another word about her. But I didn't care. My tormentor was gone; I had a reprieve on the school front. On the home front, no so much.

Teachers like the one who terrorized my class worked in schools all over Chicago and all around the country. It was many years later that the Catholic Church recognized the abuse being perpetrated on children and took a few tiny steps to correct it. The larger scandal of sexual abuse in the Roman Catholic Church would not be revealed for decades.

My teacher's disappearance did not slow my mother at all; she ramped up her textbook wars until she was fighting with the entire Catholic school system of Chicago. In meeting after meeting with administrators who oversaw school policy, she presented detailed lists of the errors and omissions she'd documented in the textbooks. Mother's objections were similar to those arising in other parts of the country. At first, she stressed the misinterpretation of American history. Later, she branched out into broad attacks on the entire curriculum.

Before long, no one in school was happy to see my mother. No matter, she refused to compromise or stand down. "I'm doing it for the children," she said.

Ironically, as my mother devoted more and more time to save "the children," she had less and less time for her children. This seeming contradiction did not trouble her in any way. She believed that God had set her path, and she followed His will. "Saving the country trumps fun and games," she said without apology.

In the summer of 1959, my mother enrolled me at Regina Dominican, the newest girls' high school in the northern suburbs of Chicago. The school had been commissioned by the Archbishop of Chicago, Cardinal Stritch, who served Chicago for eighteen years. Stritch was known for his commitment to Catholic schools as well as for his refusal to engage in interfaith dialogue, a stance that made him beloved by traditional Catholics like my parents.[2]

Cardinal Stritch died just as Regina opened its doors, but his death didn't change my mother's positive assessment of my new school. She described Regina as "orthodox" and its curriculum as "traditional." To my ears, these terms meant that my new school had passed parental muster; my father and mother would have no reason to continue their feud with the Catholic school system in Chicago.

Besides all of that, in early 1959, my parents had escalated to really big worries: international conspiracy and imminent overthrow of the United States government. Words in textbooks had to take a distant back seat . . . or so I thought.

––––––

The night before my first day of high school, I could barely sleep. I fretted about my hair, finding my classes, and whether I'd have a place to sit at lunch. By morning, I was too tired to talk and too worried to choke down my breakfast. "You're acting like a prima donna," Mother said. "Eat your meal and go to school."

That day lasted forever, but I survived. The next day and the one after that got easier. Before long, Latin declensions and conjugations made sense; solving for X became possible, and I could diagram complex sentences. New friends greeted me in the halls, and I found a group to share lunch.

One day, I looked in the mirror and smiled. "I'm a Regina girl and I'm glad." I had to give my mother credit; she'd picked the perfect high school for me.

A few weeks later, my mother announced her plan to look more closely into my education.

"Why? I thought you approved of Regina," I said.

"Don't question your mother, young lady. Bring your books home, all of them."

Soon enough, Mother and Dad had uncovered a nest of "errors, lies, and mistakes" in every one of my books.

"We have to go to the powers that be," Mother announced.

The next day, in hat and gloves, Mother strode to Regina's main office, the click-click of her three-inch pumps echoing across the tile floor. White index cards, marking dubious passages, poked from the top and sides of the books she carried. Before long, the girls in my classes noticed.

"She's here, *again*," someone would whisper. I'd groan and turn away.

At first, the Regina staff accommodated Mother, but as the year progressed, she became a nuisance. Sister Mary Kevin, the principal, and my teachers found as many ways as possible to avoid her. Calls were not returned; scheduled meetings were abruptly canceled. Even her letters went unanswered.

Mother grew frustrated and enlisted Dad's help. When he tried to ratchet up the pressure, the administration dug in all the deeper. Finally, my parents decided to take their concerns public.

During the spring meeting of the Regina Parents' Association—even though they weren't on the agenda—Mother and Dad interrupted the proceedings to give a detailed analysis of the pro-Communist, anti-American materials hiding in the textbooks. When other parents shouted my parents down, the meeting abruptly ended. Mother and Dad packed up their materials and left. No one spoke to them.[3]

When I heard about the spring-meeting fiasco, I kept saying to myself, "This has nothing to do with me." I tried to keep my head down, my grades up, and my opinions to myself. For the next few months, I thought I was successful.

Shortly before summer vacation, Sister Mary Kevin called me to her office. She spoke about her prayers for my future and the need to find a suitable place for me.

"What? You're expelling me?" I said through tears.

"Well, I'm sure you'll be happier somewhere else," Sister told me.

"I'm perfectly happy here."

"I'm sorry, dear. God bless you."

With that, I was escorted from her office to my locker. My things had already been removed and stacked neatly on the floor. Before the dismissal bell rang, I was out the door where my mother was waiting to drive me home. She said nothing about what had just happened. "I have a flock of pressing things to finish before dinner" was her only comment.

That evening, my father said nothing. He seemed to think no comment was required.

My friends said nothing. They just stopped calling.

A few days later, I tried to talk about Regina, but my mother cut off the conversation. "Your parents will choose another school for you," she said. "Stop acting like this is the end of the world."

———

Mother and Dad were not solitary warriors in the textbook battle. They joined a small but very effective group of right-wing activists who fought for curriculum changes in both public and private schools.[4] One of those school critics was none other than Robert Welch, who had made education a major part of the agenda of the National Association of Manufacturers, an ultra-conservative business group he headed in the 1950s. In 1954, the association printed and distributed more than two hundred thousand copies of its thirty-two-page pamphlet *This We Believe About Education*, and Welch himself criss-crossed the country chairing meetings on the state of American schools.[5] It's a safe bet that Mother and Dad received a copy of that pamphlet when they met Welch for the first time.

Make no mistake: Welch predicted a grim future for education. "In my honest opinion," he wrote in 1952, "when the Federal Government controls our schools—as control them it must if it supports our schools—we shall have taken the most dangerous possible step toward a tyrannical totalitarianism."[6]

This threat of tyranny had jolted my parents into action. In the process, they met and worked with several of the most influential textbook critics of the day, including Mel and Norma Gabler, founders of the Educational Research Analysts, based in Longview, Texas. The Gablers prepared long lists of objections to textbooks.

In her book *As Texas Goes . . .* , Gail Collins describes the Gablers' *"scroll of shame*, which listed objections they had to the content of the current reading material. At times, the scroll was 54 feet long."[7]

I chuckle at this image of the endless scroll, but I can't laugh at the Gablers. Those two folks changed the landscape for the adoption of textbooks, not only in Texas but in much of the country.[8]

Mother couldn't heap enough praise on the Gablers. "I just love Norma," she said. "She knows more about textbooks than anyone in the country, and Mel's a saint."

The Gablers identified specific errors in the books they attacked. Any criticism of our constitution or the Founding Fathers was unacceptable. Support for one-world government or the United Nations was unforgivable. Gun control was a major no-no, as was any suggestion of limits on ammunition. Our nation, they believed, was first and foremost Christian. Thus, any suggestion that the founders were deists was intolerable. There could be no discussion of other nations as equal to the United States. After all, our country was exceptional and a perfect embodiment of what government ought to be.

Good books also had specific characteristics. They always emphasized states' rights over federal authority. Good books trumpeted small government and the idea that we ought to spread our wonderful system all over the world. Good books taught that the Confederate generals were great patriots. Good books showed the weaknesses in evolutionary theory. Good books respected Judeo-Christian morals, emphasized abstinence in sex education, and described the principles and benefits of free enterprise.[9]

Not everyone appreciated the Gablers. As *Time* said in 1979, "Though the Gablers claim only to seek 'balance,' their criticism seems to spring from a hell-for-leather conservatism in politics and Bible belt fundamentalism."[10]

Along with the Gablers, Mother also met Phyllis Schlafly in the textbook trenches. Both women had a love affair with the nineteenth-century school primers the McGuffey Readers, and both put considerable effort into "selling" McGuffey as the answer to lagging reading skills among America's children.[11]

Mother later partnered with Schlafly on other projects, including fighting the Equal Rights Amendment and lobbying Catholic bishops to oppose the growing social justice movement centered in Latin America. I have photos of Mother and Phyllis together on their 1965 trip to Rome as part of a delegation to discuss the implications of the encyclical *Pacem in Terris* (Peace on Earth), written by Pope John XXIII two years earlier.

Mother and Schlafly never became close personal friends, and my mother was critical of Phyllis, calling her a "self-promoter." I attributed the animosity to jealousy—Phyllis became a nationally known conservative in the 1960s while Mother remained behind the scenes. I later discovered, however, that Mother's beef with Phyllis was about loyalty, not jealousy.

According to my mother, Phyllis and her husband, Fred, insisted they'd never been members of the John Birch Society, but Mother knew they'd actually joined ten months after my parents did. Robert Welch must have known Phyllis was a Bircher in 1960 when he called her "one of our most loyal members."[12]

Mother also knew that in 1962 Fred Schlafly had been invited to join the Birch National Council because my father, already a council member, told her. Mother's information (this wasn't a contention; it was a fact) proved correct. In his 2005 book about Schlafly, Donald Critchlow quotes Fred's letter declining Welch's invitation. "I know of no other more patriotic or dedicated group than your council," Fred wrote.[13]

The more that Phyllis insisted she was not a Bircher, the less Mother liked her. "Phyllis sold out to the Republican establishment," she said.

———

Forty-plus years after Mother dove into the textbook wars, I sat on a five-gallon bucket in my parents' basement, sorting a mountain of old papers. "They saved everything," I complained to the silverfish scurrying along the damp floor. "I'll be here for a month of Sundays."

Black-metal file cabinets lined three of the walls. Books, magazines, and pamphlets littered rows of shelves. In the corner, a tall stack of hard-cover books leaned against the wall. The jumble spilled over into piles on the floor. All around me was the debris of my parents' long fight against all things liberal. My brother Jay R. had already made arrangements for our parents' extensive library of conservative books, personal correspondence, and writings to be donated to a Catholic library in Virginia. I was left with the stuff no one wanted.

All afternoon I filled boxes. I found index cards, covered with Mother's nearly illegible scrawl, stuck out of the pages of old textbooks—remnants of her crusade.

I took a moment to remember my mother as she marched down the hall to confront the authorities about the errors in the books. How I wished she'd just go home and bake cookies like other mothers did. Of course, my mother never did. She moved from project to project and issue to issue for almost fifty years. Right to the end, she was a formidable crusader for everything right-wing.

I dragged boxes to the corner and stuffed books inside. The next day was trash pickup; all of this stuff was headed to the dump.

While those books went to the trash compactor, Mother's ideas were being rescued from the dustbin of history. In 2010, the Texas Board of Education adopted curriculum standards that were as far to the right as anything ever imagined for public schools. My mother, Phyllis Schlafly, and Mel and Norma Gabler—along with two generations of John Birchers and religious fundamentalists—were reemerging on the winning side of the textbook battles.

Some of the curriculum changes to Texas's books defy fact; others delete important historical figures and erase events from the timeline of American history. Still others diminish the importance of the civil rights movement while praising states' rights ad infinitum.[14] Today's students in public schools across the country are in danger of learning Creationism alongside evolution. Sex education is relegated to abstinence-only instruction, and contemporary history is a right-wing romp praising the likes of Joe McCarthy and Phyllis Schlafly herself.

Everything in the textbook controversies points to one conclusion: Mother's personal battles ended with her passing, but the textbook wars never die.

Chapter Five

Hard Right

The John Birch Society embodied a militant anti-Communist fervor. Members pledged that the battle against Communism would continue until the last American patriot had died with a sword in hand.

—DONALD T. CRITCHLOW[1]

In the summer of 1958, the Conner family left our crowded, second-floor apartment for a new home in the desirable Edgebrook neighborhood in the northwest tip of Chicago. The first time I saw our house, a brown English Tudor–style cottage on tree-lined Sioux Avenue—three whole blocks from the closest "busy" street—I knew we'd arrived. My dad had achieved his American dream: a house in the suburbs, well, almost the suburbs; five kids; a beautiful, smart wife; and a successful business. Life was good.

For me, life would be perfect if my mother and dad gave up their politics and embraced the suburban life of bridge clubs and cocktail parties. I fell asleep that first night in my new pink room dreaming about my new, improved parents.

A few days later, my pipe dream burst when Mother announced she had no more time for unpacking. "I have pressing work that must be done," she said. "I'll be in the dining room. Don't disturb me until lunch." Mother arranged her papers on the table, seated herself on a straight-back chair, and lit a Viceroy. In no time, she was absorbed.

Mother maintained a strict daily regimen. She read her correspondence, looked over the latest newspapers and magazines, and determined what material she would keep. Important articles were clipped and stuffed into manila folders. After she'd finished her reading, she started writing. Almost every day, she churned out a stack of letters to newspapers, senators, and congressmen. Sometimes, she critiqued textbooks for school administrators, principals, and pastors.

One day, two fellows arrived with new filing cabinets that landed in the corner of the breakfast room. Before long, those gray-metal contraptions bulged with Mother's precious documentation. In no time, the dining room and breakfast room were littered with boxes of filmstrips and reel-to-reel tapes. Textbooks from school districts around the country sat in stacks on the floor. Books, magazines, and newspapers crowded the top of the credenza. Mother didn't seem to notice the jumble, nor did Dad. Their focus was squarely on the dangers threatening the country, dangers they'd become more and more aware of over the last few years. They did everything they could as individuals to stop some of the damage, but they were convinced that only concerted group action would give real Americans a fighting chance.

According to my father, the existing anti-Communist groups scattered around the country were useless. "Debating societies," he called them. He longed for a national movement headed by a serious, wise leader, a man who would rouse Americans before it was too late. A man like Robert Welch.

———

I realize that the name Robert Welch means nothing to most people today. But in the 1960s, he built the largest, most effective, and most controversial right-wing organization in the country.[2] He was able to gather an impressive array of successful business leaders and retired military officers to join him, including my own father. Welch planned to build (and control) a million-man (and -woman) army to find and destroy the enemies of our country. The stakes were high. According to Welch, the United States was a few short years from being absorbed into the Soviet Union or into a one-world government under another name.

In *The Blue Book of the John Birch Society*, Welch wrote a brief version of his life story. He was born December 1, 1899, on a farm in Chowan County, North Carolina.[3] His ancestry included farmers and Baptist preachers. For four years, he attended the University of North Carolina, though he doesn't mention that he enrolled at the age of twelve. He does acknowledge a two-year stint at the Naval Academy and two years at Harvard Law. But most of his education he attributes to forty years in the school of hard knocks.

Welch went on to highlight his career in the candy business and his extensive activities in the National Association of Manufacturers. After his retirement, Welch claims that he gave up most of his income to devote all of his time and energy to the anti-Communist cause. He described himself as someone who "will climb on a soapbox to argue against the evils of socialism whenever anybody will listen."

Apparently, a lot of people listened. According to historian Jonathan Schoenwald, by the mid-1950s, "Welch was undeniably one of the best known—and well-respected—conservatives in the United States."[4]

In early December 1958, Robert Welch invited eleven men to join him in Indianapolis for a weekend.[5] For two days, Welch climbed on his proverbial soapbox where he opined about the decline of civilization, the destruction of America's Constitution, and the looming threat of Communism which he described as an "octopus . . . so large that its tentacles now reach into all of the legislative halls, all of the union labor meetings, a majority of the religious gatherings, and most of the schools *of the whole world.*"[6]

According to Welch, "The human race has never before faced any such monster of power which was determined to enslave it."[7]

On the second day of the meeting, Robert Welch outlined specific plans for a national organization dedicated to stopping the Communist advance and restoring America's constitutional purity. He named his group the John Birch Society.

If only a small number of Americans know Robert Welch, it's a safe guess that only the tiniest sliver knows John Birch. For my parents and most of Welch's associates, however, Captain John M. Birch was not unknown. Welch had memorialized him in a book written in 1954, *The Life of John Birch: In the Story of One American Boy, The Ordeal Of His Age*. In it, Welch described John Birch as the first casualty of the Cold War and an unsung American patriot.[8]

A week after the end of World War II, six days after I was born, John Birch, a twenty-seven-year-old Baptist minister and field officer for the 14th Air Force, volunteered to lead a secret mission into Suchow, China, (now written as Suzhou). The American was known in that area, having worked both as a missionary and an army officer. He was also semi-fluent in Mandarin.

After several days of travel, the group encountered Red Chinese soldiers who assumed that the men were working as spies. The Communists insisted that Birch turn over his weapons. The captain refused. Birch was bound, forced to kneel, and shot from behind. In an attempt to prevent identification, Birch's body was mutilated.

Eventually, the body was taken to a morgue in Suchow, where an American officer, William T. Miller, arranged for a public memorial. Birch was buried on a hillside overlooking the Chinese city.[9]

The facts about Birch and his death at the hands of Communists on August 25, 1945, were never clear. Did Birch provoke the Chinese? Was he on a clandestine mission for the army? Why did he argue with his captors? These questions went unanswered, and Birch's army records remained sealed.

Robert Welch determined that the failure of our government to demand an accounting from the Chinese, who were supposed to be our allies, constituted a deliberate cover-up. Welch often cited the silence around Birch's death as proof that the American people were being deliberately kept in the dark about the nature of our Communist enemies.[10]

For Robert Welch, Captain John Birch was the pure American patriot; a man willing to give up his life fighting Communists.

———

Shortly after the Indianapolis meeting, my father accepted Welch's invitation to join eighteen other men in Chicago for the second Birch Society recruiting meeting. As at the Indianapolis meeting, the men met for two days, and Welch did all the talking. My father joined the brand-new John Birch Society that weekend. He paid for a life membership for himself and for my mother, agreed to be the Chicago point man for the organization, and dedicated the rest of his life to saving the country.

"If the country doesn't wake up," Dad said, "we'll be slaves ruled from Moscow." For many years, in speech after speech, I heard him declare, "I will die before I let the Commies take my country." I never doubted that my father meant every word.

———

My father was the first John Birch Society member in Chicago; my mother was the second. Working together, they built the entire Birch structure in the city and the suburbs. Recruiting meetings were scheduled for three to four times a week. The other nights were devoted to special meetings with Birch leaders who stopped by or with folks who wouldn't become members but could help the cause in other ways—folks like our parish priests, Catholic clergy from around the city, or leaders of local civic organizations. It was not unusual for six nights in a week to be Birch nights.

While the younger kids were banished to the second floor with strict orders to play quietly, without fighting, and go to bed on time, my brother and I were drafted into service. We dragged folding chairs from the front-hall closet for the guests, emptied ashtrays, served coffee and cookies, handed out pamphlets, and collected donations. Night after night, new John Birch Society recruits were full of questions, and my parents answered every single one. The meetings might to stretch way past ten and sometimes past midnight.

Sometimes I'd nod off while the talking droned on and on. My mother, if she noticed at all, would shake my shoulder and send me to bed. "You can straighten up in the morning."

In those early days, my parents were totally engaged with the new Birch Society. Their efforts produced new members, and those new members brought in more recruits. "It was wild," Mother liked to say.

My parents never doubted their decision to join with Welch. "We chose freedom over slavery," Mother said. "It was good or evil, life or death, God or Satan."

"Your mother and I will never stop, and we'll never surrender. This is what we do. This is who we are," my father said.

As one of the older children, I was drafted into this new army and saving the country became my job too.

It was a shock when I discovered that the task was much bigger than stopping the Commies. According to my dad, the Communist enemy was only one tentacle of a two-hundred-year-old conspiracy to take over the entire planet. I couldn't imagine what a thirteen-year-old like me could possibly do against an enemy like that.

Enter the Illuminati.

I'd never heard of the Illuminati and, according to my parents, neither had anyone else. Until Robert Welch uncovered old writings and unmasked a plot to take over the world, the super-secret conspiracy group had existed in the shadows. Welch discovered the writings of an obscure eighteenth-century Bavarian canon-law professor, Adam Weishaupt, who nourished a hatred for authority. Weishaupt gathered a group of like-minded men—the Illuminati—who set out to destroy the monarchies of northern Europe. Once the kings were out of the way, the thinking went, the Illuminati planned to crown themselves the all-powerful leaders of a New World Order.[11]

The conspirators knew this plan would not be popular with the targeted governments, so they disguised themselves inside another secret organization, the Masons. Powerful princes in Europe discovered the Illuminati and tried to destroy them. After brutal attacks, including torture, murder, and exile, the powers that be believed they'd snuffed out the Illuminati forever.

But the brotherhood went deep underground and swore oaths to protect the Illuminati, even agreeing to be killed if they broke their vow of absolute secrecy. Hiding made the Illuminati strong, strong enough to disrupt the entire world.

According to Welch, the wars and revolutions over the last two hundred years had Illuminati roots. They had orchestrated the French Revolution, the

Russian Revolution, and both world wars. In Welch's mind, even the U.S. stock market crash in 1929 and the Great Depression were Illuminati-caused disasters.[12]

All of this mayhem had one goal: to bring about the New World Order.[13]

To me, the complexity of this conspiracy seemed impossible. "How did it stay a secret?" I asked. "What happened when old Illuminati died? How did Mr. Welch figure this out?"

"Enough, young lady," Mother said. "Do you think your parents would lie about something so vital?"

Dad dug in his pocket and pulled out a dollar bill, which he placed on the coffee table, with George Washington facing down. He pointed to the left side of the bill and asked, "What do you see?"

"A pyramid inside a circle," I answered.

He then instructed me to look at the top of the bill. "See, right there. It's a floating eye—and a secret code." The eye was added to the dollar bill by President Franklin Roosevelt, proof, my father insisted, that FDR was himself a member of the Illuminati conspiracy. "Roosevelt understood the symbol, and he knew conspirators around the world would recognize it, too."[14]

The words below the pyramid, in the unfurled scroll, were another key to the code. Mother copied out the Latin words for me on a piece of paper: *Novus Ordo Seclorum.*

"What does that mean?" I asked.

Dad and Mother translated in concert: "New World Order." (Though the actual translation of the Latin is "a new cycle of the ages.")

"You have to understand," my father continued. "The president used the U.S. dollar to send a specific message."

All Illuminati members knew Roosevelt's meaning, my father went on. The time had come for the biggest political coup in the history of the world: the violent merger of the United States of America into the Soviet Union.[15]

My parents went gung-ho into the conspiracy school of American politics. The story of the Illuminati and the codes on the dollar bill became key John Birch Society recruiting tools. Hardly a meeting went by that my father didn't pull out a buck and tell the tale he'd told me.

Gradually, the Birch Society refined and expanded its conspiracy theory, eventually naming the organizations that were pushing the conspiracy's aims and compiling lists of conspirators. Robert Welch got the ball rolling when he published *Proofs of a Conspiracy*, a 1798 manuscript that described the

"Order of the Illuminati whose select members became part of a conspiracy to enslave all people in Europe and America."[16]

A few years later, the book *None Dare Call It Conspiracy*, by Gary Allen, explained how the Communists, international bankers, and other highly placed bad guys, men called Insiders, aspired to the same goal of enslavement. Allen promised "to present evidence that what you call 'Communism' is not run from Moscow or Peking, but is an arm of a bigger conspiracy run from New York, London and Paris." For Allen, socialism was the "philosophy," finance capitalism the "anvil," and Communism the "hammer to conquer the world."[17]

Out of this conviction, Allen identified a web of men from a host of organizations including, but not limited to, the ones my father always mentioned. The central one, named by all conspiracy gurus, was the Council on Foreign Relations. Allen insisted that the council, founded in 1919, had only one goal: "abolish the United States with its Constitutional guarantees of liberty."[18]

Allen shared his conspiracy theories with Dan Smoot, author of the 1962 book *The Invisible Government*, and with John McManus, later president of the Birch Society. These three men were friends of my parents, and two of them, Smoot and McManus, were guests in our home.

Today, the John Birch Society continues to add to their catalogue of conspirators. They've already traced the New World Order operatives through the administrations of Presidents Carter, Reagan, Clinton, and both Bushes in volumes titled *The Insiders*. The most recent edition included fifty-five pages of names and organizations that support the conspiracy.

From the American Association of Retired Persons and the Sara Lee Corporation to Jonathan Alter and Elie Wiesel, "Insiders" are everywhere, and the conspiracy seekers are busy naming them and blaming them for every move to the Left since FDR.[19]

When the Soviet Union collapsed, so did my fear of the Illuminati and its web of conspirators. My mother and dad and the Birch Society took a darker view, insisting that the conspiracy was not defeated at all but growing stronger.[20]

"Just wait," Mother told me not long before her death. "They're still coming, and while you're busy with your fun and games, the New World Order will arrive."

———

The John Birch Society changed my parents. I didn't understand how, but I knew that my brothers, sisters, and I were constantly in trouble. We played too much, didn't finish our chores, talked back, or didn't come when we were called. These infractions, which used to warrant a "talking to," now became serious violations of the rules. All reason went out the window. Dad turned into a father who yelled and hit; Mother became his informer. When she said, "You just wait until you father gets home," we knew someone would face the heavy hand or the belt.

We kids lived by our parents' rule: "When we say jump, you ask how high."

My big brother and I tried to cover for the little kids whenever we could. We couldn't bear to watch Dad hit Larry or listen to Mother attack Janet. "We're all they've got," Jay and I told each other. "We have to protect them."

On a chilly, damp evening in 1959, I sat on a folding chair in the front hall waiting for the John Birch meeting to begin. I had asked to be excused to help with the baby, but Mother refused, saying, "People expect to see you. Remember, we're doing this for you, young lady."

My older brother, as usual, was parked in the living room. Periodically, he smiled at me or, when no one was watching, made a face or mouthed a silly comment. "No one will ever kill the joker in you," I thought.

The room was stuffed with people; their Viceroys-Camels-Marlboros created a haze of gray-blue smoke. Mother tapped the table with a pencil to get the meeting underway. Everyone stood and placed their right hands over their hearts while Dad intoned the Pledge of Allegiance.

Sometime later, over the buzz of the projector—Birch meetings usually featured an educational filmstrip—I heard Janet calling. "I need help," she said. "The baby keeps crying." I bolted up the stairs.

My ten-year-old sister stood over the crib where Mary, eighteen-months-old, waved her arms and fussed. Blue veins covered the baby's upper body, and she was shivering. "She has goose bumps," Janet said. "I can't get her warm." Janet's green eyes were huge; I knew she'd start crying any minute.

"It's okay," I said. "I'm here now."

A year before, Mary had been diagnosed with dislocated hips. We were told that she'd never walk unless she spent several years in a body cast.

In the 1950s, before the development of rigid casts, the doctor had to build a cast out of plaster of paris. While the paste was pliable, Mary's hips, knees, and feet were positioned at 90-degree angles, like stair steps. It took almost a week for the cast to dry, especially in the cold of winter.

Every few months, Mary outgrew her cast. The old one was sawed off and the doctor constructed a new one. Each time, we worried about the drying, especially after Mary struggled with a bout of pneumonia. After that, Janet and I decided to use a hair dryer to speed the process.

That evening, while I was stuck downstairs at a Birch meeting, Janet was struggling alone. "I can't hold the hair dryer and keep Mary covered at the same time," she said.

"Let me take over. You keep the blanket on her."

I propped my arms on the top rail of the crib and moved the hair dryer back and forth, back and forth, covering every inch of the cast. When I'd been over the front, Janet and I gently turned Mary on her tummy and repeated the process.

The meeting in the living room went on and on. It seemed like forever before I heard Mother calling me. When I went to the steps, she looked stern and pointed toward the floor. "Where have you been?" she asked. I quickly explained. "Go back up then," she said. "When everyone's gone, I'll be up."

Ten o'clock came and went. Finally, my brother appeared in the doorway. "Everyone's gone, and Mom and Dad want to see you," Jay R. said. "I'll help Janet."

In the living room, Mother and Dad greeted me from their usual spots on the sofa.

"Your country is calling," my father said. "You are old enough to join the fight." Dad slid a membership application toward me. "Sign on the line."

That night I became a full-fledged, adult John Bircher. I was thirteen years old.

Chapter Six

Twisted

Although Revilo Oliver remained unknown outside White Supremacist circles, his fingerprints showed up on virtually every far right tendency during the post-World War Two era.

—LEONARD ZESKIND, *BLOOD AND POLITICS*[1]

For ten years, my family and I lived in Rogers Park, a northside Chicago neighborhood of many Jews and a few Catholics. I was in the first grade when I started walking to school, a four-block hike from our apartment on Maplewood. The highlight of the trip was three blocks on Devon Avenue, a busy commercial street lined with small specialty shops, most with Jewish proprietors. Many of those folks had "come over from the old country," which, in my mind, explained why the men sported beards and the women wore babushkas.

I was around ten years old when it dawned on me that many of the snippets of conversation I heard concerned Germans, Jews, and World War II. I didn't understand a lot of the words, as the old folks often spoke in Yiddish. But I did know the English words "smoke," "ghetto," and "camps."

One day, I asked our across-the-alley neighbor, Mrs. Fishman, about what I'd been hearing. "Oy gevalt, it's bad luck to speak of the dead." Even so, she sat me down at her kitchen table, offered me a cookie and milk, and shared her story.

"My family came from Germany when I was about your age. That was years before the war, but my father worried. 'They hate us,' he said. 'We have to go to America.' He was right. First, every Jew had to wear yellow stars, and then they were rounded up and put in railroad cars. Now they're all dead. Everyone. No one is left."

One evening I asked my father about the yellow stars and the boxcars. "Those were terrible times," he said. He told me how Nazis arrested the Jews in cities and towns across Germany and Poland. The Jews were loaded into cattle cars without food or water and transported to camps to be killed. In places called Treblinka, Dachau, Buchenwald, and Auschwitz, men, women, and children were forced to strip naked. Their clothes were thrown into huge piles and their heads were shaved. Then they were gassed. After every extermination the bodies were thrown into huge ovens, called crematoriums. Day and night, smoke spewed from the chimneys.

"The ashes of the dead covered everything," my father said. "Hitler planned to exterminate every Jew in Europe. It was his Final Solution."

My father told me that American soldiers who liberated the camps at the end of the war found thousands of emaciated prisoners in striped prison pajamas. In the camp yards, piles of decomposing bodies were stacked like cord wood. "How could anyone do these things?" I asked.

"The Germans claimed they were following orders," Dad explained. "But that is no excuse. You can never do these evil things and make an excuse like that."

"What happened to the bad men?" I asked.

The worst of the Nazi war criminals were arrested and tried, my father told me. Many were put in prison, and some were hanged. "It's right for the men who did these things to be punished," Dad said.

"They should have hanged all of them," I said.

My father agreed with me.

I knew these things had happened during World War II and that the Germans had done them. I knew, as well as I knew my own name, that America had saved the world. "If we hadn't beaten those bastards, you'd be speaking German," Dad said.

I hugged my father and thanked God we'd won the war. "The Nazis are dead and gone, forever," I told myself. "They'll never hurt anyone again."

Shortly after Mother and Dad became Birchers, they met Revilo P. Oliver, a classics professor from the University of Illinois, a founding Birch member—he had joined even before my parents—and a close friend of Robert Welch's. Welch described Oliver as "one of the very top scholars in America in his field and one of the ablest speakers on the Americanist side."[2]

My parents welcomed Oliver enthusiastically, but he gave me the creeps. His long face was exaggerated by black hair glistening with pomade, bushy eyebrows, and beady eyes. He sported a mustache as wide as his mouth. When he smiled, his lip curled into a snarl. Oliver always showed up in a starched white dress shirt, tie, and tweed sport coat. I never remember him removing that coat, even in the heat of the summer.

His first name, Revilo, puzzled me, but he was quick to explain: "My name, an obvious palindrome, has been the burden of the eldest or only son for six generations."³ Revilo = Oliver. I thought that was peculiar, but it was hard to make a big deal about it when my father's given name was Stillwell.

Revilo Oliver was the only person I ever knew who was able to translate ancient Sanskrit manuscripts. Dad bragged that he could write in a dozen or more languages, some with their own alphabets. I thought my father was exaggerating until I read that Oliver's home office had "twelve typewriters, each with a typeface for a different language."⁴

For almost ten years, Oliver was a frequent contributor to *National Review*, William Buckley's magazine, and to the John Birch Society's magazine, *American Opinion*. Apparently, Oliver was allowed free rein to offer his views on politics, culture, and race. In 1956, Oliver used the pages of *National Review* to share this vision of America's future: "Naked dictatorship, the rule of uniformed thugs, and the concentration camp for all who obstinately believe in human freedom."⁵

Seven years later, in *American Opinion*, Oliver attacked the United States for "an insane, but terribly effective, effort to destroy the American people and Western civilization by subsidizing . . . the breeding of the intellectually, physically, and morally unfit."⁶

From 1959 through the summer of 1966, Oliver thrilled audiences with his stories of war, treason, and Communist subversion. He ranted against American involvement in World War II, insisting that we were pushed into the war for only one reason: Franklin Roosevelt wanted to help his Communist friend Joseph Stalin. According to Oliver, "We [the United States] had fought for the sole purpose of imposing the beasts of Bolshevism on a devastated land."⁷

Those ideas were not the worst of the stuff that Oliver preached. Not long after he turned up at our house, I began to hear a new version of World War II, one in stark contrast to everything I'd learned. Oliver called the Holocaust a "hoax" concocted by the Jews themselves and said numerous times that "there were no gas chambers and there was no 'extermination.' "⁸

Soon, my parents began to parrot Oliver. The Holocaust that I'd learned about from Mrs. Fishman and my father stopped being so terrible: The death camps turned into detention camps. Jews were taken prisoner because they were traitors to the German government, not because of their faith. The "Final Solution" became fiction, the "Holohoax," as Oliver called it, and the

Nazis were turned into loyal military men following orders.[9] "In wartime, it's kill or be killed," my father now said.

I didn't ask my father about the Jews who were sent to Auschwitz and the gas chambers. I didn't ask about the photographs and the eyewitness reports of the Americans who liberated the camps. I didn't ask about the testimonies of those who survived. I didn't ask about any of it. I thought my parents had lost their minds and that Dr. Oliver had helped them.

I remember how disappointed I was in my father for having anything to do with the awful Dr. Oliver. To me, it was obvious that he was a vicious, nasty man, and I couldn't imagine what my father saw in him.

For the first time, I doubted my dad.

———

Revilo Oliver and my father served together in the leadership of the John Birch Society for seven years. During that time, Oliver spent many hours in our living room spewing forth some idea or other while recruiting new members to the society. My parents drank in everything the man said and repeated most of it, almost verbatim, to anyone who would listen. Robert Welch continued to praise Oliver for his outstanding contributions to the cause.

In July of 1966, Oliver headlined the fourth annual New England Rally for God, Family, and Country, an annual Birch-sponsored festival held in Boston and billed as a reunion for conservative Americans. Scott Stanley, managing editor of the two Birch publications *American Opinion* and the *Review of the News*, was listed as the moderator for Oliver's speech, "Conspiracy or Degeneracy."[10] Near the end of his remarks, Oliver talked about "vaporizing" Jews as part of the "beatific vision."

Oliver's shocking statements generated an avalanche of negative press, followed by a month of internal Birch turmoil on how to respond. Finally, in early August, Welch told council members that Oliver was out.[11]

The minute Oliver left the Birch Society, he vanished from my parents' conversations. I asked what had happened, but neither my mother nor my father would say; they pretended he'd never really been a friend anyway.

Revilo Oliver lived the rest of his life as a hero to the neo-Nazi Holocaust deniers, who spread his message of hate through their books and magazines. On August 10, 1994, Revilo Oliver died of a self-inflicted gunshot wound. He was eighty-six.

In his recently published book, Arthur Goldwag says this about Oliver: "Hateful doesn't even begin to describe Oliver's racialism, which is expressed in impolitic, frankly Hitlerian terms that would shock even many a hard-core segregationist. His reflexive use of epithets like 'sheeny' and 'nigger' alone put him beyond the pale."[12]

In addition to his vile ideas and white-supremacist ideology, Oliver also introduced the John Birch Society to its single most essential belief. In his 2009 book *Blood and Politics*, Leonard Zeskind identifies Oliver as "the person responsible for introducing the idea of a conspiracy by the Illuminati into Birch circles."[13]

Thanks to Revilo, my parents embraced the Illuminati and toyed with denying the Holocaust. Personally, I wish I'd never heard of Oliver. I wish I could forget his creepy smile, slicked-back hair, and vile ideas. And I wish I could say that Oliver was the last Jew-hating, race-baiting, Nazi-loving extremist my parents brought home for supper.

Sometime during their lurch to the right, my parents decided that dinner was the ideal time to teach us kids about Communism. They no longer mentioned Nazis or the Holocaust; Mother and Dad made sure that we understood that Communists were the real evil monsters.

Before long, I could name all the Communist tyrants: Karl Marx, the father of Communism; Joseph Stalin, the scourge of Russia; Nikita Khrushchev, the current Russian gangster. In Asia, it was Kim Il-sun, the demon of North Korea, and Ho Chi Minh, the leader in North Vietnam. Finally, the newest member of the club was Fidel Castro, the Cuban revolutionary just ninety miles off our coast.

"These Commies make Hitler look tame," Dad said.

The ultimate fiend was Mao Zedong, the dictator of China. The scope of the murder and mayhem he'd unleashed on his own people was unimaginable; seventy million Chinese dead from starvation and mass murder.[14]

Statistics weren't vivid enough for my parents, however. They used the dinner hour to paint detailed pictures of the horrendous things Mao ordered. Over chicken and dumplings, we heard about prisoners hacked to pieces by guards wielding machetes. Some unfortunates were forced to sit on chairs with seats of spikes. Their tormentors jostled the chairs until the victims were impaled. Thanks to my father, I learned how prisoners were forced to drink so much water that they died. From the specifics of sleep deprivation to the agonies of starvation, my parents shared it all.

Most of the time I could drown out the stories by pretending I was somewhere else. My sister and I used to call that "flying." We'd see ourselves hovering above the table just far enough away that we couldn't hear anything.

That worked, most of the time. But some stories we could not escape; they were seared into our memories.

One night, Mother described the atrocities in a village where Mao's henchmen rounded up the women and girls, stripped them, and tied them to stakes. Nearby, the guards built fires and heated coals until they were red hot. Those coals were shoved into the vaginas of the victims. "You could hear the screams for miles," Mother said.

Another evening, Dad explained execution quotas. In some villages, every man, woman, and child was killed. In other places, children reported their parents for crimes against the state. The children were then forced to kill their own parents.

"Remember this," Mother said, "the day may come when you will have to turn on your father and on me. What will you do then?"

Around the table, silence. Finally, I took the risk to answer. "No matter what, I'll never hand you over to a firing squad," I promised. My brothers and sister agreed.

Mother, however, wasn't convinced by our vows. "Don't be too sure, children," she said. "Until the worst happens, you never really know what you'll do."

The worst did not happen, but that never stopped my parents. They were positively sure that every secret Commie and every liberal Democrat was working around the clock to turn the United States into Russia, North Vietnam, or, worse yet, China. No one in Chicago had been butchered by machete-wielding revolutionaries yet, but disaster was definitely coming.

Chapter Seven

Moving Up

*The paranoid spokesman sees the fate of this conspiracy in apocalyptic terms—
he traffics in the birth and death of whole worlds, whole political orders, whole
systems of human values. He is always manning the barricades of civilization.
He constantly lives at a turning point: it is now or never in organizing resistance
to conspiracy.*

—RICHARD HOFSTADTER[1]

Our home buzzed with John Birch activity. Day after day, Mother was consumed with whatever project hit number one on her priority list. Sometimes,
she enlisted the help of other Birch members who were eager to participate.
Many weekends, I was recruited for the latest project. When my mother said,
"You're on deck," I knew I'd be spending my Saturday stuffing envelopes and
licking stamps.

What we did in Chicago was duplicated in chapters across sixteen other
states. From Illinois to Florida, New Hampshire to California, the John Birch
Society rallied scores of loyal Americans to take on the conspiracy and defeat
the Communists.

In 1959, just as the Birchers were getting their organizational legs, President Dwight Eisenhower—in the third year of his second term—invited Soviet premier Nikita Khrushchev to visit the United States. If all went well, a
presidential visit to Moscow would follow. According to David Halberstam,
President Eisenhower dreamed that these meetings could "end the worst of
the Cold War," if Ike were able to negotiate a limited test-ban treaty, which
would be "the triumph of his presidency."[2]

For Robert Welch and his newly minted Birch Society, Eisenhower's
efforts were a call to action. Believing that "peaceful coexistence" with the
Communists was impossible, the Birch leadership organized its first "front"
group, the Committee Against Summit Entanglements (CASE), to publicize
its objections to the proposed meetings.

CASE produced a full-page ad headlined, "Please, President Eisenhower,

Don't!" urging the president to postpone Khrushchev's September visit until the Communist leader proved that he was "no longer the enemy of freedom and of ourselves."[3] Over the summer, almost one hundred newspapers across the country ran anti-summit ads. Each ad included a petition with space for ten signatures and directions for mailing the completed form to the White House.

The ad campaign did not stop Khrushchev's visit, but it did accomplish a major goal: prominent conservatives who were not John Birch members endorsed the campaign, contributed money to fund the project, and signed their names to the CASE ads. Barry Goldwater, William Buckley, and the libertarian economist Ludwig von Mises all signed, as did my father and dozens of other Birch leaders. In all, sixty-four names were printed in the national ads.

The success of that ad campaign set up the Birchers for their next battle: stopping the summit entirely. In January 1960, Welch unveiled the slogan that would drive the next six months of effort: "The summit leads to disaster."[4]

"It is the most important, most comprehensive, and most dangerous of all the planned Communist advances now looming before us," Welch wrote in February.[5] In May, in a last-ditch effort to stop the summit, Welch instructed Birch members to write postcards and letters to the White House with the message, "Dear President Eisenhower — If you go, don't come back!"[6]

Welch quantified the stakes in the battle: If the Communists "finally take us over," he wrote, ". . . they will murder at least forty million of the most independent and family-loving Americans . . . fight while we still can."[7]

I was a good little fourteen-year-old Bircher, and every month I tried to follow Welch's directions. I read my *John Birch Society Monthly Bulletin* and wrote as many letters and postcards as I could. I didn't recoil when Welch outlined his vision for the future, complete with death statistics. My parents had told so many graphic stories of torture and killing that Welch's warnings seemed tame in comparison.

On May 1, 1960, the Soviets shot down a U-2 spy plane and captured the pilot, Francis Gary Powers. The political fallout forced the cancellation of Eisenhower's trip to Moscow; the possibility of any accord with the Russians was kaput.

The John Birch Society claimed victory, despite the reality that they had nothing to do with the aborted visit. Still, the new grassroots organization had sent, according to Welch, six hundred thousand postcards to the White House.[8] That, in itself, was a victory. The Birchers were on their way.

In the fall of 1959, right in the middle of the summit project, Mother called me into the dining room. On the table, piles of pamphlets, letters, envelopes, and stamps waited. Mother scurried around checking the supplies. She stopped for a sip of cold tea and looked at me. "You're on deck," she said.

"The summit?" I asked.

"No," she answered. "Today we're saving Christmas."

"Saving Christmas . . . from what?"

"The United Nations," she told me.

The John Birch Society, she explained, had uncovered a plot to replace the baby Jesus with an international celebration of brotherhood. Before anyone was the wiser, traditional Christmas ornaments and trees would be replaced with United Nations insignias and flags.[9]

"The Christmas tree at Marshall Fields will be no more," Mother said.

To thwart this assault on our Savior's birthday, the Birch Society had published *There Goes Christmas.* "All the Communist plans are exposed, right here," Mother said, tapping the booklet's cover.

I was put to work on the booklet assembly line and stuffed *There Goes Christmas* into envelopes addressed to a slew of folks. Everyone from our family Christmas-card list to the members of the local country club was sent a copy. By the time the project was over, I swore everyone in Chicago must have received one.

"This is a war on Christmas," Mother said. "You watch. Before long, they'll write it like this: *Xmas.* That's the clue. They're x-ing Christ out of his own birthday."[10]

———

Playing on a potent mix of fear, patriotism, and religious fervor, the John Birch Society became the right wing's rising star. Before long, the society had units in thirty-four states and was collecting dues from more than sixty thousand members.[11]

The growth proved that Welch's top-down, authoritarian model featuring rigid control from the main office was working. The small cells, which the society called chapters, made membership personal, and the activities detailed in each monthly bulletin kept everyone focused in the same direction at the same time.[12] A Birch leader's manual put it like this: "There is no room in the John Birch Society for dreamers, drifters or deadwood."[13]

Welch bestowed a new name on all of his patriots: *Americanists.*[14] They were the real Americans, battling the bad guys who lived inside our own government, the men Welch had christened "Insiders." Insiders were not themselves Communists, and they'd never be caught at party meetings, but they controlled and financed the card-carrying Communists.[15]

Across the country, the Americanists (Birchers) hammered home their message: the Commies are coming; in fact, they're already here. Thousands of people believed what they heard and joined. Those new members went out and recruited their neighbors and friends.

After hearing the society's growth figures, my father was cautiously optimistic. "If this keeps up, we may be able to beat these bastards," he said to my mother.

Mother put it a little differently: "We're taking our country back."

At our house, the Birch parade marched on, picking up new members every week. Our chapter grew to thirty members, enough to split into two. Then, those two chapters split. It didn't take long before Chicago boasted four chapters. Then eight.

———

In the spring of 1960, my father joined a small group of men chosen by Robert Welch to serve as his advisors. That inner circle, the National Council, had one major responsibility: to pick the next Birch leader "if and when an accident, 'suicide,' or anything sufficiently fatal is arranged for me by the Communists," Welch said. Other council functions included "showing the stature and leadership of the Society" and giving "your Founder the benefit of the Council's advice and guidance."[16]

One historian studying the Birch Society described the council as "ornamental, designed to impress through its collection of powerful Americans united behind Welch's beliefs."[17] I'm sure my father would have argued— loudly—against that assessment. He held his council seat as a sacred trust and a singular personal accomplishment. "I gave my all," he said. "With no regrets."

During his thirty-two years on the National Council, Dad rubbed elbows with some of the right wing's most interesting and infamous fellows. He met decorated former military officers, including Colonel Laurence Bunker, who had been a personal aide to General Douglas MacArthur, and Lieutenant General Charles B. Stone, who had served in China as the commander of the 14th Air Force. Dad became close friends with Clarence (Pat) Manion, former dean of Notre Dame Law School, and William (Bill) Grede, a Milwaukee industrialist. Before long, my father knew successful business owners, doctors, lawyers, and even a former IRS commissioner, T. Coleman Andrews.[18]

In the first few months of his council tenure, Dad befriended a dynamic Serb, Dr. S. M. Draskovich, who had immigrated to the United States after World War II and built the Serbian Cultural Club on Chicago's north side.

My father and Dr. Dan, as we called him, served together on the council for over six years. Their relationship came to an abrupt end when Dr. Dan hatched a scheme to unseat Welch from his leadership position and take over the society himself.[19]

Over the years, Dad knew several congressmen, a candidate for president, a young physician shot down in a Korean Air disaster, a leader of the Mormon Church, authors, publishers, and former FBI agents. Most of those Birch council members, whether scoundrels or saints, are buried deep in the recesses of American history, known only to politics junkies, history wonks, and Birch kids like me. There is one exception, however, a Birch council member whose name booms across today's political landscape. That name is Koch.

Before Koch became synonymous with vast wealth and unlimited corporate power, the family patriarch, Fred Koch, amassed a small fortune in the oil-refining business. When my father met him, in 1960, Fred was the president of Rock Island Oil and Refining Company, a private firm headquartered in Wichita, Kansas.[20] Dad was drawn to Fred for two reasons: he hated the Communists and he hated the labor unions.

Fred Koch had something most people in the United States did not have: a firsthand, on-the-ground experience of Joseph Stalin's Russia. He'd seen Communism for himself in the early 1930s as he traveled across Russia overseeing the installation of fifteen oil refineries, systems that played a significant role in building the Soviet economy. The money Koch was paid made him a wealthy man, and a quiet one. It took almost thirty years before he went public with his Russian experiences.[21]

In 1960, a little over a year after he'd become a founding member of the John Birch Society, Fred published *A Businessman Looks at Communism*, a harsh critique of the Communist system. The book became a hit in the growing anti-Communist movement. According to Koch himself, "Over two and a half million have been printed and circulated in one form or another."[22]

Koch's book outlined the steps the Communists planned to take over America: "Step one: Infiltration of high office of government and political parties until the President of the U.S. is a Communist . . . even the Vice-Presidency would do, as it could be easily arranged for the President to commit suicide."[23]

Step two was a general strike, which "could bring our country to its knees." Wrote Koch, "Labor Unions have long been a Communist goal. . . . The effort is frequently made to have the worker do as little as possible for the money he receives. This practice alone can destroy our country."[24]

As much as my father aligned with Koch on Communism, on the issue of labor unions, they were clones. "As long as there is breath in my body," Dad vowed, "there will never be a union in my company. I'll board it up first. Fred sees it like I do, one hundred percent."

I never visited my dad's Southside factory, but I do remember him talking about firing any employee who talked union or union organizing. Over the years, several efforts to organize Dad's companies did get as far as a vote, but my father prevailed every time. The Banner Mattress Company was never a union shop. Nor was the Conroth Company or Modern Sleep Products.

Fred Koch's views on Communism were universally accepted within the Birch Society as gospel, including his bleak vision for the coming Communist takeover of the country. The United States "looks like it is going down the Communist drain," Koch wrote. " . . . It will probably happen so quickly that most people will never realize what is happening to them."[25]

Fred Koch died in 1967, leaving his company and his fortune to his four sons—Freddie, Charles, David, and Bill—who spent the next twenty years warring over the estate. Eventually, David and Charles emerged with control over Koch Industries, one of the largest privately held corporations in the country.[26]

The Koch brothers have enormous personal fortunes, at least $60 billion in net worth as of September 2012.[27] They've invested millions and millions of those dollars in their favorite right-wing, libertarian, anti-government causes. David identified himself as the wallet behind Americans for Prosperity, the big umbrella organization for Freedom Works and the Tea Party. Charles founded the Cato Institute, a powerful think-tank specializing in selling right-wing policies on everything from taxes to entitlements.[28]

In their book *The Betrayal of the American Dream*, Donald L. Barlett and James B. Steele described David and Charles's legacy from their dad as a "burning hatred of governments of all types."[29]

———

Every few weeks, my father received a large manila envelope from Birch headquarters containing materials for the next meeting. Everything was stamped confidential, intended for council members only, but as Dad shared with Mother over dinner, I listened to their conversation. Most of the information I forgot as soon as I heard it, but one evening, I paid more attention.

"Listen to this," Dad said to my mother. "Bob [Welch] says that our federal government is already, 'literally in the hands of the Communists.'"

My father proceeded to read the names of senators who Welch included in that Commie cabal. Most of them I'd never heard of, but I did recognize one: John Kennedy, the junior senator from Massachusetts. "Every one of those men," my father read, "is either an actual Communist or so completely a Communist sympathizer or agent that it makes no practical difference."[30]

"That means we'll have another Commie in the White House if Kennedy ever becomes president," Dad said.

"What do you mean by 'another'?" I wondered.

"Hush, young lady. These are adult conversations. Someday, when you've read more, you'll understand," Mother said.

My father loved the game of golf. As winter turned to spring, he'd take a stance—in the living room or the kitchen, it didn't matter. He called the process "grooving his shot." After he positioned his feet, gripped his imaginary club, and straightened his left arm, he'd swing. Not once, not twice, but over and over. I knew he was dreaming of perfect drives leading to one-putt greens.

I could not believe that any cause, even saving the country, would keep my father from his Saturday round. But once he joined the Birch council, he spent at least one weekend a month at a meeting. Sometimes, when he complained about the impact the meetings were having on his score, Mother cajoled him: "There will be no golf when the Commies come. Besides, you're making such wonderful contacts, dear."

Chapter Eight

The Black Book

I want no part in this. I won't even have it around. If you were smart, you'd burn every copy you have.

—Senator Barry Goldwater, after reading *The Politician*, Robert Welch's secret manuscript[1]

Chicago simmered in the summer doldrums. Up and down our street, kids ran through sprinklers. When the Good Humor truck arrived, they traded their nickels for ice-cream treats.

The heat and humidity encouraged an explosion in the pest population. One afternoon I opened the metal garbage can and found handfuls of white, squiggly worms crawling over the paper bags. I screamed for Jay R. "They're maggots," he said. "Baby flies."

I ran to the house, grabbed a bottle of Lysol, and poured it all over those awful things. "When are we getting out of here?" I whined.

"Not this year," Jay said. "They just canceled Gloucester."

That summer, everything was about the John Birch Society. Dad's position on the National Council had added a new urgency to Chicago recruiting efforts. After all, the city now boasted a national leader.

More and more people wanted to hear my father speak. The crowds had outgrown our living room, so alternative meeting places were found. One perfect spot was the hall at Our Lady of Perpetual Help Catholic church in Glenview, which could accommodate several hundred people.

The pastor, Father John Dussman, a good friend of my parents and an avid Bircher himself, welcomed the meetings. Father suffered no qualms about the separation of church and state, and used the *Clarion*, his weekly parish bulletin to endorse everything Birch. "The conspiracy is afoot," he wrote in one Sunday's bulletin. ". . . It dubs itself liberalism & always its hidden purpose is the enslavement of human will to an Almighty State instead of Almighty God."[2]

My parents had set ambitious goals for Birch membership, hoping to create a network of five hundred members in two dozen chapters by the end of December 1960. For the most part, things were "progressing nicely," as Mother said.

Once in a while, however, a hint of trouble surfaced. I overheard my parents whispering about a rumor that wouldn't die and a book that didn't exist. From their conversations, I figured out that this imaginary book contained details that could never be revealed about secret Communists in the government.

"It's a rumor," Dad said. "It won't amount to anything."

"I hope you're right," Mother answered.

Several times, Birch members actually asked about the secret book. Dad never hesitated to answer: "There is no book. There never has been." That was enough for me. I never dreamed my father would lie.

On Monday, July 11, 1960, Mother and Dad prepared for a big meeting at Our Lady of Perpetual Help. I was shocked when mother announced that I did not have to come. "You've heard your dad many times," she told me. "Stay home with the little kids."

While I watched TV in the basement with Jay R., Larry, Janet, and Mary Elizabeth, two hundred people filled Our Lady of Perpetual Help's hall. I had no idea, until the next day, exactly what had transpired, but I imagined the meeting being like every other one I'd attended. Father Dussman offered a prayer and an enthusiastic introduction. Then my father took the microphone. Dad went right into his usual remarks, the same ones I'd heard a dozen or more times. He talked about the Communist empire and its growing influence in our country. He decried Fidel Castro in Cuba and the evil intentions of the United Nations.

I figured that Dad attacked the federal government, taxes, and creeping socialism. His vivid descriptions of their lives when our country merged into the Soviet Union scared the audience into silence. By the time my father begged the loyal Americans seated in front of him to join the John Birch Society and save their country, the audience burst into loud, sustained applause.

At this point, my mother was waiting at the literature table knowing she'd sell books and sign up new members as soon as the question-and-answer session finished. It was a big crowd; she would be busy.

As Dad relaxed and took a sip of water, he removed his sport coat and invited questions from the audience. As usual, someone asked, "Who was John Birch?" Others wondered, "Why is the John Birch Society better than other anti-Communist organizations?" and "Are Republicans more anti-Communist than Democrats?"

Dad was prepared for these questions; they were the same ones he heard almost every time he spoke. This was his favorite part of every speech, debating the skeptics and turning an adversary into an ally. He was good at it and he knew it. My father had learned his debate techniques back at Northwestern University as a member of the varsity debate team. In his Birch talks, he employed the very same tactics he used so well back then. After fifteen minutes or so, Dad announced that he'd take a last question.

That night, however, things went off the rails when a woman, seated in the middle of the hall, waved her hand. When Dad nodded to her, she jumped to her feet and asked about the "secret book."[3]

My father gave his standard response. "There is no such book."

"Really?" the woman said. She reached into her satchel and produced an 8½" x 11" spiral-bound manuscript written by Robert Welch, the Birch Society's founder. She turned to pages she had marked and began to read: "Eisenhower's motivation is more ideological than opportunistic . . . he has been sympathetic to ultimate Communist aims, realistically willing to use Communist means to help them achieve their goals, knowingly accepting and abiding by Communist orders, and consciously serving the Communist conspiracy, for all of his adult life."[4]

The room was deathly quiet. The woman, who never identified herself, paused for just a few seconds and then continued reading: "My firm belief that Dwight Eisenhower is a dedicated conscious agent of the Communist conspiracy is based on an accumulation of detailed evidence so extensive and so palpable that it seems to me to put this conviction beyond any reasonable doubt."[5]

The audience gasped.

Everyone in the room that night understood what that sentence meant; according to Robert Welch, the president of the United States was a traitor to his country.

Over the next few weeks, I learned that Robert Welch had begun his book, which he titled *The Politician*, as a letter to a friend. He kept adding more and more material until the manuscript grew to three hundred pages. The mimeographed manuscript was only released to select friends or political allies, and each copy was numbered. Recipients had to promise, in writing, to keep both the book and its contents confidential. By 1960, five hundred numbered copies of the unpublished version had been distributed.

My father eventually revealed that he'd possessed a copy of *The Politician* for four years. He never did tell me where he hid it.

The book was finally published by the Birch Society in 1963 as *The Politician*, but in Birch circles, it's usually called *The Black Book* because it had a black cover.

That night in Glenview, the idea that President Eisenhower was a Communist was too radical for the audience to accept. Many of the men who were in the audience had served under General Eisenhower, and everyone knew men who'd given their lives in World War II. Welch's claim that Eisenhower was a traitor and had been for all of his adult life was an outrage.

The audience grew angry: angry with Robert Welch, who'd written those words, and angry with my father, who'd spent ten minutes denying they existed.

Confronted with the evidence, my father had to admit that the manuscript was real and foolishly tried to justify the secrecy. According to an FBI informant who reported on the meeting, my father insisted that "the book was only for those who had been properly guided within the Society."[6]

The audience burst out laughing. My father put down the microphone and walked away from the podium. No new members joined the John Birch Society that night.

In the next few days, my parents talked at length about the meeting in Glenview. At first, they decried the anonymous heckler who had disrupted the meeting with her unfounded attacks. The whole story came out two weeks later when my dad arrived home with the evening paper tucked under his arm. He slapped the *Daily News* on the table where Mother was seated. "Take a look at Mabley's column on page three," he said.

Jack Mabley was a hometown favorite: a hard-hitting newspaperman willing to tackle Mayor Richard Daley's political machine.[7] Like most Chicagoans, my parents considered Mabley tough and honest. In fact, he was the only reason they even bothered with the *Daily News*. Otherwise, they were strictly *Tribune* people.

Mother spread out the paper on the table, turned to page three, and began reading. "'Bares Secrets of Red-Haters,'" she said.[8] "What's this?"

"He got a hold of *The Politician*," Dad said. "Probably from that woman in Glenview."

Mother immediately realized the trouble this kind of publicity could create. "Look at this," she said, tapping the paper. Right there—in a major Chicago newspaper with a large circulation—were stunning quotes from Robert Welch, the same ones from the meeting in Glenview: "My firm belief that Dwight Eisenhower is a dedicated, conscious agent of the Communist conspiracy is based on an accumulation of detailed evidence so extensive and so palpable that it seems to me to put this conviction beyond any reasonable doubt," and, "There is only one possible word to describe his [Eisenhower's] purposes and actions. That word is treason."[9]

That word "treason"—haunted the John Birch Society for years.

The next day, Mabley continued his expose with a piece entitled "Strange Threat to Democracy." In the second installment, the columnist recounted the story of my father's actions during the meeting and his bizarre explanation about the "secret book."

Mabley wrote, "Recently a meeting in Glenview was disrupted when the book was brought up in open discussion by someone in the audience. . . . Stillwell J. Conner, leader of the meeting, had told a member that giving the book to a member of the Society before he became 'qualified' was like telling a first-year medical student to go out and cure cancer."[10] Mabley went on to enumerate Welch's beliefs about the Communists inside our government: Roosevelt and Truman were Communist pawns, but it was Eisenhower's election that altered the entire equation. "The Communists have one of their own actually in the Presidency," Welch wrote.

The Jack Mabley expose was picked up by papers far beyond Chicago. Within a few weeks, criticism of the Birch Society spread across the country, from the *Milwaukee Journal* to the *Los Angeles Times* and *Time* magazine.[11]

After the Mabley bombshell, the Chicago media clamored for interviews with my dad. Following Welch's personal directive, my father refused all requests. No matter, reporters showed up at our house, and the phone rang off the hook.

"What's going on?" I asked.

"Your father is standing up for the truth," Mother said.

"Then why did he lie about the book?" I asked.

Mother came across the room toward me. "You dare to question your father," she said as she slapped my face. "Go to your room. I can't even look at you right now."

———

In early 1961, the John Birch Society reversed its blanket refusal to speak with the media, and my father made himself available to the Chicago media. Dad's interview with Frank Reynolds, the news anchor of WBBM Channel 2, a CBS affiliate, made him the Birch Society's public face in Chicago.[12]

My dad spared no effort to protect the John Birch Society. In an interview conducted April 3, 1961, Dad discussed "his willingness to testify in Congress about the society's beliefs," saying, "There is nothing sinister about the group." He declared that "he would *not* plead the Fifth Amendment under questioning."[13]

The Birch stories unleashed a firestorm from pundits and politicians across the political landscape. Criticism from the Republicans was particularly brutal, not a shock as Eisenhower was a Republican. Barry Goldwater and William Buckley, who had received copies of the manuscript years earlier, distanced themselves from Welch immediately. *Time* labeled the response "Thunder Against the Right" and called opponents "The Birch-Barkers."[14] Those articles were just the first in what would become a multiyear effort to neutralize the Birchers.

Long after the Mabley columns had appeared, I learned more of the mystery surrounding the infamous book. Like all the other folks who had a copy of *The Politician*, my father had signed a confidentiality agreement stating he would never reveal the book's contents. Dad made one exception to this rule: my mother. But, in every other case, he kept his promise to Robert Welch by lying, even to me.

I never found out who the woman in Glenview was or how she got a copy of the controversial manuscript. My father swore he'd never seen her before that meeting, and he never saw her again.

In 2007, I discovered that the FBI had investigated the John Birch Society as part of its Subversive Trends of Current Interest Program. In a report filed on September 16, 1960, agent J. A. Meyertholen described not only the Glenview meeting but a later one where my father threatened another woman who asked about the same book. According to the agent, "If she ever revealed the nature of the book, he [Conner] would promptly discredit her and deny the existence of the book and its contents."[15] The agent hinted in the comments section of his report that "there is an element of deceit in the manner of recruiting people" into the Birch Society and that "fortuitous revelation" of *The Politician* could have been deliberate.

Years after the controversy around the book subsided, Robert Welch admitted to a Birch audience that he had really wanted the manuscript to "gather dust."[16]

The uproar around *The Politician* had a brutal impact on my parents. The Birch Society acknowledged that reality in the 1965 publication of their pamphlet *Responsible Leadership through the John Birch Society*. "Since the very early days of The John Birch Society, Jay Conner and his wife, Laurene, have been two of its most knowledgeable, unwavering and dedicated members. They have probably suffered more personally harmful effects from their unceasing support of the Society than any other member of our COUNCIL, and they have taken it all in stride without a word of complaint."[17]

What happened to us kids . . . not on anybody's radar.

Chapter Nine

Stirring the Pot

Not only did the newspaper attacks cause acute embarrassment to many of our members in the areas affected; but to some it caused serious distress, danger to their jobs, and many reactions from neighbors and relatives for which embarrassment was too mild a word. Some of our staunchest friends and strongest supporters, especially among our Coordinators and members of our COUNCIL, were badly hurt. . . . Nor is the end of such cruel unfairness . . . even foreseeable.

— ROBERT WELCH, SEPTEMBER 1960[1]

A week after Jack Mabley's articles were published, I woke in the middle of the night with a terrible headache. I tiptoed into the bathroom for aspirin, swallowed three, and inched my way back down the hall. An hour later, I was still staring at the crack that snaked across the ceiling. "You have to talk to them," I told myself. "It's August."

Two months earlier, my parents' textbook antics had gotten me kicked out of Regina, but, as yet, they had not said a word about a new school. All summer long, I'd been fantasizing about Carl Schurz, the public high school closest to my house. What the place was like, I had no idea, but I found one compelling reason to enroll. "They never expel anyone," Jay R. told me. "No matter what you do."

Schurz High had one other positive characteristic—it was really, really big. Hardly anyone would know me or my parents. As the weeks rolled on and the John Birch Society attracted so much publicity, anonymity became more and more appealing to me. "There could be lots of kids named Conner," my brother said. "No one will connect you with Dad."

The next day, I broached the subject. But the minute I mentioned Schurz, Mother and Dad erupted. They decried the abominations in the "godless, co-educational public schools." They yelled about hoodlums in leather jackets, boy-girl parties without chaperones, and (gasp) sex education.

My public-school fantasy died in an avalanche of "no daughter of mine" and "you be careful, young lady." A few days later, I was enrolled at Marywood, a small Catholic girls' school in Evanston. Luckily, it was an easy commute for me: eight miles on the #10 bus.

The first day of school was like all the other first days I'd experienced; I was nervous and worried. Luckily, the "Marywood ladies," as the nuns dubbed their students, had little interest in the new kid. Only a few pointed and giggled and one person whispered, loudly, about the "Birch kid," but on the whole it was bearable.

On day two, three girls made space for me at their lunch table. Mary T., Kathy, and Pat carried on a lively conversation about the most pressing topics of the day: boys, boys, and, well, boys. I loved those girls instantly.

Those three precious girls were my best friends for the rest of high school. Despite the Birch scandal, which made me a target for criticism in school, my friends stood by me. They defended me, fixed me up on dates, loaned me clothes, and cooked up elaborate schemes to get me out of my house whenever I was grounded. Thanks to them, I survived three of the most tumultuous years of my life.

When I graduated from Marywood, in 1963, I swore that I'd never lose track of those "forever" friends. But I was seventeen; I had no idea how life would shove all of us in different directions. Today when I think of those girls, it's with gratitude and great big smile.

One Friday evening in September of 1960, the seven Conners sat at the dining room table gobbling halibut, rice, and green beans. The scratching of forks on china was the only sound until the grandfather clock in the hall chimed seven times.

As soon as we finished our plates, Mother directed Janet and me to clear the table. "Don't dawdle, girls," she said. "Scrape and rinse. You can do the rest later."

"Why isn't anyone talking?" Janet asked as we piled dishes on the counter.

"I don't know, but let's not rock the boat," I said.

"Get back in here, girls," Mother called. "Your father has something to say."

We had barely slid into our seats when Dad started in. Despite the valiant efforts of the Birchers, Dad announced that the United States was lost. "We've only got two years, tops, before the Commies are in complete control," he said.

I looked across the table at my brother Jay R. He was looking down, but I could still see him roll his eyes and grin. I put my hand in front of my mouth to hide my yawn, before floating away into an afternoon on West Egg with Nick Carraway and his friend Jay Gatsby.

Mother's voice shook me out of my daydream. "Get going, right now. Our guest will be here in the morning," she said.

"What?" I asked Janet as we hustled out of the room.

"The big muckety-muck is coming," she said. "We gotta move the boys."

On that note, Janet and I helped our brothers transport their belongings to the basement, the move we made every time overnight company came. Up and down we went, carrying pillows and sheets, blankets and books, and several changes of clothes.

"Lucky ducks," Janet said. "They've got TV and a fridge."

"Maybe we'll be able to sneak down for a show with them," I told her.

"*Lassie*?" she asked.

We'd barely cleared breakfast the next morning, when Mother called me into the living room. "Your father and I have serious issues to discuss with Bob. You're on deck."

"But I have plans with my friends," I said.

"Your friends can wait." She turned on her heel and marched to the front door. Over her shoulder, she called, "Get the coffee ready."

A minute later, I got my first look at Robert Welch. He wore a charcoal-gray fedora that almost covered his eyebrows and a baggy, beige trench coat—I guessed it was a London Fog, just like my dad's. In one hand, he carried his overnight grip and a briefcase. In the other, his cane. I figured he'd be all decked out in a white dress shirt and striped silk tie, and when his coat came off, that's exactly what he was wearing.

After introductions, my father took Welch and his belongings up to the boys' room while Mother and I arranged coffee, cookies, and clean ashtrays in the living room. "Stay and listen," Mother said. "And don't interrupt."

While we waited for the men, Mother reminded me of Welch's personal achievements: home-schooled child prodigy; lover of ancient languages, higher mathematics, and poetry; college graduate at sixteen; midshipman at the Naval Academy with a perfect 4.0 grade point average.

She retold the story of little Bob, the precocious child, who'd devoured nine volumes of *The History of the World* by age seven and become a chess master not long after.[2] It was that boy who'd grown into the candy man who'd invented the Sugar Daddy and become the world's foremost expert on the international Communist conspiracy.

Over the next few hours, the idealized Welch gave way to the sixty-one-year-old man coughing and hacking in my living room. He had to be very allergic—a situation not helped by the smoke haze that hung from the ceiling. My parents, unfazed, puffed away on their cigarettes. Every so often, Welch lit his cigar and belched out some smoke of his own.

Smoking and coughing did not deter conversation. The three adults seemed to talk constantly and often at the same time. I had nothing to add, which was just as well; I had not been invited to contribute anyway. Welch barely acknowledged my presence, except for a thank you when I passed cookies or freshened his coffee.

By the end of the first day, when my parents and Welch left for dinner at Edgewater Golf Club where Dad was a member, I thought about what I had heard. That's when I realized that Welch's visit was an effort to bolster Dad and Mother in the face of Jack Mabley's attacks.

Conversation continued after they returned from the club, and when I fell asleep, the meeting downstairs was still in full swing. Several times, I was awakened by raised voices, one of them belonging to Welch. I was surprised. Up until then, I'd only heard the intellectual Welch. That night, another side appeared, the aggressive Welch.

I figured out very quickly what the argument was about. Welch did not want anyone from the Birch Society giving interviews; my father disagreed, quite vehemently. I fell asleep while the arguing continued.

In the morning, there was not a hint of the night's disagreement. The adults ate breakfast, chatted about Bob's wife, Marian, and his golden retriever, and skimmed the newspaper. In the middle of the morning, Welch packed his grip, wished me well in school, and thanked my mother for her hospitality. While I helped wash dishes and straighten the house, Dad drove Welch to Midway Airport, where he boarded his flight back to Boston.

I never heard a word about the Welch-Conner argument. But in a few months, I'd know the winner.

Until the fall of 1960, my parents pretended that the John Birch Society was not political. "We're all about education," Mother said.

"The society does not endorse candidates," Dad added.

These claims seemed pretty far-fetched to me. From the beginning, the society had been up to its neck in politics, something Robert Welch himself did nothing to hide. "We would put our weight into the political scales in the country just as fast and far as we could," Welch said when he founded the society in 1958. Those words were no secret; they were in every edition of *The Blue Book* since its publication in 1959.[3]

Propelled by those words, Birchers jumped into the 1960 GOP presidential primary in support of their dream candidate: Barry Goldwater, the junior senator from Arizona. Goldwater embodied everything the Birchers loved; he was anti-Communist, anti–big government, anti–civil rights, pro-military, and anti-welfare.[4] Barry was *the* man.

Robert Welch embraced Goldwater as both a friend and a patriot. "I know Barry fairly well," Welch wrote. "He is absolutely sound in his Americanism, has the political and moral courage to stand by his Americanist principles, and in my opinion, can be trusted to stand by them until hell freezes over. I'd love to see him as President of the United States, and maybe someday we shall."[5]

Technically, I guess Welch could claim he didn't tell anyone to vote for Barry Goldwater, but I doubt Birchers missed the message in his words.

In the summer of 1960, when it was clear that Richard Nixon would be the Republican nominee, many right-wingers, my parents included, refused to lift a finger to get him elected. Mother shut the checkbook, and Dad rebuffed every plea from the GOP for help.

Mother and Dad were not alone in their disgust with the prospect of a Nixon candidacy. Robert Welch was equally as negative. In September's bulletin, he was still arguing against the GOP and the "left-wing pressures *within* the Republican Party."[6] He went on to say that those pressures would "so steadily increase as to smother all efforts . . . to make Americanist views effective."

Obviously, Welch was not defining this election as a clear choice between the good guy on the GOP side and the bad guy on the Democratic side. The Birchers were taking aim at the Republican Party itself. The GOP establishment understood that they had to respond. The potential that the Birchers and their right-wing allies would boycott the election and hand the presidency to John Kennedy loomed large.

Only one person on the political stage could bring the right wing back into line: Barry Goldwater himself. The GOP leadership pressed Goldwater for a full endorsement of the Nixon–Henry Cabot Lodge ticket. Anything less would guarantee a GOP loss.[7]

Goldwater delivered for the party and endorsed Nixon. "We are conservatives," he said to the assembled delegates at the Republican National Convention in Chicago. "This great Republican Party is our historic house. This is our home. . . . Let's grow up, conservatives. If we want to take the Party back, and I think we can someday, let's get to work."[8]

The party crossed its fingers and hoped that Goldwater had pulled the reluctant Right back into the fold. But even a month before the election, it was unclear whether the Goldwater contingent was going to turn out for Nixon.

Robert Welch hemmed and hawed about Nixon. He analyzed the events of the Chicago convention and scolded Goldwater for ignoring the chance to launch a third party, the American Party. "There had been created for him [Goldwater] a rendezvous with history which it was a tragedy for him not to keep," Welch wrote.[9]

Welch mused that a Goldwater–Strom Thurmond ticket for the new American Party, if announced from the podium during the GOP convention, would have "electrified the nation," carried most of the South, and "made a terrific showing in November." The third party would not win in 1960, Welch admitted. But its success would pave the way to take the White House four years later.[10]

The remaining section of the September bulletin was devoted to various scenarios of how Birchers "might" vote in the upcoming election. For sure, Welch didn't say which lever to pull, but he did put in a plug for a campaign button that said, "Goldwater Says Don't Dodge; Vote Nixon and Lodge."[11]

While Welch pined for a third party and the right wing refused to fall in love with Nixon, my father took a more pragmatic approach. "Hold your nose and vote Dick," he said to Mother at dinner. "Otherwise, it'll be JFK."

The day after the election, it was JFK, but only by a tiny 113,000-vote margin.[12] For a whole lot of right-wingers, the GOP loss was proof of fraud. Mother claimed that Chicago had made Kennedy the president by allowing dead people in Cook County to vote. My father blamed Lyndon Johnson's shenanigans in the Lone Star State.[13]

After the inauguration, my father took a black-and-white approach to Kennedy's presidency—if JFK was for something, Dad was against it.

Opposing Kennedy meant more than fighting his policies. It meant that Kennedy had to be a one-term president, a daunting project as the young president was very popular. At the same time, however, the people who hated Kennedy were becoming more organized and more determined. It didn't hurt that they'd already found their anti-Kennedy in Barry Goldwater.[14] It also didn't hurt that they had allies in Robert Welch and the John Birch Society, considered by at least one historian as "the premier example of right-wing activism in the early 1960s."[15]

———

Though most of the Right moved on to fighting Kennedy, my father still smarted from the debacle at Our Lady of Perpetual Help. It had been six months, but he still worried that the storm about Eisenhower and the infamous secret book showed no signs of dying down. "The society has to fight back," Dad often said. But he seemed to have no answer to the question how.

Welch had offered my father his personal support. The entire council had congratulated Dad for his perseverance in the face of the smear. But that support, as appreciated as it was, did not hold back the waves of criticism that just kept on coming.

My Chicago aunts and uncles—except for the one uncle who was in the society—rebuked my father for his Birch involvement. Before long, we didn't attend family parties. I don't know if the invitations never came or my parents declined them, but I do know that my cousins who attended Marywood turned the other way when they spotted me in the halls.

That was small potatoes compared to the criticism swirling around the society all over the country. Welch admitted in February of 1961, "We have given up all hope of avoiding publicity, either good or bad."[16] In March, he described increasing "smear campaigns," including one in Chicago. "Good patriots are . . . being informed that The John Birch Society is Communist . . . two of Chicago's leading citizens are being specifically named as Communists on the basis of their membership in the Society."[17]

I have no idea who those two Chicagoans were; certainly my parents could not be the targets. Not long after that bulletin appeared, however, Robert Welch changed his mind about society leaders giving press interviews. My father was relieved; he had worried for months that the society would be engulfed and destroyed by all the negative press.

Mother and Dad believed Welch's theory that the society had originally been targeted for annihilation on direct orders from the Communists in Moscow.[18] Following that directive, "the whole Liberal-slanted press of America . . . went all out in a continuous and extensive smear campaign against the Society which created a furore [*sic*] for many weeks," Welch wrote.[19]

According to my father, standing by while that Commie-driven smear campaign did its work had been foolhardy. The only chance the society had was to tell the truth, loudly and often, on every television and radio show and in every newspaper and magazine. "Take the fight to the American people," Dad said.

Once Welch gave the green light for interviews, Dad made himself available to all of the local press. Then, he agreed to go national with an interview for *Life* magazine.

"Millions of Americans will finally see us as we are," he said. "Real patriots."

"This'll turn the tide," Mother believed.

A few days before the interview, Mother told me to take out my only Sunday suit and give it a good brushing. "You'll wear it for the photos," she announced.

"Me? Why me?"

"People expect to see the Conner children. You and your brother will be dressed when everyone arrives," she instructed. "Be ready to answer any questions."

"What should I say?"

"Be polite," Mother said.

All night long, I worried about the reporter and his questions. "Please ignore me, please," I prayed.

The next day, I planted myself next to my brother while the *Life* crew busied themselves with my parents. After an hour or so of waiting, the photo shoot began. At first, no one paid a bit of attention to me; then, I was pulled away from Jay R. and stuck on the other side of the room. "Better balance," the photographer said.

"I want to be with my brother," I said to the man. "Please."

The fellow stepped away and I followed him.

"Claire, stay where you were," my mother called out. "Now."

I obeyed.

The actual photography took a long time. It was "one more, please" and "another one" and "let's try that again." At first, I stood up tall, sucked in my tummy, and tried to keep my eyes open. After a dozen "one more, pleases," I no longer cared how I looked. I just wanted everyone to go away.

Apparently, my parents had a similar reaction to the experience because they never mentioned it afterward. When I asked about the publication date, Mother was noncommittal. "It'll be in when it's in," she said. "Don't pester me about it."

———

One day in early May, I came home from school, pushed open the front door, and found my mother seated at the dining-room table, surrounded by piles of newspaper clippings, books, and reprints. A cigarette burned in the overflowing ashtray, one of the forty or more she lit in the course of a day.

On the credenza, I spotted the new issue of *Life*. Mother looked up. "The Birch article is in it," she said. "It's a doozy."

I picked up the magazine, dropped my books and jacket on the breakfast table, and plopped down on the bench. On the cover was a photo of astronaut

Alan Shepard being lifted from his space capsule into a Marine helicopter. I turned to the table of contents and glanced down the page. The fourth high-lighted article was "The John Birch Society," page 124. "Oh, God," I said. "There it is."[20]

According to the summary, the story described the "new and highly controversial political phenomena [sic], the John Birchers, violently anti-Communist and opposed to publicity." Above the title, a miniature Jay R. stared out at me—my brother, my sixteen-year-old brother—captioned "Dedicated Bircher."[21]

"A dedicated Bircher?" I thought. "He can't even drive."

The feature opened with a two-page photo—the one that had been taken in our living room. Twelve John Birch Society members stood with hands over hearts pledging allegiance to the flag. Six people were on each page. My parents and my brother were on the first page. I was on the second.

I studied my picture. I was focused straight ahead, eyes wide, mouth open forming some word of the pledge. I looked serious, stiff, and scared. No one looking at the photo would miss the poof of my hair and the white corners of my upward-slanting glasses.

Reality hit: my picture was in *Life* magazine, and *Life* was everywhere, in homes, newsstands, libraries, doctors' offices, schools. My friends, my friends' parents, my teachers, even my priest would see this, and they'd recognize me. I wanted to scream, "My parents made me!"

I read every word of the article. Then, I read it again. *Life* cloaked its crit-icisms of the society in questions wondering if "members are truly construc-tive American patriots" or "people who feel that flag-waving and what their critics call witch-hunting are substitutes for intelligent service to the nation."

The author went on to describe Welch's charge that "important figures in American public life have abetted the Communist conspiracy" as "incon-testably scurrilous." That word sent me to Webster's, where I read: "scur-ril-ous *adj.* 1. grossly or obscenely abusive: *a scurrilous attack.*"

"Uh-oh," I thought. "This is not good."

"The John Birch Society has its roots in the frustration that many Ameri-cans feel at seeing the nation baffled, thwarted and humiliated in the cold war," *Life* continued. Then the Birchers were accused of "condemning a few devils" so the United States could "be magically restored to some nostalgic Utopian condition."

In the next pages, Birch friends and foes faced off. Ohio senator Stephen Young called Welch a "Hitler." Attorney General Robert Kennedy called the Birch Society "humorous." Even a few protestors marching outside the

Belmont offices of *American Opinion*, the society's magazine, were pictured. The largest sign read: "In John Birch Society Everyone Not Far Right Is Left." Boston's Cardinal Cushing said, "I know that Welch is a man dedicated against Communism. I know nothing of the society."

I puzzled over that remark. How did the cardinal, who lived in Boston, know nothing of the John Birch Society, headquartered less than ten miles away? The magazine also included an essay on the death of John Birch in China, followed by a full-page photo of Robert Welch. I laughed; he looked exactly like the man I had met in the front hall of my house—same hat, same coat, same cane, and same cigar. Well, I hoped it wasn't the exact same cigar. Welch described himself to the reporter as a man having "one wife, two sons, a Golden Retriever dog and 14 golf clubs—none of which he understands but all of which he loves."

That was the only nugget of humor in the entire six-page spread. As the shock of actually seeing myself in a national magazine wore off, I began to realize that the Birchers did sound odd, extreme, and even . . . dangerous. "How's that possible?" I thought. "I'm just a kid."

Over a lot of scotch, Mother and Dad dissected the article. While their analysis stretched on and on, I turned down the chicken, put the beans on low, and cut wedges of cheese for my hungry brothers and sisters. Finally, my mother appeared at the kitchen door. "Serve the dinner," she said. "Hurry, everyone's hungry."

My father sat at the head of the table. His cheeks were ruddy, his lips thin and stretched. His eyes darted around the table while the fork in his hand drummed an erratic rhythm on the placemat. I sensed trouble.

I looked across the table at my brother. He lifted his finger to his lips, reminding me to say nothing. I saw the signal and sent him a tiny smile of recognition. I gave Larry's hand a quick squeeze. I knew Jay R. was passing a signal to Janet. Janet would take care of Mary.

I worried for Jay—he'd take grief at school, just like I would. And we'd be navigating rough waters at home. Good thing we had each other.

Suddenly, Dad erupted. "The goddamned liberal press smeared us again." He raged on about extremism, loyalty, and conspiracies. "We are patriots!" he screamed. "Do you hear me? *We are patriots!*"

Dad paused for a minute and took another sip of scotch. "Your Mother and I have dedicated ourselves to saving this country," he continued. "We will do just that and no one—I tell you, no one—will stop us. By God, I'll stay in the fight until my dying breath. We do this for our God and for our country!"

No one moved. No one said anything. I had to remind myself to breathe.

Mother broke the silence. "Children, we are under attack. You father and I have no time for trouble with any of you. Disobey and you will be punished."

Then she spoke directly to Jay R. and to me. "People will talk," Mother said. "It's up to you two to defend your parents and the Birch Society. We expect your complete cooperation."

In the morning, mother's warnings followed me out of the house, onto the bus, and into my history class. My current-events teacher, Sister Anna Raphael, loved controversy, and I knew she'd be talking Birch that day. She never missed an opportunity to be "up to date," as she liked to say. As I expected, she passed around the issue of *Life* so everyone could take in the photo. The giggles and the snide whispers stung so much; I put my head down on my desk and pretended I was on another planet.

Luckily, I had my three friends. "People will forget," Kathy told me. "In twenty years, no one will even recognize you." I prayed she was right. But in 1961, I could barely think about next week, let alone twenty years down the road.

Meanwhile, on the national front, the publicity in *Life* had added fuel to the fire of Birch criticism that had been raging all year.

Between early 1961 and the middle of 1962, *Time* ran thirty-three articles about Birchers, while the *New York Times* published over 250 articles, another dozen or so on Robert Welch, and another twenty that connected the Birchers to Southern opposition to the civil rights movement. JBS was also prominent in articles elsewhere about the rising right wing.

In the *Chicago Tribune*, there were over 150 JBS mentions, including a number of feature articles. The *Boston Globe* reported on the Birchers more than 300 times.

In March of 1961, *Time* described the Birch Society as a "tiresome, comic-opera joke" and *The Politician* as "Welch's *Mein Kampf*."[22] A month later, *Time* reported on Welch's speech in Los Angeles, where 6,658 people in the Shrine Auditorium heard him declare that "some 7,000 members of the U.S. clergy were Communists or Communist sympathizers."[23]

On April 2, 1961, my father offered a ferocious defense of the John Birch Society at a meeting in Chicago. The *Chicago Tribune* quoted him as saying, "I would be glad to answer, under oath, and with a polygraph strapped to me, the question of whether there is anything secret, sinister, or un-American about the John Birch society. My answer would be a flat no."[24]

Later that month, the *Tribune* covered a Chicago meeting where an organizer for the JBS, Kent Courtney, hoped that "the group will start a third political party."[25] It's a safe bet that my father was one of the Birch leaders in that room.

"Birch Unit Pushes Drive on Warren" hit the front page of the *New York Times* on April 1. In that article, Bryton Barron, a paid Birch coordinator, explained that Chief Justice Earl Warren had "voted 92 per cent of the time in favor of Communists and subversives" and so deserved to be removed from the bench.[26]

An April editorial in the *Times* called the JBS the "latest publicized addition to the lunatic fringe of American life."[27] The piece continued, "John Birchers are busily looking for Communists in the White House, the Supreme Court, the classroom, and, presumably, under the bed."

One attack in particular really smarted. The U.S. assistant attorney general declined to investigate the Birchers, saying, "The cadre of the John Birch Society seems to be formed of wealthy businessmen, retired military officers and little old ladies in tennis shoes."[28] This sarcastic smack hung on for years. I was still hearing about "little old ladies in tennis shoes" when I was in college.

Most of the attacks, however, were not funny. In early 1961, Robert Welch acknowledged that in two weeks more than a hundred newspapers had run articles hostile toward the society. One editorial in the *Los Angeles Times* described the Society as "bitterly critical and condemnatory."[29]

In his book about Barry Goldwater, Rick Perlstein depicted the situation like this: "By April of 1961, you had to have been living in a cave not to know about Robert Welch and his John Birch Society. The daily barrage of reports left Americans baffled and scared at this freakish power suddenly revealed in their midst. It also left some eager to learn where they could sign up."[30]

Despite the hostile environment, Robert Welch agreed to appear on *Meet the Press*, two weeks after the *Life* magazine article dropped. During the interview, Welch refused to walk back his accusations of treason against President Eisenhower. Instead, Welch framed the entire controversy as a "brazen violation of *my* property rights." He insisted that the book *The Politician* was his property and releasing it without his permission had constituted an invasion of his personal property rights.

Later in the interview, Welch claimed that he was able to "smell out a communist." And in the concluding segment, he defended the nonprofit educational status of the JBS, asserting that it took no part in political campaigns. He went on to admit, however, that two-thirds of the membership had worked for Goldwater during the 1960 primary.[31]

After that appearance, my father blamed the liberal press for conspiring against Welch. "Always gotcha questions," Dad said. "They could make God himself sound like a fool."

At the time, it seemed that my father harbored no concerns about Welch. Everything I heard at home indicated that Dad, along with the entire JBS council, composed a staunch, unwavering Robert Welch support squad.

It came as a big shock to me when Robert Welch exposed, in great detail, a plot to remove him as JBS leader. Writing in the February 1962 society bulletin, he described the effort as one of the Communists' "steps in the projected destruction of the John Birch Society," followed by five pages of details about who, what, and when.[32]

Welch traced the effort to get rid of him to a "prominent publisher of a conservative magazine," who was suggesting that the JBS was a "wonderful group of people, if they would only get rid of Bob Welch and his dictatorial control."[33] I was sure this was a slam at Bill Buckley and his *National Review*, even though Buckley wasn't specifically named.

Welch described what happened next in the effort to remove him from leadership: "It spread to a few strongly anti-Communist members of both the [U.S.] House and the Senate, and even to a few members of our COUNCIL."[34] In June and September of 1961, proposals were made that Welch "step aside and let somebody else take over . . . so as to give it [JBS] a new 'image' not affected by the smears against myself."

The council, after lengthy discussion, realized that "the proposal was unrealistic," Welch wrote. " . . . Even the very few who thought otherwise have now to feel that at least it is impractical."

Welch was firmly in control. As he said, "A monolith is a pretty firm body. Do you know any other body in America today that now shows signs of being able to stand up permanently against their external pressures and *internal infiltration?*"[35]

In April of 1962, JBS released a statement that had been approved by the council: "We have every confidence in Robert Welch and never for a moment have thought of replacing him or rejecting his leadership. We have not been frightened nor discouraged by the frantic efforts of the conspiracy to destroy him and the Society and are resolved more than ever to support him and the principles upon which the Society is built until the battle is won and the Communist menace has passed."[36]

Twenty-one members of the council approved that resolution. Six thought it went too far. I never knew how my father voted.[37]

All of this internal hullabaloo did not keep my dad from his Birch activities. On February 25, 1962, he spoke at the forum of the Unitarian Church of

Evanston.[38] I thought that was amazing; my father always called the Unitarians "the one-worlders' church."

Then, in late June, Dad moderated a daylong seminar on Communism and "Americanism" in Chicago. Two thousand, yes, two *thousand*, people packed the Flick-Reedy Auditorium, where they learned that the JBS was "the best program to save America from insolvency, socialism and surrender."[39]

Despite enduring almost two years of scrutiny and criticism, my father remained the Chicago face of the John Birch Society.

Chapter Ten

The Uncivil War

A month after *Life* hit the newsstands, I was still studying my picture. Did I look fat? Did I look cross-eyed? How would I ever get my hair into a smooth pageboy? The longer I looked, the more I hated my suit. I decided it made me look dowdy and stiff.

I fretted, secretly. One day I discovered that my mother was also fretting. "We've been victimized," she said. "They used the worst possible shot. Look at your father's arm. It's not anywhere near his heart."

I understood. I hated my picture because I looked fat and ugly; my mother hated the picture because Dad looked un-American. His right hand should have been over his heart during the Pledge—anyone who saw the picture would know that.

When Mother mentioned her concern, my father argued with her. "I don't give a damn," he said. "The pictures mean nothing. The real smear is in the editorial."

That night, I read the editorial carefully. In "The Unhelpful Fringes," the Birchers were characterized as extremists led by an "extremist [Robert Welch] . . . who believes that forms of government don't matter much, since all government is dangerous to liberty; the quantity is what matters."[1]

Birchers were denounced as desperate and pessimistic, a group using a "patriotic foam of uncompromising war on Communism, at home and abroad." According to *Life*, the basic problem for the Birchers was "how to combat a monolithic Soviet enemy with an 18th Century-style minimum government and budget." The society was summed up in the word "lunacy." I had to admit that Dad had this one pegged right: the real criticism of the JBS was not in the photos; it was ninety-two pages earlier in the feature editorial.

Wow, was I grateful that Sister Anna Raphael had focused on the photographs. It also helped that school was out for summer vacation. I told myself that the uproar around the JBS would die down before school started in the fall. It just had to.

The June 10 edition of the *Chicago Tribune* dashed my pipe dream. On page six, I read, "Hint Pentagon to Reprimand Gen. Walker: Chiefs Get Report on Anti-Red Drive."[2] Any good Bircher, especially one living in the

Conner house, understood the significance of that headline: the Kennedy administration had the Birchers' favorite general in its crosshairs.

Edwin A. Walker, a two-star army general and a JBS member, had enjoyed a storied military career as a combat veteran of both World War II and the Korean War. In 1959 he was named commander of the 24th Infantry Division in Germany, where he developed his "Pro-Blue" troop training program, designed to educate soldiers about the evils of Communism. Walker incorporated Birch materials into this program and advised his soldiers how to vote.[3] According to witnesses, Walker also accused both former President Truman and Eleanor Roosevelt of being "pinko," a common euphemism for having Communist leanings. The general's comments and the contents of his "Pro-Blue" program made the front page of the *Overseas Weekly*, a tabloid that Walker described as "immoral, unscrupulous, incompetent, and destructive." Shortly after the article was published, the general was suspended from duty.[4]

The Walker saga escalated all throughout the summer. Finally, the general was admonished by the Department of Defense for failing to "heed cautions by superior officers to refrain from . . . controversial activities," leading the JBS to scream about muzzling the military.[5]

Historian Jonathan Schoenwald explained the reasons behind uproar: "After the disappointment of Eisenhower's relatively liberal presidency, conservatives expected JFK's tenure to be even worse. But no one believed their government would go so far as to discharge anticommunist generals whose job was fighting communism."[6]

In his book *Cruising Speed*, Bill Buckley put it more colorfully: "General Edwin Walker . . . betrayed a Birchite ignorance of any distinctions, shored up by his indecipherably documented certainty that everyone in sight was an agent of the Communist Party."[7]

For Americans today, General Walker and his "pro-Blue" program have been relegated to the dustbin of American history. But in 1961, he was a headliner. His plight—as a brave anti-Communist destroyed by his own government—resonated with the Right. For many, including my parents, Walker was proof positive that un-American elements lurked high in the government, high enough to destroy the career of a general in the U.S. Army.

All summer I watched and listened as my dad defended Walker and the JBS against all critics. For Dad, there was no other option; he'd never abandon that "great cause" of his life, as he called the Birch Society. He'd sworn, many times over, to live for—or, if necessary, die for—that cause. As I'd gotten older, I'd dismissed a lot of my father's rhetoric as overly dramatic, but by the end of August, I saw another reality: my father was paying a high price for his JBS obsession.

My first clue was Rolaids. Rolls and bottles in the bathroom, on his bedroom dresser, in the corner of the kitchen counter, on the dining-room table. He also had a stash of prescriptions for his "fussy belly" and Alka-Seltzer for quick relief from indigestion.

I noticed his nervous mannerisms, usually preceding a fit of temper: drumming fingers, pursing lips, narrowed eyes. I heard him pace the floor in the living room and raise his voice to my mother. Sometimes he forgot to kiss Mother before taking his place at the table—a dramatic departure from the norm.

One day, I overheard him arguing on the phone. "No, I won't," he said. "God damn it, I won't compromise for a few bucks and you know it." He slammed the phone down and looked over at me. "Don't eavesdrop again," he said.

I figured that Dad was talking to one of his business partners and things were not going well. "Thanks to that socialist in the White House, the economy stinks," was Dad's mantra. Kennedy made a perfect scapegoat, but I wondered about the impact of the JBS. It seemed to me that being the face of an organization labeled as crackpot couldn't be helping.

I felt sorry for my father, and I tried to stay out of his way. Dad was volatile even on the best day, but when things were bad, he was a tinderbox. School couldn't start soon enough for me.

———

I lived in a white world.

Everywhere I went, from school to church, the country club to the grocery store, I saw almost all white faces. The only exceptions were the women who worked as maids, a few busboys at the country club, and the handymen who did odd jobs.

I was a good citizen growing up in the Land of Lincoln. I knew that Honest Abe was born in a one-room log cabin, became the sixteenth president of the United States in 1861, and was shot to death by John Wilkes Booth six days after the Civil War ended. I knew that the North fought to keep the union together and end slavery, while the South fought for states' rights. I could recite every word of the Gettysburg Address and sing the first three stanzas of "The Battle Hymn of the Republic."

And I could write everything I knew about being black in America on the palm of one hand.

By the time I was sixteen, I had known, by name, only four African Americans: Maddie and Alberta, our maids; Olie, the housekeeper in Gloucester, and her husband, Brooks.

Growing up, I was expected to call all adults Mr., Mrs., or Miss followed by their last name. So Robert Welch was always Mr. Welch, our family friend Ellen White was always Mrs. White, and so on. "It's courteous and respectful," my mother explained. "Children do not address adults by their first names." The rule did not apply to African Americans, however. They were always called by first names; I did not even know their last names.

I heard white people use the n-word in casual conversation, but Mother said the word was vulgar. Mother preferred "colored" to describe black Americans. I thought myself highly evolved because I used "Negro," just like my teachers did.

This question of what to call African Americans ignored the real issue: African Americans in the South—and in many parts of the North—were second-class citizens. As a white girl, living on Chicago's affluent North Side, I had no experience of second-class.

All of that changed in the fall of 1961. My teacher for junior English, a laywoman with a love of fiction, introduced me to her "restricted" shelf. On it, she had a collection of extraordinary books, each camouflaged with a carefully folded brown-paper cover. On the spine, she had printed "Honors English." She and I made a bargain: as long as all of my grades were As or Bs, I had access to that treasure trove. Bad marks in geometry or chemistry would cost me my reading privileges. I made sure that didn't happen.

My teacher never told me in advance what book she'd selected. One time it was *Catcher in the Rye*; another time, *1984*. Of all the books she shared with me that year, the one that moved me the most was John Howard Griffin's *Black Like Me*. I read the first two sentences of the preface: "This may not be all of it. It may not cover all of the questions, but it is what it is like to be a Negro in the land where we keep the Negro down,"[8] and I knew my parents would be enraged if they ever discovered that I'd read this book. From past experience at Regina High, I knew they'd take their fury out on my teacher and me. So I read *Black Like Me* in study hall and stowed it in my locker for safekeeping.

Griffin, a white writer from Texas, dyed his skin black and for thirty-seven days traveled through Louisiana, Mississippi, Alabama, and Georgia to experience life as a black man. After a month of struggling for his basic needs—a restroom, a drink of water, a meal, a place to sleep—Griffin wrote, "My skin was dark. That was sufficient reason for them to deny me those rights and freedoms without which life . . . becomes a matter of little more than animal survival."[9]

I'd never struggled to find a restroom or a drinking fountain. I'd never been refused a table in a restaurant or a seat on the bus. I couldn't grasp being beaten for no reason or being threatened for looking at a white person. No one had ever said to me, "What're you doing in here, nigger?"[10]

Griffin made me feel those things. He also forced me to discard many of my notions about being black in America. Before *Black Like Me*, I thought that anyone could make it in America with hard work and perseverance. I imagined African Americans living like I did, well, except for smaller houses and smaller bank accounts. I had seen Chicago's skid row and tenements, but I assumed that only drunks and bums fell that far. Where they landed was their own fault.

When I finished *Black Like Me*, I wondered if Griffin was right when he said, "I like to see good in the white man . . . but after this experience, it's hard to find it in the Southern white."[11] That Griffin didn't indict the Northern whites gave me some comfort.

After reading Griffin's book, I paid more attention to the women who worked in our house three days a week. For the first time, I noticed the Ace bandages wrapped around Alberta's knees. One day, I saw her, on all fours, washing the kitchen floor. She was humming. When she realized I was standing by the doorway, she stopped.

"What is that?" I asked. Alberta sat back on her heels and in a haunting alto voice sang, "Swing low, sweet chariot. Coming for to carry me home." I realized that I did know that song, but I'd never heard it sung like that. When she finished, she picked up her rag and went back to scrubbing. Later, I wondered if she needed help getting to her feet, and I was angry at myself for not offering my arm.

Our maid Maddie had large arthritic knots on the joints of her fingers, and I knew the ironing had to be hard on her. I'd heard Mother scold her about a scorched handkerchief or pillow case, and I worried if Maddie would be let go. But I said nothing.

Mother could have hired younger maids, but she never did. Every Monday, Tuesday, and Friday, for as long as we lived in Chicago, Maddie and Alberta rode the bus from the South Side, came in our back door, and went to work.

One afternoon, I saw Alberta and Maddie getting on the CTA bus heading home just as I was getting off my bus from Evanston. I watched as the two women dropped their coins into the fare bucket and go to the back of the bus.

They stood while the bus pulled from the curb. Plenty of seats were empty, but the women didn't sit.

That was the day I stopped placing all racial problems south of the Mason-Dixon line. I began to wonder what was happening in Chicago.

———

I wasn't entirely clear about race and inequality, but I was sure of one thing: I could not discuss my feelings with my parents. They were coming from a very different place, the one I'd heard at scores of John Birch Society meetings.

From the very first meeting of the JBS, in 1958, Robert Welch had talked about racial issues being "fomented almost entirely by the Communists to stir up such bitterness between whites and blacks in the South . . . that small flames of civil disorder would inevitably result. They could then fan and coalesce these little flames into one great conflagration of civil war."[12]

Those "little flames" included the confrontation in Little Rock, Arkansas, in September of 1957 between Governor Orval Faubus and President Eisenhower. Faubus used the Arkansas National Guard to keep nine African American students out of Central High School, but the president federalized those troops, put them under the command of General Edwin Walker—yes, that same Walker—and deployed them to keep those students safe.[13] Eventually, the Arkansas schools were integrated; President Eisenhower got himself some enemies, including Robert Welch; and General Walker became "credible" to right-wingers when he talked about civil rights.[14]

In *The Politician*, the scathing attack on Eisenhower that thrust the JBS into the national headlines, Welch wrote, "A most interesting subject for detailed study would be Eisenhower's role in connection with the segregation storm in the South; his part in bringing about that storm, in subtly promoting its increasing violence, and in steering it towards the ultimate objective of his Communist bosses who planned the whole thing far in advance."[15]

Welch castigated Eisenhower for Little Rock and further argued that the situation arose as a result of Ike's greatest sin: the appointment of Earl Warren as chief justice of the Supreme Court. The magnitude of that choice had become clear in 1954 when Warren handed down the *Brown v. Board of Education* decision, which held that racially segregated schools were inherently unequal. For Welch, this ruling was "the most brazen and flagrant usurpation of power that has been seen, in a major court in the whole Anglo-American system of jurisprudence, in three hundred years."[16]

The vitriol against Warren evolved into the JBS "Movement to Impeach Earl Warren." On January 1, 1961, Welch announced this new project, writing, "We are aware that the whole Supreme Court is a nest of social-ists and worse. . . . A *successful* impeachment of Earl Warren would 'put the fear of God' in the whole pro-Communist hierarchy that already controls our government."[17]

My parents and the members of our local chapter embraced the Im-peach Earl Warren project enthusiastically. Meeting after meeting that year explored the horrors of forced integration of schools and the terror of the federal government trampling on the right of the Southern states to segregate African Americans in their own schools. Mother and Dad gave full-throated support to all the Jim Crow laws, including keeping public spaces segregated. Private spaces like restaurants, movie theatres, motels, and shops had the absolute right to keep their whites-only designations.

The Birch Society was not alone in defending the segregated South. In 1960, *National Review*, William F. Buckley's magazine, editorialized, "In the Deep South the Negroes are, by comparison with whites, retarded ('unad-vanced,' the NAACP might put it). Any effort to ignore the fact is sentimen-talism and demagoguery. Leadership in the South, then, quite properly, rests in White hands."[18]

In the first months of 1961, Welch crisscrossed the United States, urging his followers to get on the Impeach Earl Warren bandwagon. "If we cannot impeach Earl Warren," Welch said, "I doubt we can save America."[19]

Welch never said that Warren was a Communist. But he came close. During an interview in Tulsa, where he had been the keynote speaker at the Christian Crusade Convention, he was asked whether he thought Warren was a Communist. "I have no idea," he said. "I have no way of knowing. We're not going to run down specific facts—that's the F.B.I's job—but we can draw an over-all conclusion."[20]

In the same interview, Welch suggested that the move to impeach War-ren was behind most of the criticism of the JBS. "Somewhere behind the scenes," he said, "a button was pushed and a violent and wild attack was begun on us."[21]

The biggest push in the Warren project was a petition drive, planned to be so gigantic that it would force Congress to initiate impeachment pro-ceedings against the chief justice. The goal was ten million signatures, to be gathered before January of 1962.[22] That gave the JBS six months to do the impossible: collect signatures from almost 10 percent of the eligible voters in the entire country.

This petition drive became the be-all and end-all of activity in our house. Mother mustered as many JBS members as she could to go door-to-door. She called and counted and called some more, but the results were underwhelming.

What happened in Chicago must have happened all over the country. January came and went; Welch never reported on how many signatures were collected. Mother gathered up the remnants of the petition drive and stored them in our basement closet. My parents echoed Welch's insistence that the continuing media attacks on the JBS arose from the Impeach Warren project. "The god-damned liberal press is trying to kill the society," Dad said.

The empty chairs on Birch meeting nights proved the attacks were working. Sometimes Mother waited in the living room for hours, arranging and rearranging the handouts and scratching notes to herself on her clipboard before she would accept the reality—no one was coming. Birchers were wilting under the heat of the negative press. I couldn't blame them: they'd signed up to save the country and ended up being tagged as crackpots and cranks.

My parents grew more paranoid. They attributed the newest Birch attacks to those "secret" Communists Welch had mentioned in the founding meeting of the JBS. "One of the hardest things for the ordinary decent American to realize is that a secret Communist looks and acts just like anybody else, only more so. . . ," Welch wrote. "Highly placed secret Communists . . . are something with which we are absolutely loaded."[23]

My father believed that these "secret" Communists were organized in "secret cells" and just when they were needed, they'd be activated. Welch believed that we had six years before the Communists took control; but my parents were less confident. They were among those folks Welch described as "alarmed that they [the Communists] may actually take us over in six months' time."[24]

I knew—even though it was hard to admit—that I was moving in a different direction. I didn't worry so much about Communists coming in six months, or in six years. I worried that my parents would discover my secret: I wasn't their perfect little Bircher anymore. I had ideas, ideas that put me in the other camp—the bleeding-heart, left-wing, liberal camp. *Black Like Me* had started something. . . .

For the first time in my life, I had indigestion. When my stomach was upset, I chewed Rolaids or chugged Pepto-Bismol right out of the bottle. I had headaches so often that I kept even more aspirin in my purse and next to my bed. I had trouble sleeping. "You have black circles under your eyes," Mother said. "Stop reading at night."

Chapter Eleven

Here We Go Again and Again and Again

While my friends got in trouble for typical teenage shenanigans: drinking, ditching school, dinging up the car, I got in trouble for ideas contrary to Conner family dogma. Early in my junior year, I inadvertently brought down the wrath of the Sioux Avenue thought police by doing my homework.

That year, my religion teacher was enamored of Pope John XXIII and spent several days discussing his sixth encyclical, *Mater et Magistra* (*Mother and Teacher*). In this letter to the faithful, the Pope "urged wealthy nations to "balance the differences between excessive production and misery and hunger." Pope John went on to decry the plight of workers who are "paid wages which condemn them and their families to subhuman conditions of life."[1]

At the end of the discussion, we were assigned to write an essay on practical ways to fight poverty. I wrote about using food surpluses, through the Food for Peace program, to feed hungry children in Africa, Asia, and Latin America. I applauded President Kennedy for doubling food grants to needy Americans at home and expanding programs to reduce starvation abroad.[2] When Sister returned my essay, I smiled at my A, stowed the paper in one of my three-ring binders, and forgot all about it.

Several weeks later, Mother and Dad called me to the dining room. "Sit," Dad told me. "What the hell is this?" He pushed my poverty essay across the table toward me. The two scowling faces told me I was in big trouble.

I had no idea where they'd found my paper, but I knew better than to ask. My father, in his role as inquisitor, demanded my complete attention. "You listen to me, girlie," he hissed. "I want an explanation."

I could feel a headache behind my right eye.

"You are not fit to be our daughter," Mother said.

I felt tears and wiped my eyes.

My father pounced. "You know how I feel about crying. Stop right now or I'll give you something to cry about." He stood and started to unbuckle his belt. "What were you thinking?" he screamed as he stalked toward me.

My father belonged to the 1950s school of child-rearing, where using a hand or belt to make a point was neither unusual nor shocking. Like so many parents, he relied on the biblical principle spare the rod, spoil the child. That night, I had no doubt my father might hit me; he had many times before. My only chance was to stop the situation from escalating by being polite and calm and praying that my mother would stop him before he lost all ability to step on the brakes.

For my part, I tried to explain how I *felt:* children were dying; the United States had more food than we needed, and we should share it. I did not realize that the word "feel" was red to a charging right-wing bull.

"You feel?" my father interrupted. "What do you *know?*"

"She knows nothing," Mother answered. "Or she'd know that government is never the answer. Private charity is the only moral way to help the poor."

"And you defend foreign aid? Foreign aid has always helped the Communists," my father said.

Dad was repeating what Robert Welch had always said: "This pouring of American billions into foreign countries, to make things easier for the Communists . . . is exactly what the Communists wanted the American government to do. The one surest [*sic*] way in which foreign aid could be ballyhooed successfully, and made permanently acceptable to the American taxpayer, was to present it as a means of opposing Communism."[3]

My father continued. "It's all unconstitutional," he said. "Our framers never intended anything like this." His voice was escalating. Bright pink streaked his cheeks. His tongue darted across his narrow lips.

"I didn't mean anything," I said. "I just *felt* so terrible when I saw the pictures of those starving babies. What if they were American babies?"

Dad slammed his open hand on the table. "I don't care what you *feel*, goddammit, tell me what you *know!* What do you know?"

Dad stood right over me. I braced myself. He leaned into my face. "Answer me, I'm running out of patience."

Finally, my mother said, "Stop, Jay. I don't want you getting any more upset tonight. You know how these scenes irritate your digestion, dear."

My father took a breath and stared at me. After a long pause, he hissed, "Do not try my patience anymore or you'll wish you'd never been born."

———

Many people have a hard time squaring my parents' views with the Catholic Church's positions on social justice. But, in fact, they had a simple justification: a principle called "subsidiarity." This Catholic tenet says, "Nothing should be done by a larger and more complex organization which can be done as well by a smaller and simpler organization. In other words, any activity which can be performed by a more decentralized entity should be."[4]

According to right-wing Catholics in the 1960s and right-wing Catholics today, "This principle is a bulwark of limited government and personal freedom. It conflicts with the passion for centralization and bureaucracy characteristic of the Welfare State."

For many years I pondered this principle against the backdrop of starvation, famine, and increasing poverty. I have yet to meet any right-wing Catholics who could explain why their beloved principle of subsidiarity had never worked.

———

The uproar over my too-liberal essay was short-lived but long-remembered. I took care to store anything remotely controversial in my locker at school. I also tried to erase "I feel" from my vocabulary and replace it with "I think." For a while, I was successful.

In January of 1962, the Birch Society unveiled a new project, one that would become a signature effort for decades: Get US Out! (of the United Nations).[5] "The United Nations has always been an instrument of Communist global conquest and was designed for that purpose," wrote Robert Welch in his announcement of this effort, emphasizing that "the United Nations should not be reformed, but abolished. You don't reform the rats and fleas that spread the bubonic plaque, you wipe 'em out. The guiltily responsible personnel of the United Nations are far worse."

For this new project, Welch enlisted my dad as one of the national spokesmen. In the next few years, Dad traveled across the country to headline anti-UN gatherings. His stump speech, one I heard several times, touted JBS talking points: The UN is a Communist plan to socialize the world. Alger Hiss, an American Communist and member of the State Department, was the main author of the UN charter. My father dubbed the UN as "the house that Hiss built."[6] In addition, he explained, the UN has not been an instrument of peace but rather has facilitated an enormous expansion of the Communist empire. Dad peppered his speech with numerous examples, including the Soviet occupations of Albania, Hungary, Yugoslavia, Rumania, Bulgaria, and Poland, as well as its domination in North Korea, Manchuria, East Germany, Tibet, and Cuba. All of these examples, my father reminded his audiences, occurred after the UN Charter was ratified, in 1945.[7]

Dad took strong exception to the structure of the UN, including, the use of the Security Council veto to ensure that a socialist or Marxist would always be at the head of the organization. Dad insisted that the ultimate goal of the UN, a goal stated by Secretary of State Dean Rusk, was this: "The UN stands, finally, as a symbol of the world order that will one day be built."[8]

Dad always closed with the same words: "We do not need more government; we need less. We do not need the UN Charter; we need the United States Constitution. We do not need the House that Hiss Built; we need the mansion bequeathed by our forefathers. We need to get the United States out of the UN and the UN out of the United States."[9] As his last word rang out, the audience would jump to its feet and applaud. It was not uncommon for the standing ovation to go on for several minutes.

For several years, my father gave this speech in venues across the country. On November 16, 1963, he spoke at the Melodyland Theatre in Anaheim, an auditorium with a 2,300-seat capacity. I don't know if the place was full that night, but I do know that Dad's speech was published by the John Birch Society and distributed in large quantities across the country.

In school, my teacher Sister Anna Raphael announced a class project for current events: a debate for the whole school and parents on the topic "Should Red China Be Admitted to the United Nations?"

This was a hot issue in America that year. Just a few months earlier, after a full-court press by the United States, Red China had been denied a UN seat.[10] Despite that setback, however, the conventional wisdom was that the issue would surface again in 1962. Sister knew all of this and realized that the issue would generate a lot of interest; her project was sure to be a success.

"Oh, God," I thought. "Please, don't assign me to the team."

I could never be on the *Yes* side of the debate. My parents would come unglued if I argued in favor of Communist anything. On the other hand, I didn't want to be on the *No* side. I knew I'd be seen as the Birch spokesperson, and I just didn't want the soapbox. I wanted to be invisible this time.

I saw one way to avoid the assignment: get out of the room.

Luckily, I didn't have to fake feeling ill; I really did have a pounding headache. I reached into my purse for an aspirin, raised my hand, and asked to be excused. In the restroom, the safest hiding place in the whole school, I locked myself in one of the stalls and waited until the end-of-class bell. Then, I merged into the hall crowd and snuck to my next class. For the rest of the day, I stayed as far away as I could from Sister Anna Raphael's room.

"Congratulations," I told myself as I settled on the bus. "You dodged that bullet."

When I got home, Mother was working away at the dining room table surrounded by piles of books, magazines, and newspapers. How she found anything in the perpetual jumble, I had no idea, but she could always put her finger on what she needed. It was uncanny.

I greeted her and headed to the stairs. As I put my foot on the first riser, she called me back. "Sister Anna Raphael phoned about the debate, dear. I gathered some material for you," she said. "There's plenty more if you need it."

"Damn," I thought.

Dinner immediately became the "Why We Hate the United Nations" hour. Mother and Dad pounded away on every bad idea that had its origin in some UN policy or agency. By the time they were finished, I knew all the points in Dad's speech by heart. Then it was a refresher course on all the horrors of Red China under Chairman Mao, including a rewind of the hot-coals story.

"You need to include these details," Mother said.

"Sister won't appreciate that one," I told her.

Undeterred, my mother wrote the gory details on index cards, underlining the points she thought most relevant.

For my parents, the idea of Red China holding membership in the United Nations was ghastly—an affront to freedom and decency. Given the horrendous things Mao did in China, who could possibly disagree?

I became a walking dictionary of all things UN. In addition to knowing the dirt about Alger Hiss, I also knew that there was no mention of God in the UN Charter.[11] I could discuss the secret agreement that the secretary-general always be either a one-world socialist or Marxist/Communist, and I could show the proof: Trygve Lie, a Norwegian socialist; Dag Hammarskjold, a Swedish socialist; and U Thant, a Burmese Marxist. I could talk about the UN plans for complete disarmament of the United States, praised in State Department booklet #7277, *Freedom From War*, along with the plan to disband our military and replace it with a "United Nations Peace Force."[12] And I knew that the United States was paying the lion's share of the bill for all of this.

I had no doubt that I'd find a way to include the views of Barry Goldwater since he had said, "Now is the time for the United States to declare openly that if the United Nations votes to admit Red China, our government will suspend all political and financial support of the United Nations."[13]

I knew all of this and I still didn't want to be in the debate. Sister Anna Raphael, aware of my reluctance, assigned Kathy Durso to be my partner. Kathy, ever the optimist, spotted the plus in the situation: we needed a quiet place to practice.

"Eureka," she said. "We'll have to work at my house all weekend. It's too busy at your place."

I gathered my notes and headed to Lincolnwood. As soon as I dropped my materials in Kathy's room, her mom served up a plate of her fabulous spaghetti and yummy garlic bread. "You can't work on an empty stomach," she insisted. Kathy's mother had always welcomed me. I didn't care that my parents decided to dislike the Dursos; I never missed an opportunity to visit. Many a weekend, if I wasn't grounded, I was at Kathy's.

One of my fondest memories is of Dr. Durso sitting across the table from us, drinking his cocktail and teasing Kathy and me. More times than I can count, he said, "You know, you really are my favorite girl."

"Yes, I am, Dr. D.," I always said.

I never told Kathy or her parents how my parents derided them, calling them "low-class Italians." Mother and Dad put the Dursos on a par with Greeks, "Indians," "Orientals," Jews, and, of course, Negroes. While I hated these slurs, I told myself to keep my mouth shut and get out of the house.

Kathy and I goofed around as much as we worked on our speeches, but we were ready by the night of the debate. We spoke, without notes, and we had so much detail, thanks to my mother, that we overwhelmed the other team. I don't think it hurt that public opinion wasn't favorable to Communists, but we were still tickled when we were declared the winners.

My parents, who hardly ever ventured out to my school activities, were there. "You girls were sharp as tacks," Mother said.

Dad put his arm around me. "You were excellent," he said, "a natural debater, just like your old man."

That night I was proud; I'd lived up to my parents' expectations and I'd been true to myself. I was sure Red China didn't belong in the UN, and I'd argued forcefully for my position. I wasn't ready to toss out the UN completely, but in all honesty, I could understand why my parents thought the organization was hopeless. On the subject of the United Nations, we had reached détente.

When I was a kid, I knew quite a few old people—or people I defined as old. From what I could tell, a lot of them smelled sour, worried about their aches and pains, and despaired of the younger generation. My great-aunt Agnes— my grandmother's youngest sister—was different. She spent her days playing cards, watching her housemate Miss Ernest dig in the flower garden, and telling stories about her career as an executive assistant in downtown Chicago.

When my mother announced that Aunt Agnes had invited me for tea, I threw on my Sunday dress, brushed my hair, and raced across the yard to the little bungalow next door. My aunt and her friend were my favorite old people.

Aunt Agnes taught me to play gin and canasta, for money, while I sipped a concoction she called "Cambric" Tea—tea, sugar, milk, and (in her cup) a dash of "something stronger." From my aunt, I heard family secrets, like the name of my mother's first boyfriend (Dick Thunder) and why Grandpa didn't like my dad at first (Dad was too "fast" for his oldest daughter, Mary Laurene).

I always had to swear that I'd keep everything that she said a secret from my mother and my grandmother. "They lean to the German side of the family," Aunt Agnes said. "Not prone to stories. Me, I take to the Irish."

Sometimes, her stories turned to the "dark days," when money was scarce, poor people stood in long, snaking bread lines, and beggars came to the back door for table scraps. "Old people ate out of garbage cans," she told me. "We tried to help when we could, but times were hard."

Because of my aunt, I realized that the Great Depression was not an abstract history lesson. My aunt had lived it. My grandparents had lived it. My parents had lived it. I understood that every adult I knew had lived it.

Despite the hardships of the Depression, my parents hated every single program passed by President Roosevelt as his New Deal. They railed against Social Security and unemployment compensation for creating "socialism" and making people "dependent on government." For my father and my mother, it was always and only about their notions of the Constitution, our Founding Fathers, and tiny, tiny government.

One afternoon in June of 1962, I found myself fussing with my mother about the Birch meeting that was set to begin in a few hours. I didn't want to attend; she insisted. "The future of the country hangs in the balance," Mother said. "You will be on deck and ready to participate. Or do I need to call your father?"

"I'll be there," I said.

"Yes, young lady, you will," she added. "And get some letters written before dinner."

I went into my bedroom, shut the door, and opened the latest issue of the Birch Society bulletin. On the first page I read Robert Welch's latest analysis of current events. "The dominant feature of life in the United States today is confusion," he wrote, insisting again that the United States would be a police state in three or four years unless the Birchers rode to the rescue.[14]

"Et cetera and et cetera," I thought. "Every month, the same story. Bad government, bad president, coming disaster. I'll just write a couple of letters."

The "Agenda for the Month" told me where to start: "The King-Anderson Bill–Gateway to Socialized Medicine." This was the latest Birch project, and Mother would expect me to write at least one letter opposing this bill.

I picked a name from Welch's list of target congressmen and added the standard address, House Office Building, Washington, DC. I used Welch's own words as my reason to oppose the bill. "The King-Anderson Bill is simply one significant part of the whole intensive drive of the Kennedy Administration to continue and complete the conversion of the United States into a socialist nation. *It is basically an extension, in form, as well as in degree, of Social Security.*"[15]

I signed my name, folded the letter, and slid it in an envelope. Next, I wrote to some guy I'd never heard of, a Dr. Blasingame, to thank him for the courageous stand of the American Medical Association against socialized medicine.

Later that evening, a big crowd turned out for the meeting, more than usual. Over the last months, Birch attendance had bounced back, and, judging from the crowd in the living room, the looming threat of socialized medicine was enough to pack the place. I took coats, passed coffee, and handed out materials. When everyone had settled, Mother led the Pledge and then announced, "We'll get right to it."

She dropped a 33 rpm record on the stereo. "For those of you new to the cause, this is a recording done over a year ago," she explained. "It outlines perfectly the danger of the new push to force government health care on the elderly. Listen carefully and then we'll discuss the issue fully."

In a few seconds, the voice of a rising right-wing star—the dashing, engaging, and charming Ronald Reagan—filled the room. I'd heard this record, *Ronald Reagan Speaks Out Against Socialized Medicine*, several times before, so I already knew his main point: Americans would never vote for socialism directly, but we could be taken in by things labeled liberalism.

One of those bad liberal things was the current push to impose "statism" through medicine. Americans could fall for this plot because medicine seemed so "humanitarian," but Reagan knew better. Medical coverage for old people would be the "foot in the door" to socialized medicine.

Real Americans had to wake up and stop this abridgment of freedom. If we didn't fight hard enough, in sad days to come, old people would sit around and tell their children what it was like in the good old days when "men were free."[16]

As Reagan's voice faded, several Birchers clapped enthusiastically.

Mother picked up on Reagan's themes with additional information on the perils of government health care. "The elderly in America are just fine under the current system," she explained. "Government health care is unnecessary, expensive, and anti-American. It costs too much and threatens our freedom."

While the arguments against government-run health care continued, my mind drifted to a story my friend Bob had told me. When he was a toddler, his father took him to a big hospital in the city to visit one of his relatives. The little boy held his father's hand tight as they walked a long, noisy, crowded corridor. "In here, son," Mr. Besse said. "This is Aunt Maude's ward."

Bob gripped his father's hand tighter. "I don't like it here," he said.

"I know. But we have to stay awhile. She's old and sick. We're all she's got. Everyone else is in Sterling, where she used to live. You know, with Grandpa Besse."

"Send her back there," little Bob said.

"We can't," his dad explained. "This is the only place for her."

Mr. Besse led his son along a row of hospital beds. They stopped in front of a shrunken old lady curled on her side. She never moved or spoke, just moaned. After a few minutes, Mr. Besse leaned over, kissed Aunt Maude on the cheek, and turned toward the doorway.

"To this day, I remember the smell and the moaning," Bob had told me. "Those poor people languished there until they died. Without money, charity wards were their only option."[17]

I looked at the folks in the living room and assumed that none of them would die in the charity ward of Cook County General Hospital. Hating government-run health care was easy when your doctor made house calls and your hospital stays were in private rooms.

I snapped out of my thoughts as Mother was quoting a letter Reagan had written in 1960 to Richard Nixon about the up-and-coming John Kennedy. "Reagan knew the score," Mother said. "He recognized JFK for what he is. 'Under the tousled boyish haircut,' Reagan said, 'it is still old Karl Marx.'"[18]

———

Eighteen years later, just before Halloween, I parked myself in front of the TV to watch the debate between President Jimmy Carter and Republican nominee Ronald Reagan. Late in the discussion, when the issue of health care took the spotlight, Carter reminded the audience of Reagan's long-standing opposition to Medicare: "Governor Reagan began his political career campaigning around this nation against Medicare."[19]

The president then moved to a full defense of national health-care reform. "Now, we have an opportunity to move toward national health insurance, with an emphasis on the prevention of disease, an emphasis on out-patient care, not in-patient care; an emphasis on hospital cost containment to hold down the cost of hospital care for those who are ill; an emphasis on catastrophic health insurance, so that if a family is threatened with being wiped out economically because of a very high medical bill, then the insurance would help pay for it. These are the kinds of elements of a national health insurance, important to the American people."

Carter completed his argument with these words, "Governor Reagan, again, typically is against such a proposal."

Before I could clap my hands in agreement, Ronald Reagan looked over at the president, smiled, and said, "There you go again."

By the time Reagan had finished his response, even I, who knew better, almost fell for the idea that he supported Medicare and always had. Then, I remembered the velvet voice on that scratchy record urging all Americans to oppose Medicare. "If you don't do it," Reagan said, "one of these days, you and I are going to spend our sunset years telling our children and our children's children what it once was like in America when men were free."[20]

Chapter Twelve
The End of the World

In August of 1962, my brother Jay R. stuffed clothes and books in his suitcase while I thumbed through his record albums. "I love this one," I said when I came to the Kingston Trio's . . . *From the Hungry i*. May I keep it?"

"Sister of mine," he said smiling, "my albums are yours, until I get home next summer. Then, of course, they are mine again."

With that, Jay R. intoned one of our favorite Kingston Trio hits, "The Merry Minuet," a happy little tune about nuclear war and pestilence. "They're rioting in Africa . . . ," he sang, and I joined right in. Together, we did all the verses and ended on a flourish: "What nature doesn't do to us, will be done by our fellow man."[1]

"You're such a jerk," I teased my college-bound brother. "And I'll miss you."

"I'll miss you, too, but not to worry—as long as no one pushes the button, I'll be home for Christmas."

Over the next few weeks, I had plenty of opportunity to think about my brother's "button" comment. Soviet premier Nikita Khrushchev seemed determined to flex every muscle he had, up to and including the threat of nuclear war. On September 12, 1962, the *Chicago Tribune* reported on its front page that the Soviet Union had "warned the United States that an armed attack on the Marxist outpost in the Caribbean [Cuba] would plunge the world into a nuclear war."[2]

As the tensions between our country and the USSR escalated, news reports, magazine articles, and everyday people talked about A-bombs, H-bombs, nuclear annihilation, and doomsday. People were on edge; people were afraid. Except at my house.

My father put it like this: "There are worse things than nuclear war."

"What could be worse than blowing up the earth?" I asked.

"That's just what the Communists want you to think."

"Dad, nuclear war would be disastrous for all of us."

"You're talking nonsense," he retorted. "We don't know what would happen."

"We do," I told him. "Look at Hiroshima and Nagasaki."

Dad shrugged and turned away.

My father's views came directly out of the JBS school of history. Just like Robert Welch, Dad believed that "the conspiracy" had placed a web of "Insiders" deep within our government, where they steered American foreign and domestic policy toward Communist objectives. They accomplished this with a sleight-of-hand trick Robert Welch dubbed "the principle of reversal."

Here, I'll let Welch speak for himself: "Although our danger remains almost entirely internal, from Communist influences right in our midst and treason right in our government, the American people are being persuaded that our danger is from the outside, from Russian military superiority. And under the excuse of preparing to match that military might, of defending ourselves from this threat of outside force . . . we are being stampeded into the biggest jump ever toward, and perhaps the final jump right into socialism and then the Communist camp."[3]

Thus, the conspiracy is tricking us into "greatly expanded government spending for missiles, for so-called defense generally," while "hammering into the American consciousness the horror of modern warfare, the beauties and the absolute necessity of peace—peace always on Communist terms."

The goal of all of this: to "make us domestically a communized nation" and "pull us right into the world-wide Communist organizations, ruled by the Kremlin."[4]

Think of it this way: our government does anti-Communist things that are really pro-Communist, but we the people think they're anti-Communist because the pro-Communists in the government said so. So, military spending is just what the Communists want us to do and nuclear war is not nearly as bad as the Commies say.

When looking at current tensions, my parents leaned on one other Birch commandment: "Better Dead than Red."

For me, however, a child born under the mushroom cloud, I saw things differently. Thanks to my teachers and John Hersey's *Hiroshima*, required reading in my high school, I knew the exact moment the world had gone nuclear—August 6, 1945, at 8:15 a.m. Japanese time.[5] I'd followed as Hersey shared the stories of six citizens of Hiroshima as they endured the nuclear blast and the subsequent illnesses that plagued them. I could imagine the burns, the puss, and the purple blotches caused by radiation exposure. By the time I finished the book, I believed that atomic weapons should never have been built and were too terrible to ever use again.

What I thought had no impact on world leaders. Once Stalin got himself an atomic bomb, the nuclear arms race with the United States was on. When we built one new warhead, the Russians built two. When we "improved" our atomic bomb, the Russians built a hydrogen bomb. Before I was sixteen, the United States and the Soviet Union had enough atomic stuff to kill every living thing three times over.[6]

My parents and Welch believed that we'd been tricked into this arms race. I didn't really care who started it or why. I was afraid that one side would push "the button," the other would retaliate and . . . my brothers, my sisters, my parents, and I would be vaporized.

———

For as long as I could remember, every Tuesday morning at ten, the air-raid sirens went off. The screaming sound sent my classmates and me into the hallway, where we stretched out on our stomachs and folded arms over head. I pressed my check to the cold floor, shut my eyes, and waited. The piercing whine of the siren went on and on and on. When the short blasts of the all-clear finally sounded, I pulled myself to my feet, smoothed my uniform, and filed back to class. "You're safe," I reassured myself. "This is not real."

Sometimes, at the direction of my teacher, we did the "duck and cover," stuffing ourselves under our desks for protection from a nuclear explosion. Every year until I graduated from eighth grade, I saw *Bert the Turtle*, a short movie that taught American children to "duck and cover" in case of nuclear attack.[7]

I don't remember when I began to wonder, "Can my desk really keep me safe from nuclear destruction?" I also don't remember when I answered with a big, fat no.

Following a 1961 plea from President Kennedy to Americans to "prepare for all eventualities," surviving a nuclear attack became big business.[8] People ordered and built personal air-raid shelters and stocked them with dry food and emergency radios.[9] Families were reminded to get first-aid kits and radiation detectors. For citizens who could not afford their own safe rooms, a network of fallout shelters were prepared.

The experts said, "The next world war could be nuclear and it could be fought in the United States," and Americans believed them.[10] Regardless of the experts, I'd reached my own conclusion about nuclear war: I didn't want to live through the end of the world.

———

In the fall of 1962, reports surfaced about unsettling developments in Cuba. Several thousand Russian soldiers had arrived on the island nation along with tons of supplies. It was assumed that most of those supplies had a military use. The chorus of American voices demanding pushback against the Russians grew.

In mid-October, one of our U-2 reconnaissance planes flying over Cuba photographed what looked like missile silos under construction. Soon after, President Kennedy canceled a campaign trip because of "illness." We didn't know it at the time, but U.S. intelligence agencies had confirmed that Soviet ballistic missiles, missiles that carried nuclear warheads, were being installed in Cuba. It didn't take high-level intelligence to realize that the United States was the main target.[11]

When the Soviet missiles became public knowledge, my parents decided that the whole crisis was a smokescreen. President Kennedy would be made to look like a good anti-Communist, pro-American leader while he secretly opened the door to more Communist power in our hemisphere.

"Another example of the principle of reversal," my father said.

"Another Bay of Pigs in the making," Mother added.

My parents had never trusted Kennedy, but they had become even more certain of his anti-Americanism when 1,300 CIA-trained Cuban freedom fighters were stranded during the Bay of Pigs invasion in April of 1961.[12] From then on, they had ratcheted up their unrelenting anti-Kennedy rant.

They called the president a Commie-dupe, a traitor, a coward, and a liar. And that was just for starters. My parents hated Fidel Castro and John Kennedy in equal measure. Castro for being a Communist and Kennedy for, well, being a Communist too.

Regardless of what they said, however, it became evident that a real crisis was unfolding in the Caribbean. I parked myself in front of the basement television on October 22, 1962, to listen to the president's address from the Oval Office.

From the beginning, Kennedy laid out a strong and terrifying message. After outlining the steps taken to verify the presence of Soviet offensive missiles in Cuba, Kennedy said: "This urgent transformation of Cuba into an important strategic base—by the presence of these large, long range and clearly offensive weapons of sudden mass destruction constitutes an explicit threat to the peace and security of all the Americas."

As the president continued to outline the depth of the Soviets' deception about the weapons, I realized that this situation could easily explode into a world war or world destruction. The calmness of President Kennedy did nothing to soothe me. In fact, it scared me; it was so stark and so definitive.

"Missiles in Cuba add to an already clear and present danger," Kennedy said. "We will not prematurely or unnecessarily risk the cost of worldwide nuclear war in which even the fruits of victory would be ashes in our mouth; but neither will we shrink from that risk at any time it must be faced."[13]

Later that evening, I couldn't fall asleep. I stared at the ceiling while the lyrics of "Merry Minuet" played in my head. I missed my brother so much; I wanted to sing with him, hug him, and be with him if the worst happened. The next day, the naval blockade of Cuba began and orders to sink any ships attempting to run the quarantine line were given.[14]

In school, we were back to the old "duck and cover" drills. I knew that a missile strike anywhere near Chicago would kill us all, but the adults seemed to think that something was better than nothing. I dutifully stuffed myself under my desk, bent from the waist, and covered my head. It was hot and uncomfortable and quiet, except for the occasional nervous giggle.

Later that day, I went to Confession. As a good Catholic girl, I was terrified of dying with unforgiven sins on my soul; the Catholic sacrament of Penance promised to wash me clean. Afterward, during Mass, I knelt and prayed for my family and my country. I begged for blessings on the president. I hoped God had some brilliant strategy ideas for him—no one else seemed to.

That day, President Kennedy authorized the loading of nuclear weapons onto our bombers and the DEFCON (the defense readiness condition) level was raised to 2, the highest it had ever been.[15] "This really is it," I told myself. I fell asleep with my rosary in my hand.

In the morning, when I wasn't dead, I worried even more. "Will it be today?"

I watched television whenever I could. The reports didn't ease my worries, but I had to know. When we learned that Kennedy had received a proposal from Russia that could diffuse the situation, my parents went into hyperdrive.

"See, he's giving in," Mother cried. "We are doomed."

"They'll kill us anyway," my father insisted. "Nothing can stop the Commies now."

Finally, on Monday, October 29, after a week of public skirmishes and behind-the-scenes negotiations, our president agreed to remove old missiles we had in Italy and Turkey, and Khrushchev agreed to dismantle the missiles he had in Cuba. Diplomacy had won a big Cold War battle.[16]

Everyone in the country breathed a sigh of relief—well, not quite everyone. After the crisis, my parents were even more disgusted with John Kennedy. They believed that he'd surrendered to Khrushchev and that those missiles were still in Cuba, loaded and ready to strike.

"The whole Cuban Missile Crisis was fabricated," Mother said.

"Kennedy is a Commie through and through," Dad added.

———

As far as my parents and their Birch friends were concerned, the Bay of Pigs and the Cuban Missile Crisis were the ultimate proof that the president was both a traitor and a coward. My father contrasted the words and actions of the Kennedy administration with the words of a "real" American, Barry Goldwater. At JBS meetings, Dad would read whole sections of *The Conscience of a Conservative*, Goldwater's conservative manifesto. As much as his prescriptions for America resonated with the Birchers, the last section of the book, "Our Goal Must Be Victory," seemed to be everyone's favorite.

In it, Goldwater emphasized the need for the United States to take the offense against the Communists with weapons of our own choosing, especially "small, clean nuclear weapons."[17] He knew we had to be powerful, no matter the cost—in lives or money.

In a nod to anti-Communists everywhere, Goldwater said that the United States "should withdraw diplomatic recognition from all Communist governments" while we "encourage the captive nations to revolt against their Communist rulers."[18]

Goldwater might have co-opted this plan to foment revolution from Robert Welch, who had called for JBS "undertakings on the international front."[19] Those "undertakings" would be "the setting up, or helping to set up, one by one and very carefully, governments-in-exile out of the most respected and solidly anti-Communist refugees from satellite nations." If no such leader was available for this task, Welch suggested establishing "revolutionary committees."[20] These groups, according to Welch, would be "rallying points for a far more energetic opposition to Communist maneuvers and propaganda."[21]

Welch didn't go quite as far as Goldwater, however, who believed that "our strategy must be primarily offensive in nature" and that "we must—ourselves—be prepared to undertake military operations against vulnerable Communist regimes."[22] We could even move a "highly mobile task force equipped with appropriate nuclear weapons to the scene of the revolt."[23]

Like my father, Senator Goldwater never shirked from war talk. "Any policy that successfully frustrates the Communists' aim of world domination runs the risk that the Kremlin will choose to lose in a kamikaze-finish," Goldwater said.[24]

Dad usually ended his pro-Goldwater pep talks with this quote: "For Americans who cherish their lives, but their freedom more, the choice cannot be difficult."[25]

"Barry is absolutely right," my father always said. "'War may be the price of freedom.'"[26]

———

One evening shortly after the Cuban Missile Crisis, my parents called me into the living room. "Your father and I have something important to discuss with you," Mother said. I'd barely taken a seat when they got right to it.

"Something important" was this—Dad's business was struggling and money was tight. It was time to look at expenses, including the costs of educating five kids. They reminded me, as if I didn't know, that my brother was in a Catholic college, my sister and I were in a Catholic high school, and the two little kids were in a Catholic grade school.

"Something has to give," Dad said.

In a minute, it became clear what they could not afford—my college education. My mother spelled it out, "Don't expect any money from us. You'll have to figure this one out, alone."

Making sure I understood just what no money meant, the two of them ticked off every college expense: tuition, room, board, books, transportation, and clothes, while declaring "No" to each one.

"Does Jay R. know about this?" I asked. "What happens to him?"

"He's all set," Mother said. "We have him covered."

I sat in the living room staring at the hideous floor-length flowered drapes. Then I looked at my hands shaking in my lap and tried to swallow the lump in my throat. When I started to sob—deep, sad sobs—I couldn't stop.

Mother and Dad made no effort to comfort me. Not a word, not a hug, nothing. Instead, my father got angry. "Young lady, you know how I feel about tears," he said.

"Stop playing the martyr," Mother added. "Go upstairs."

Sometime later, I finally stopped crying. I tried to figure how much money I would need for my first year of college. One thing was clear: I needed more than my 75-cent per-hour weekend job could bring in. I needed a scholarship, the bigger the better. Most of all, I needed a big miracle—not quite Moses parting the Red Sea, but close.

The next morning I didn't stop at my locker or grab a Coke in the senior lounge. I was looking for advice, advice I couldn't get from my friends. I had to learn everything I could about college scholarships, the bailiwick of Marywood's guidance counselor.

Mrs. Waldron listened to my situation while she passed me tissues to mop up my tears. After a few minutes, she pointed out, gently, that crying would not fix my problem; I needed a plan. She reminded me to focus on school; high grades and high test scores made all the difference in landing scholarships. She also recommended public schools in Illinois; they were the only ones I could possibly afford. Finally, she'd make sure I had great recommendations from my teachers.

By the time I left Mrs. Waldron's office, I was still terrified, but ready to give it the "old college try."

"I can do this myself," I thought. "Just watch me."

At the same time that my parents were refusing to pay even a dime toward my college education, they were demanding that I enroll at the University of Dallas, the school they had selected for me, the same one they had selected (and financed) for Jay R., now a freshman there.

To me, the whole arrangement was completely unjust, unfair, and mean, but my parents didn't give a damn. As Dad said, "Either go to the University of Dallas or don't go to school at all. You decide."

"We found the finest conservative Catholic school in the country for you," Mother said. "It's for your own good."

My parents were convinced that this tiny Catholic school—fifteen miles outside of Dallas—would save me from the clutches of the liberals, Communists, and non-Catholics who peopled the secular universities. I'd be purified with huge doses of orthodox Roman Catholicism and correct political thought.

"Our job is to save your mind and your soul," my father said.

"Your father knows what you need," Mother added.

My parents had committed to the University of Dallas without ever seeing it. Instead, they relied on the recommendation of Robert Morris, the university's former president and one of my father's "associates in the cause," as Mother referred to him. I knew what that meant—Morris was a Bircher.[27]

Morris had taken the reins at the University of Dallas in 1960, but his tenure was short and rocky. He spent so much time speaking at Birch rallies around the country that he neglected the needs of the struggling school.[28] Two years after he arrived, the Board of Trustees sacked him.

My dad didn't care. "UD is the only decent school out there," he maintained.

I had a long list of reasons why the University of Dallas was not the school for me, reasons I pointed out every chance I got. The university had only 275 students, making it smaller than my high school. It was not accredited, offered only a few degrees, and had almost no social life. Worse yet, without a car, I'd be stranded in the boonies of Irving, Texas.

The final argument against the school: my brother was a student. I tried to explain how much I didn't want to be "Jay R. Conner's little sister," especially on a campus with such a tiny student body. My parents were not moved. They loved the university, period.

When I fretted to my school guidance counselor about this, she reminded me to focus. "A scholarship offer will change their minds," she said. I followed her advice: I finished my college applications, took my SATs, and waited.

Early in March of 1963, I caught the early bus. I had several big assignments and wanted to get a start on my homework. When I opened the front door, I saw Mother camped at the dining room table doing research about something or other. "There's a letter for you on the credenza," she told me.

I grabbed the envelope. The first line of the return address was Otto Kerner, Governor. Curious, I slid my thumbnail under the envelope flap, took out the sheets, and began to read.

I'd been chosen as an Illinois State Scholarship winner, one of 1,800 students in the whole state offered a monetary stipend.[29] I rifled through the enclosures: a letter of acceptance, details of the scholarship, and an explanation of renewal requirements. Then I returned to the letter and read it again, word for word.

Reality began to sink in: this award would pay for college, four years of college. It covered $600 per year—$600. I'd need some spending money and clothes, but I could figure that out. I knew I could.

A couple of hours later, I sat at the dinner table basking in the joy of having a bright future. I paid attention when I heard my mother say, "She got mail from Kerner, the governor. He's liberal scum, that one."

"I want to see it now," my father said.

I waited. In the corner the grandfather clock tick-tocked. My heart pounded in my throat. Mother read the letter and passed it to my father. He read it and passed it back to her.

While I waited, I worried. My father couldn't stand the governor, a situation made worse when Kerner had called the Birchers "dangerous" and then added, "Whatever they are doing and saying is a dangerous thing."[30] Of course, the remarks had been carried in the Chicago papers just a few months earlier. I prayed that my dad would look past the Democratic governor and his anti-Birch stand, and think about me.

"Why was I kept in the dark about this?" Dad asked.

"The guidance counselor and teachers at school recommended me," I explained. "I didn't think I'd win."

Dad's lips were pencil thin, his jaw tight. His face clouded over, and he inhaled deeply. "No child of mine will ever be in that school. I don't care if they're giving away five-dollar bills for four dollars. You know how awful that place is. Dr. Oliver has talked about it hundreds of times."

"How could you?" Mother said to me. "You are a disgrace."

In no time at all, I was begging. I promised to meet my dad's Birch friend Dr. Revilo Oliver on campus. I promised to take only classes he okayed. I even promised to come home every other weekend. I promised anything I could think of. Finally, I blurted out, "If I'm paying, why can't I decide?"

I could hear my father breathing. The seconds passed.

Dad's hand slammed on the table. "Enough!" he screamed. "You are going to the University of Dallas or you'll be out on your ear. Another word and I'll make you regret it."

I knew my father's rages, and I knew he'd get his way, with his belt if necessary. Then, when he was finished, I'd face months of disapproval and recriminations. My mother would support and enforce everything my father ordered.

When my father ordered me to my room to compose a letter declining the scholarship, I obeyed. When he insisted on reading what I wrote, I handed it over. The next day, I left the envelope addressed to Governor Kerner on the dining room table. My mother stamped it and put it in the mail.

I never said another word about the University of Illinois.

Chapter Thirteen
Civil Rights Marching

The black-white matter is still the Great American Obsession.

—Studs Terkel[1]

I resigned myself to reality: in the fall, I'd either be a freshman at the University of Dallas or I'd be in Chicago under my parents' thumbs. With that in mind, UD looked a whole lot better. But, I needed money. That meant a job that paid a lot more than my current part-time retail gig in the neighborhood clothing shop.

Over Easter vacation, I walked up and down Devon Avenue, talking to every manager in every shop. "Nothing now. Try again in a month," was the refrain I heard.

As much as it wounded my pride, I asked my father for help. In a couple of days, he sent me to a friend of a friend who had a few openings.

"What's the job?" I asked.

"Something on the phone," Dad said.

"Where?"

"Downtown in the Greyhound bus station," he told me.

"What does it pay?" I wondered.

"More than you make now."

The next day, I was in the line at the Greyhound bus station on the corner of Clark and Randolph in the heart of Chicago's Loop. A dozen other people were waiting to interview for the information operator position. I worried: I had no skills or experience that applied, even remotely, to bus schedules or fares. I knew nothing of switchboards, and I'd never been on a Greyhound bus, but I needed this job. I swore to the station manager that I'd work hard and learn fast. I nearly fainted when I heard, "You're hired."

My head started to spin when I heard the salary, $2.47 per hour plus overtime. This job gave me a 325 percent pay jump. I decided to tell Dad the good news minus one little detail: I'd just landed a union job.

I went to work a week before I graduated from high school. For the first time in my life, I had a full-time job downtown, punched a clock, and worked with tattooed motorcycle guys, military vets, single women, and many African Americans. I learned right off the bat that a lot of folks didn't think I deserved my job—I was a rich, white kid from the suburbs. I didn't try to correct them; I just worked hard, asked questions, and took advice. Before long, people stopped giving me grief and started helping me.

Thanks to new friends at Greyhound, I learned that "going South" always meant Memphis. I learned that many people were terrified that the racial unrest in the South would spread to Chicago. I learned about an influx of "Negroes" from New Orleans, many traveling to Chicago on free tickets given to them by the White Citizens Councils.[2]

All through that summer of 1963, while I worked to earn enough money for college, the country was grappling with a civil rights movement that would not be silenced and a preacher from Georgia who had a dream.

———

My parents had gotten their views about African Americans and the civil rights movement from Robert Welch, an old Southern boy. He'd always thought the Negroes had it good in the United States, a view he explained in a pamphlet published in the early 1960s, *Two Revolutions at Once*.

In it, Welch claimed that "educational opportunities [for Negroes] have tremendously improved" with "some states [in the South] spending as much as fifty percent of their total school budget on Negro schools, while deriving only fifteen percent . . . from taxes paid by the Negro population."[3] He claimed that job opportunities for the Negro had "markedly increased despite a determined undercover effort by the Communists to prevent this trend." This assertion was unproven, but that didn't stop Welch from repeating it. Welch even believed that "separate but equal" had been "gaining substance in the matter of equality and losing rigidity in the matter of separateness."

In 1963, Welch was still insisting that "separate but equal" was "surely but slowly breaking down, with regard to public facilities, wherever Negroes earned the right by sanitation, education, and a sense of responsibility, to share such facilities."[4]

As jarring as these words are today, they worked well for the John Birch Society in the 1960s—so well that, by 1965, JBS could boast more than one hundred chapters in Birmingham, Alabama, and its surrounding suburbs. The *New York Times* reported that "the society is capitalizing on white supremacy sentiment, as well as on a general social, religious and political conservatism in the south."[5]

As a Birch kid, I wasn't a bit surprised. The JBS had been fighting the civil rights movement since its founding, and the events of 1962 and 1963 added even more grist to their racist mill.

In the fall of 1962, chaos erupted in Mississippi when the federal courts ordered the admission of James Meredith, a twenty-nine-year-old Air Force veteran, to the University of Mississippi.[6] The Ole Miss Rebels and segregationists across the former Confederacy were not about to sit quietly by while a "colored" man soiled the 144-year whites-only history of the university. Ross Barnett, Mississippi's governor, didn't help matters when he vowed that "no school in our state will be integrated while I am your Governor."[7]

President Kennedy sent sixteen thousand federal troops to quell the rioting in Oxford. One of the protestors was General Edwin Walker, John Bircher, friend of my parents, and right-wing hero.

Walker had resigned from the Army almost a year earlier. In no time, he took up the cause he called "constitutional conservatism." In speeches across the country, Walker denounced the Kennedy administration's "no-win" foreign policy toward the "world Communist conspiracy."[8]

Walker's accusations alarmed members of the Special Senate Preparedness Subcommittee, which had called him to testify. In April, giving his Senate testimony, the general challenged the loyalty of then secretary of state Dean Rusk and of Walt W. Rostow, head of policy planning at State. When questioned about calling these men Communists, Walker said, "I reserve the right to call them something worse such as traitors to the American system of constitutional government, national and state sovereignty and independence." A small melee occurred after the hearing when the general punched a reporter trying to ask a question.[9]

Following the hearing, Walker became "the flag-bearer for the entire conservative movement," according to Jonathan Schoenwald.[10] In our house, he was simply "The General."

Just a few months later, Walker was in the thick of the troubles in Mississippi. He even called for Americans from every state to march to Mississippi and help Governor Barnett keep James Meredith out of Ole Miss.

The situation in Oxford rapidly deteriorated, leading to two deaths and over two hundred injuries. According to *Time*, about two hundred were arrested, including General Edwin Walker.[11] During the melee, Walker proclaimed that court orders allowing integration were part of "the conspiracy of the crucifixion by Antichrist conspirators of the Supreme Court." One man close to Walker said, "There was a wild, dazed look in his eyes."

My father said, "The General spoke the truth, and they made him *sound* crazy."

Following the Oxford situation, which the JBS labeled the "Invasion of Mississippi," Robert Welch said, "We are now reaching the point in the Communist timetable where it is necessary for the Central Government in the United States to demonstrate . . . how dangerous and futile it will be for the people anywhere, or their local governments, to resist that central power."[12]

In January of 1963, my parents found themselves a new hero—the newly elected governor of Alabama, George Wallace. He won them over after declaring, in his inaugural address, "I draw the line in the dust and toss the gauntlet before the feet of tyranny, and I say segregation today, segregation tomorrow, segregation forever."[13] Wallace went on to threaten a "Dixiecrat rebellion," *Time* reported. "We intend to carry our fight for freedom across the nation. . . . We, not the insipid bloc of voters in some sections, will determine in the next election who shall sit in the White House."

"George Wallace is a true statesman," my father said.

"We have to stand with the governor now or it'll be Chicago," Mother added.

Five months later, I pulled the latest *Life* magazine from the stack of mail and headed upstairs. My parents condemned *Life* as a left-wing piece of crap, though like millions of Americans they subscribed. I didn't care about the politics; I loved the photos. That week, Nelson Rockefeller and his new wife, Happy, graced the cover.

My parents loathed Rockefeller for his liberalness and for his divorce and quickie wedding. "He's disgusting, and she's a harlot," my mother said of the couple.

"Rockefeller's a Commie, period," Dad said.

"Who cares?" I thought as I daydreamed through the magazine, skimming the stories and the ads. When I came to page twenty-five, I woke up.

In a grainy, black-and-white, uncaptioned photo, three civil rights protestors braced themselves against a building.[14] Their soaking wet clothes hugged their bodies. One man appeared to be shielding the woman next to him from the fire hoses that had been turned on them. In other shots, police dogs tore the clothes off young boys as they tried to run away. "Bull" Connor, the Birmingham police commissioner, described the scene saying, "I want 'em to see the dogs work. Look at those niggers run."

I fell back on my bed and covered my eyes. "This cannot be happening in my country," I told myself. I knew my parents and the JBS would be totally supportive of Bull Connor and his methods. I also knew that there was nothing I could say to change their minds. The best thing for me was to shut up and earn enough money to go to Dallas.

Shortly after the Birmingham riots, Governor Wallace refused to comply with federal orders to integrate the University of Alabama. The situation escalated until President Kennedy called out the National Guard and forced the governor to stand down.[15] The schools in Alabama were eventually integrated, but not before Wallace had emerged as an icon for racists and right-wing extremists everywhere.

As African Americans continued to ride, sit in, and march for their civil rights, the JBS ramped up its rhetoric around the movement. Welch reminded all members that the whole idea of civil rights was conceived by the Communists to "foment racial riots in the South."[16] The goal, Welch insisted, was "to break off one part of the United States after another until they [the Communists] have converted it into four separate Communist police states."[17] All of this would be made possible by "brutal, ambitious and heavily armed Negroes operating in guerrilla bands, perpetrating vicious atrocities on their fellow Negroes." And, lest the white folks relax, Welch continued, "These guerilla bands will be murdering the whites, too."

Thanks to Welch, my parents were terrified. So was I, but my fear was for the safety of the protestors who wanted nothing more than the same rights white Americans had.

———

Late in August of 1963, while my parents were on their annual summer vacation in Gloucester, Massachusetts, I carted a drink, a peanut-butter sandwich, and the *Chicago Tribune* to our basement rec room. I scanned the front page and noticed a column about a protest march in Washington to be held that day.

Curious, I snapped on the TV and switched the channel to CBS. It took some time to adjust the rabbit ears, but gradually I got the picture focused. On the screen, thousands of people stood shoulder-to-shoulder in front of the Lincoln Memorial. The crowd was so enormous that it spilled along both sides of the Reflecting Pool and stretched nearly to the Washington Monument.[18] I'd never seen anything like it.

It was August 28, 1963. The March on Washington was underway.

I watched as Dr. Martin Luther King Jr. stepped to the podium. I'd heard a lot about Dr. King. I'd heard he believed in a Negro country inside the United States. I heard he encouraged violence against whites. I'd heard he hired thugs to terrorize black folks who disagreed with him. I'd heard he was as bad as they came.

But until that day, I'd never actually heard him.

From his first words, I was riveted. When he talked about the "fierce urgency of now" and "meeting physical force with soul force," about his "dream rooted in the American dream," that "sons of former slaves and sons of former slave owners will sit at the table of brotherhood," that children would "not be judged on the color of their skin but the content of their character," and "little black boys and little black girls will join hands with white boys and white girls as brothers and sisters," chills ran up my arms.[19] When the throng burst into "We Shall Overcome," I stood in my basement, all alone, and sang with them: "We shall overcome some day."

I touched my face. It was damp. Until that moment, I hadn't realized I was crying.

Chapter Fourteen

A Big Texas Howdy

To the radical conservatives, Dallas had become a kind of shrine, a Camelot of the right. . . . We who lived there began to feel that we were in the middle of a political caldera, a grumbling, reawakening fascist urge that was too hot to contain itself. I wonder what might have happened in Dallas if Kennedy hadn't died there.

—LAWRENCE WRIGHT[1]

A few days after Dr. King's March on Washington, Robert Welch sent an urgent letter to all JBS members. In it, he wrote, "It appears that the March on Washington was just one big bust! And that not even all of the exaggerated and glowing reports of the Liberal press could make it anything else. Maybe we could take a little credit for this outcome, through having helped to maintain both patriotism and common sense in some quarters where they were being extensively undermined."[2]

I didn't read Welch's missive when it arrived. I was on the Greyhound bus bound for Dallas, a trip that would take me south to Memphis and then across Arkansas and down into Big D. Gradually, Chicago melted into the suburbs; then there was no city at all, only cornfields as far as I could see.

As we pulled into a scheduled stop, the driver announced off-bus time for snacks and restrooms. At first, I turned my nose up at the crappy food and the filthy ladies' rooms. Before long, I grabbed whatever passed for a meal and peed standing up. By the time we hit Memphis, I had made a vow: "No Greyhound again, ever. Free ticket or not." When I stepped off the bus in the Dallas terminal, dirty and exhausted. I craved a hot shower and a real bed, but first I needed water.

Directly in front of me on the terminal wall were two drinking fountains. Above one hung a sign—WHITE ONLY—with an arrow pointing down. A foot away was another—COLORED ONLY.

As I waited my turn, in the white-only line, I had to pinch myself. I'd never, ever seen this in Chicago. "Good god, it's segregated, just like Alabama and Mississippi."

I retrieved my suitcase from the belly of the bus and retreated to the edge of the crowd. Standing on tiptoes, I scanned for my brother, who was nowhere to be seen. I sat down on my suitcase to wait.

Before long, a boy sporting a ten-gallon hat, tooled boots, and the biggest belt buckle I'd ever seen, strolled up to me. "Howdy and welcome to Big D!" he said. "Can I offer you a lift, little darlin'?"

While I was totally tongue-tied, the guy stood over me staring. Finally I blurted out, "I'm waiting for someone."

"I'll just wait along with y'all," he offered.

"No, you won't. Go away."

Fifteen minutes later, another fellow approached me. "I'm waiting for someone," I said before he opened his mouth.

"I know. Your brother sent me," he replied. "My name is Bob. My friends call me Socks."

"Maybe, but I don't know you."

This boy took my skepticism in stride. He invited me to follow him to the phone booth while he called my wayward brother. "Jesus, Claire," a still-groggy Jay R. said. "Socks is my friend. He's okay."

"What are you doing in bed in the middle of the afternoon?"

"Shut up and get in his car," was my brother's response.

Thirty minutes later, I got a look at my new home. The University of Dallas was housed in a dozen cement-block, flat-roofed buildings plopped on a thousand acres of scrubland. A few spindly trees hung over the walkway. Beyond that dirt and tufts of dry grass stretched to the horizon.

"This is really ugly," I said.

"You'll get used to it," Socks promised.

"I hope not."

Socks hauled my stuff into the dorm and gave me directions to the student center, which was called the SUB. On his way out, he stopped and called, "Claire, don't take a shower without shoes."

"Why?"

"Bugs."

I quickly learned what he meant by bugs. The construction around campus had unearthed hordes of multi-legged creatures that scurried around looking for new homes. Scorpions, beetles, and other creepy crawlies appeared in closet corners, shoes, and damp towels.

Before that fall, the only tarantulas I'd ever seen were behind plate glass in the Lincoln Park Zoo. Imagine my shock when a big hairy one showed up in my desk drawer. Having no idea what else to do, I screamed.

Without any fanfare, one of my new friends, a homegrown Texas girl, captured the thing in a towel and tossed it out the window. "You'll get used to them," she told me. "They're all over Texas."

"No, I won't."

Already the university had two strikes against it: the ugly campus and the huge bugs. Then came strike three: the rules, or, more accurately, the rules for women.

Sunday through Thursday, freshman girls had to be in the dorm by 8 p.m. for a two-hour, monitored study time—no music, no talking, no exceptions. Every night at 10:30, we gathered in the hall for mandatory prayers. At 11:30, it was lights out.

On the weekend, we could stay out until 11 p.m., unless we used one of our half-dozen late passes, tickets to an extra hour of freedom. Come home late, however, and the guilty girl would be grounded. Or, in UD talk, "campused."

The boys, however, were exempt from all of this. As one male upperclassman told me, "Being of the superior sex has its privileges."

The double standard riled some of us, but arguments for equal treatment fell on deaf ears. The nun, who was our dorm moderator, explained, "The rules are for your own good. You are girls, after all."

"For this, I could have stayed home," I told my roommate.

In the early weeks of class, I tried to untangle the mysteries of Greek tragedy while piecing together a vision of the Judeo-Christian tradition. My spiral notebook overflowed with words, scribbles, and arrows; feeble attempts to capture big ideas and specific details from each lecture. Usually, note taking kept me too busy to ask any questions.

One morning, in my Western Civilization lecture, the professor declared that the thirteenth century was, "without doubt, the greatest century in human history."

Without thinking, I blurted out, "Would the serfs agree?"

The professor pulled himself to his full height and stared down his nose at me. After a long pause, he called me a perfect example of "terminal ignorance." Only stupid people, he pointed out, lacked respect for the political, cultural, and spiritual magnificence of the High Middle Ages.[3]

Embarrassed, I put my head down and went back to scribbling notes.

Some days later, I sat cross-legged on my bed staring at a manila envelope with a typed parcel post label from my mother. Mother's package included the September *John Birch Society Bulletin* and a brief note in her nearly illegible hand. She reminded me to read Welch's latest, study hard, and make contact with Dad's friend General Walker. On a separate slip, she'd typed the General's address, 4011 Turtle Creek Boulevard, and his home phone number.

I settled back against the pillows and lit a cigarette. "I'll take a peek so I can tell her I did."

In the first section of the bulletin, Welch outlined the religious preferences of the JBS members: 60 percent Protestants, 40 percent Catholic, and 1 percent Jews. "We are aware that this adds up to 101%," he noted. "But that is because any attempt at greater precision would be a sham." Then, he launched into an explanation of "Operation Confusion," the Pavlovian techniques used by the Commies to make "gibbering political idiots out of the American people."[4] Being totally confounded, I skipped the rest of that section.

A couple of pages later, photographs caught my eye: front and side shots of a parade float. It was a galley ship, aptly named *Freedom*, bearing the slogan "Row the Oars for Freedom" and the logo of the John Birch Society along the base. This entry had taken the first-place ribbon in the Dallas Independence Day parade that summer.[5]

"Dallas loves JBS," Mother had scribbled at the top of the page.

Following the pictures of the floats, Welch outlined the ongoing Birch agenda. The first item: recruiting new members. Impeaching Earl Warren, the JBS's endless impossible dream, held forth at number two. The Supreme Court's recent decisions rejecting school prayer and bible reading had reinvigorated this project. Welch wrote, "When the impeachment is finally accomplished—when that blockbuster is landed right across the front center of the whole leftwing advance—the Communist apparatus behind that advance will begin to crumble like a house of cards."[6]

Then, it was on to getting us out of the UN with a campaign of postcards, bumper stickers, and billboards, as well as opposing the Nuclear Test Ban Treaty. For seventeen pages, Welch wove a story about Soviet power, including this nugget, "Soviet 'military might' has been used and is being used primarily in the propaganda and diplomatic fields and never on any battlefields." Despite this rather amazing assessment (without any facts or charts or expert testimony), Welch opposed all disarmament and all treaties on the basis that the USSR always lied about its intentions, making any treaty agreements impossible.

"What on earth do the Soviets need any real military strength for (instead of the mere shell for propaganda purposes), when they have ours available and completely at their service?"[7] Welch asked. He answered his own question with another: "If the Soviets have so much military strength, why do they *never* use it?"

According to Welch, the Soviets really didn't have either a nuclear arsenal or much of a weapons program. He said that the "cases of military material . . . on the docks of Leningrad contain nothing more deadly than the worn-out bodies of long dead automobiles."[8]

All of this was astounding, but Welch really outdid himself in eighteen pages about civil rights. He was sure that "the rioting [in Oxford and Birmingham] was deliberately caused and precipitated by a bunch of hooligans sworn in as federal marshals, obviously in accordance with designs formed in Washington . . . the Communists are running the whole show."[9]

This bulletin included a full-page photo from 1957 of Dr. King at the Highlander Folk School under the headline "Martin Luther King . . . at Communist Training School."[10] This photo was part of the "proof" that all civil rights legislation served Communist goals.

The Highlander Folk School was founded in the 1930s as a base for labor activists working in Appalachia. Years later, it provided training for civil rights activists who worked all across the South. Dr. King was just one of many civil rights leaders who attended seminars at the Highlander School.[11] The John Birch Society believed that the school was founded by Communists in order to further Communist goals.

In that bulletin, Welch exhorted JBS members to action: "Many of you think that the Negroes should have too much sense, or should be too appreciative of a lifetime of good will on the part of their white neighbors, to fall for the Communist claptrap that converts them into enemies. But I ask you, good people of the South, to remember how you yourselves have been led to accept and support the socialist policies of the New Deal and the Fair Deal . . . which were inspired by the Communists to serve long-range Communist purposes."[12]

On page after page, Welch decried President Kennedy and his "fake" anti-Communism. The president was never really anti-Communist and people claiming otherwise "know that they are lying." Kennedy was doing everything to "help the Communists, not to harm them," Welch said.[13]

By September of 1963, it was clear that Kennedy was the JBS's public enemy number one. Not only was the president not an anti-Communist; he was helping the Reds at every turn.

These words sound shocking today, especially given what was about to happen only a few weeks later, but, at the time, those 144 pages of Birch propaganda did not shock me. It was the same old song and dance that I'd been hearing since 1958. Welch had added a few new names to his gallery of bad guys, and the Birchers had undertaken a few new projects, but the basic ideas remained the same: the Commies were coming—no, wait—they were already here.

Finally, Mother sent me a clipping from the *Los Angeles Herald-Examiner* about a big Birch event honoring Robert Welch. The headline screamed: "2000 Hail Welch as 'Great Patriot.'"[14] I did some quick calculations: two thousand people at $50 per plate = $100,000. Mother had added another of her little notes. "Your father attended. It was glorious."

That made me mad; not a dime for me, but my father could go to California for a Birch meeting. "Damn you," I said as I threw the bulletin and Mother's notes on the floor.

A year before I arrived at UD, the board of trustees had hired a new president, Dr. Donald Cowan, the man who would put the school on the map. He and his wife, Dr. Louise Cowan, fashioned UD's core curriculum, which focused on literature, philosophy, and history. Before UD students could declare a major, we had to plow through Homer and Shakespeare, learn how to structure a proper syllogism, and spend some time with Aristotle and Aquinas.

After I graduated, UD racked up impressive academic accomplishments, including qualifying for a Phi Beta Kappa chapter, one of only fifteen Catholic universities with the prestigious honor society on campus. The university also pioneered its signature Rome semester, giving 80 percent of students the chance to live and study in Italy. In 2012, *U.S. News & World Report* ranked UD as fourteenth-best among regional universities in the West.

Of course, in 1963, when I was hired as Dr. Cowan's student-worker, all of that glory was years away. The university had not yet received its first accreditation or a significant endowment. Dr. Cowan was swamped with phone calls and meetings and everyday disasters—plumbing, construction delays, problem students and faculty.

I worked under Dr. Don's secretary, who used me for routine office tasks: drafting letters, typing envelopes, answering the phone, and filing. Lots and lots of filing.

One afternoon, the carbon copy of a letter to the White House appeared on the top of the to-be-filed pile: Dr. Don's invitation to President Kennedy to visit our campus during his upcoming presidential trip to Dallas.[15] I was surprised; Kennedy was wildly unpopular on campus. Much of the faculty and a lot of the students blamed him for the Bay of Pigs fiasco and for playing nice with the Commies. If the president did stop at the university, I figured he'd find only a handful of supporters.

"Will you applaud?" I asked myself. My question led to no easy yes or no answer. I had turned away from my parents' opinions on civil rights, making me more sympathetic toward Kennedy. At the same time, I worried about the Communists ninety miles from Miami and thought the president needed to take a hard line with Fidel Castro. I appreciated the president's resolve during the Cuban Missile Crisis and believed he'd saved the world from nuclear disaster. At the same time, I'd heard rumors that he was unfaithful to Jackie. On balance, I leaned toward the president, but I would not have described myself as a big fan.

Though I was *comme ci, comme ça* about the president, Dallas had made up its mind. It took only a glance through the editorials, columns, and letters to the editor in the *Dallas Morning News* to realize that Kennedy personified everything the right-wing town hated. No doubt, Kennedy was diving into hostile waters on this trip.[16]

As the days to the president's visit ticked down, Dallas civic leaders grew alarmed about the rabid anti-Kennedy sentiment. A chorus of folks asked people to be "Texas nice" when the president came to town. The city police chief, Jesse Curry, appeared on television urging respect for Kennedy: "Law enforcement agencies in this area are going to do everything within their power to ensure that no untoward accident or incident occurs."[17]

On November 17, the lead editorial in the *Dallas Morning News*, "Incident-Free Day Urged for JFK Visit," quoted civic leaders asking Dallas to welcome the president. "These good citizens will greet the President . . . with the warmth and pride that keep the Dallas spirit famous the world over," the president of the Chamber of Commerce declared.[18]

At the University of Dallas, the specter of a Kennedy visit sparked action. A group of students who were organizing a chapter of Bill Buckley's new group for college activists, Young Americans for Freedom, planned a campus-wide protest. One of the leaders, an avid fan of everything conservative (except the JBS), asked me to help with the posters. I refused.

"Why isn't the *Birch baby* helping?" he said. "You must know Kennedy is no good."

When I was invited to go to Dallas the next morning, I jumped at the offer. I'd see the president and grab some non-cafeteria food. Another plus: President John F. Kennedy gave me the perfect reason to cut class.

———

Around 12:30 the next afternoon, while I crossed Main Street, John Kennedy's motorcade turned right onto Houston and left on Elm toward the Triple Underpass. Five minutes away at the Dallas Trade Mart, 2,500 dignitaries waited to lunch with the president.

Unknown to me, at that moment, Nellie Connally, the wife of Texas governor John Connally, turned toward Kennedy and said, "You certainly can't say Dallas doesn't love you."[19] A second later, a bullet hit its target. Another shot and the thirty-fifth president of the United States was dead.

While hell broke out just a few blocks away in Dealey Plaza, my friend and I were maneuvering through the crowd toward our car. We had decided that it was too congested downtown to either eat or shop; to compensate, we headed to a favorite burger joint, Kip's on Mockingbird Lane, home of the Big Boy. I had never tasted a Big Boy and had no idea where Mockingbird Lane was, but my friend was undeterred. "I'll get us there," he said. "You find music on the radio."

"Easy," I laughed as I tuned the dial to 1190 KLIF, the popular Top 40 station.

Instead of music, however, I heard about "the dastardly deed done" and "a priest summoned to Parkland Hospital."[20] Then it was "no official word that the President is in critical condition at this time," followed by "Father Huber has administered the last rites to the President."

Fifteen minutes later, at 1:45 p.m.: "The president is dead, ladies and gentlemen. The president is dead."

In the recaps that followed, I could only absorb a smattering of the reports: "Everyone fully exposed . . . three bursts from a rifle . . . wild pandemonium . . . shots rang out at Elm and Houston . . . priest summoned . . . blood rushed to Parkland . . . orderly crowd except for one person who pumped bullets into the president . . . manhunt across Dallas . . . Kennedy is dead."

"I don't understand. Who did this?" I asked.

"Everyone hated him," my friend said.

"Did you?" I asked.

"No. You?"

"My parents hate him with a purple passion," I said. "But I don't."

"I'm surprised. I thought you were a Bircher."

"My father's the Bircher," I said. "I don't know what I am."

By the time we got back to campus, I needed aspirin more than food. Then, when I phoned home and my father terrified me with the idea that Birchers could be implicated in this disaster, I reconsidered my choice of drink. "Bourbon, that's what I really need," I thought.

Having no booze, however, I had to settle for a Coke and a candy bar, the two major food groups available in the rec-room vending machines. I arranged my treats and myself on one of the sofas and picked up that day's *Dallas Morning News.*

No one else was in the room. In fact, the whole dorm was as quiet as a tomb. I imagined that everyone was as shocked as I was; the unthinkable had happened. Whether you liked Kennedy or not, he was dead, and Dallas had a big black mark next to its name.

The *News,* the archconservative Dallas daily, had a reputation for savaging President Kennedy, a reputation enhanced when Ted Dealey, the paper's publisher, attacked the President during a luncheon at the White House. Dealey said, "We can annihilate Russia and should make that clear to the Soviet government. . . . You and your Administration are weak sisters." The country needed "a man on horseback," but "many people in Texas think you are riding Caroline's tricycle."[21]

This episode enshrined Dealey as a hero across the right-wing world, and his newspaper claimed a high spot in the pantheon of anti-Kennedy media. William Manchester wrote, "As the most venerable voice in Dallas, the *News,* under Dealey's leadership, had made radical extremism reputable."[22]

Kennedy recognized the growing power of the Far Right. He realized the threat it posed to his presidency and the country at large. Two years before his death, Kennedy pushed back against the conspiracy-minded, saying that they "call for a 'man on horseback' because they do not trust the people. . . . They find treason in our churches, in our highest court, in our treatment of water. They equate the Democratic Party with the welfare state, the welfare state with socialism, socialism with communism."[23]

The speech did nothing to quiet Kennedy's critics; it may have inflamed them even more. In Dallas, where the right wing ruled, the anti-Kennedy drumbeat increased.[24] Given this, I was not surprised to see a big anti-Kennedy ad in the paper that day, but, given the terrible events, the thick, black border seemed to resemble a funeral announcement more than a political ad.

An ominous tone marked the content: twelve WHYs marched down the page followed by accusations about the policies of President Kennedy and his administration, including: "Why have you scrapped the Monroe Doctrine in favor of the 'Spirit of Moscow'?" and "Why is Latin America turning either anti-American or Communistic, or both, despite increased U.S. foreign aid, State Department policy, and your own Ivy-Tower [*sic*] pronouncements?"[25]

This language sounded so JBS that I was grateful when someone I'd never heard of, a Bernard Weissman, was listed as the ad sponsor. A "non-partisan group of citizens who wish truth"—the American Fact-Finding Committee— had placed the thing in the paper. "No one can pin this on the Birchers," I told myself with relief.

As much as that terrible Friday devastated the nation, it rocked Dallas to its core. Even a newcomer like me could feel the usual rah-rah-rahs of the place give way to hand-wringing and questioning. People worried that the nastiness of Dallas politics had somehow, however unintentionally, contributed to Kennedy's death.[26]

When Lee Harvey Oswald was identified as a Communist, Dallas caught a break.[27] Civic leaders could place all blame squarely on that lone madman with Soviet ties. But when live television recorded Jack Ruby gunning down Oswald in the basement of the police station, the city suffered another black eye. The sheriff tried to defuse all criticism when he said, "If somebody wants to commit a cold-blooded murder and you don't know he intends to do it, it is almost impossible to stop it."[28]

In early December, Robert Welch offered his own interpretation of Kennedy's killing. "The assassination of the President was not only to have been blamed in a general way on the spirit of hatred supposedly created by the so-called 'right wing extremists' . . . the wholesale arrests of anti-Communists was to have been carried out just as rapidly as possible," he wrote.[29]

The formal inquiry into the assassination was set in motion five days after the tragedy when President Johnson named Chief Justice Earl Warren to head the investigation. Every detail of the events before, during, and after November 22 was studied. The Warren Commission interviewed 552 witnesses, studied 3,100 exhibits, and published 888 pages of findings. Supporting documentation filled another 26 volumes.[30]

Among the items the commission studied was the infamous "Wanted for Treason" poster that had appeared all over Dallas; the same one I'd picked up on November 22 and identified as something my father might have written. The Warren Commission found the man who created the handbill, Robert

Surrey, a right-wing activist and associate of Major-General Edwin Walker, who still lived in Dallas.[31]

Once again, the General— darling of the Dallas media, hero of the John Birch Society, and my father's friend—was in the news. Thank God I'd never gotten around to calling him.

The inflammatory handbill, with its links to General Walker and, by extension, to the John Birch Society, did not faze my father. He simply refused to acknowledge that there was such a thing at all. When I mentioned it, I was told to "stop telling tall tales."

In 1964, my mother sent me an oversized booklet titled *The Assassination Story*, a compilation of articles published in the *Dallas Morning News* and *Dallas Times Herald* between November 15 and December 11, 1963. It was the work of R. A. Surrey and his American Eagle Publishing Company, and I learned later that this was the same Surrey who'd printed the infamous "Wanted for Treason" handbill. No surprise, *The Assassination Story* did not include a picture of or any reference to the handbill.

The Warren Commission also took an interest in the full-page "Welcome Mr. Kennedy" ad in the *Dallas Morning News*. After a lot of clarifications, misstatements, and restatements, Bernard Weissman finally admitted that the cash for the ad had been given to him by Joe Grinnan, a coordinator for the John Birch Society. Weissman explained the Birch connection this way: "To get anywhere in Dallas . . . you had to cotton to the John Birch Society because they were a pretty strong group, and still are."[32]

My father refused to discuss the Warren Commission, dismissing the entire investigation as another diversion in the Communist plan to take over America. When I asked him about the Weissman ad, he snapped, "The Communists killed Kennedy. End of story. Do not mention this again."

Chapter Fifteen

Crossfire

The Republicans are more and more taking their ideas from the reckless radicals of the far right and echoing the efforts of those extreme agitators to breed fear and suspicion in our society.
—John M. Bailey, chairman of the Democratic National Committee, 1962[1]

Our opinion is that Robert Welch is damaging the cause of anti-communism. By the extravagance of his remarks he repels, rather than attracts, a great following."
—William F. Buckley Jr., 1962[2]

We cannot allow the emblem of irresponsibility to attach to the conservative banner.
—Senator Barry Goldwater, 1962[3]

Two days after President Kennedy was buried at Arlington National Cemetery, President Lyndon Johnson, who'd been sworn into office ninety-nine minutes after John Kennedy died, addressed a joint session of Congress. In his speech, he pushed for passage of the civil rights legislation Kennedy had championed. "We have talked long enough in this country about equal rights. We have talked for a hundred years or more," Johnson said. "It is time now, to write the next chapter—and to write it in the books of law. I urge you again . . . to enact a civil rights law . . . to eliminate from this nation every trace of discrimination and oppression that is based upon race or color."[4]

I knew that my parents, their Birch friends, and a lot of white Southerners would take President Johnson's endorsement of civil rights legislation as a personal threat. Robert Welch had already painted a nightmare scenario of Communist-inspired race riots, insurrection, and, ultimately, civil war. I could imagine my parents thinking they'd have to fight against the federal government, the Communists, and a mob of African Americans.

Before I left Dallas for Christmas vacation, I promised myself that I'd avoid any arguments with my parents. Luckily, Jay R. would be home, too; he was so much better at keeping Mother and Dad happy. "I'll say what you say and do what you do," I told him.

"That'll be the day," he said.

"I'll try. You'll see."

My promises didn't come to much. As usual, avoiding a fight with my mother or my father was nearly impossible. By Christmas Day, I was tired, depressed, and more than ready to go back to Dallas, but I faced another two weeks in Chicago.

The morning after Epiphany—the day the Wise Men found the Christ child—Mother ordered me to put away our Christmas things. "Get Mary and Larry to help you, and save the tinsel."

My sister Janet had already been given her chores, and Jay R., as usual, had disappeared in time to miss all the fun. So, I was "on deck," as my mother liked to say.

I didn't point out the obvious: saving tinsel was a colossal waste of time. I just shut up and showed the little kids how to remove each strand from the tree and drape it over cardboard. "We're saving it," I told them. They rolled their eyes. While they were working, I brought down storage boxes from the attic.

When I returned, I found my brother Larry with a book, my sister Mary with a new toy, and a huge knot of silver on the floor. "What happened in here?" I asked. Larry shrugged and pointed to Mary. Mary pointed back.

"This is going to be a really long day," I thought. I grabbed the mess and marched off to the garbage can.

"Save that," Mother called.

"How?"

Mother didn't answer. She turned back to doing whatever she was doing. In a few seconds, I heard the tapping of her pen and humming. Mom couldn't sing a note and her humming was way off-key, but I recognized her rendition of "The Yellow Rose of Texas."

"Christmas is definitely over," I thought.

I knew without listening that Mother had swapped Christmas music for war music—Civil War music to be exact. I knew without looking that her music choice was *The Confederacy*, a two-record set of the music of the South.[5] And I knew, if I waited a minute, Mother would cry; she always cried for the boys in gray.

Even though Mother was a Yankee, she'd fallen in love with the idea of the old South and its hero, General Robert E. Lee. "A true American patriot who lived his principles," she said of the West Pointer turned Confederate.

Mother believed that the northern states had oppressed and abused the Southern states until war became the only option. "The South fought to save their way of life," she explained. "It was a war for Southern independence."

She even found justification for the Confederacy in the U.S. Constitution. "It was all about states' rights," she said. Somehow, she spun the Tenth Amendment into approval for secession, rebel government, and bombarding Fort Sumter.

Even more disturbing were her notions about slavery. Mother often argued that "slavery was really a welfare system. The slaves were taken care of, and they were baptized."

Arguing with her was futile.

That day, when I heard Mother humming, I turned away and tackled the Christmas cleanup. I stowed the ornaments and lights in their boxes. I crawled under the Christmas tree, unscrewed the stand, and lifted the little balsam out of the putrid water. I wrestled the thing out the front door and down to the street, leaving a trail of dry, brown needles behind me.

"You have to sweep," Mother shouted. "Don't track that in here, and take off your shoes."

"I need water first," I told her. "Then I'll finish."

Mother followed me into the kitchen. Before I got near the sink, she ordered me to take a seat. "We sent you to Dallas to learn the truth and now you sound like a liberal."

"What are you talking about?"

"You sympathize with the coloreds," Mother explained. I stared at her without answering, and she raced on. "All of this civil rights agitation is a threat to the Southern way of life," she insisted.

"Damn, Mother," I interrupted. "What would you know about the Southern way of life?"

Mother wagged her finger at me. "Don't take that tone with me, young lady. You know nothing."

"Yes, I do," I blurted out. I proceeded to tell her what I knew: Colored-only drinking fountains and white-only restaurants and bars. Maids working twelve-hour days for hardly any money. Police arresting African Americans for loitering. Two kids sharing a tattered textbook. "There are two halves of the South, Mother. One for you and me, and one for those with black skin.

Your American dream, the one you love so much, hasn't arrived in Dixie, or in Dallas."

My mother shrugged. "People have the right to decide how they treat their coloreds."

"Easy for you to say, Mother," I fired back. "You're white. You have no idea how blacks are treated."

"You are impossible," she said. "I give up on you."

That day confirmed what I suspected: my parents and I were in different universes. I believed that my country would stand stronger and taller when all Americans were guaranteed equal rights. My parents believed that expanding civil rights threatened their country. Our views would never be reconciled.

After that confrontation, Mother didn't let go. She continued to preach about the evils of civil rights legislation, using her favorite right-wingers to bolster her case. I ignored most everything she said about George Wallace, the governor of Alabama; I'd already dismissed him as an ass after his "segregation forever" speech.

I did listen for a minute when Mother brought Bill Buckley, the editor of *National Review* and one of the rising conservative thinkers, into the mix. But I was shocked and disappointed to hear that Buckley believed whites to be the advanced race. As such, whites had to "take all necessary measures to prevail, politically and culturally," he said.[6] In my humble but increasingly self-assured opinion, that malarkey put Buckley in the same category as Wallace.

Mother also quoted Barry Goldwater, right-wing oracle: "The problem of race relations, like all social and cultural problems, is best handled by the people directly concerned. Social and cultural change, however desirable, should not be effected by the engines of national power."[7]

"This is serious," Mother told me. "You need to listen to your mother."

I reminded myself to shut up. This was no time to provoke my mother. I needed her help. All through vacation, while Mother and Dad were talking politics, I was contemplating my dwindling bank account. After a real "come to Jesus" moment, I'd had to face the fact: the dollars I had would barely cover my next semester at school. Any unexpected expenses and I'd be broke.

I fretted about my cash flow while I noticed how much money flew out the door in support of my parents' pet causes. I'd seen Mother write checks to the *Dan Smoot Report* and the Manion Forum, the Liberty Lobby, and the Conservative Society of America.[8] Each one of these organizations was part of the broad Birch network and sported close connections to Robert Welch and other members of the council. Some of these folks, like Dan Smoot and Clarence Manion were active members. Others, like Liberty Lobby and Conservative Society of America were fiercely anti-Communist. All of them got regular contributions from my parents.

Mother had even sent money to the Christian Crusade, despite Reverend Billy James Hargis's biblical bombast and fierce anti-Catholicism, two things Mother despised.[9] "This is no time to argue theology," she explained. "Hargis is a Birch champion." I knew what that meant: Hargis was a personal friend of the society and of my parents.

One afternoon, after I watched my mother write a check to the John Birch Society for $150—a sum that would have been a huge help to my budget—I spoke up. "Mother, I need to talk to you," I said. "School costs more than I expected, and I'm running out of money. Will you help me?"

"How much?" she answered without looking up.

"One hundred fifty dollars would be great. Please?"

"No, and don't bother me again," she said. "Your father and I made it clear—you have to fund your own education. We are fighting for our lives here."

"Will you, at least, get Dad to apply for a National Defense Loan?"[10]

"Your father won't disclose information to the Feds, you know that."

That evening, my father had to add his *no, no, no* to Mother's. "Why would you even ask?" he demanded. "You know we have no extra money."

"I'm in trouble. I thought you might help."

"For the last time, don't ask again," he said.

"At least fill out the loan forms."

"I won't, and that's final," Dad said. He went on, growing more and more agitated with every word. "You think you have problems? Your mother and I are fighting for the future. Now even Buckley is on the attack."

"Bill Buckley?" I asked.

"You heard me."

"I thought he was your friend."

"Was," Mother added. "Not anymore."

"What happened?"

"He's a damn traitor," Dad said.

Wow! This was a titanic shift. In 1955, my parents had heralded William F. Buckley Jr. as an intellectual powerhouse and a rising conservative sage. Mother couldn't get enough of Buckley's first book, *God and Man at Yale*, in which he accused the educational establishment at his alma mater of being both anti-God and anti-free enterprise.[11] "A brilliant mind," Mother said of her new favorite.

The story of Bill's discovery by Dr. Willmoore Kendall, a cantankerous politics professor at Yale, was part of the Buckley mythology. Kendall had recognized Buckley's enormous potential and encouraged him to hone his public-speaking skills until he became Yale's most formidable debater. Kendall mentored the young man throughout his Yale years and Buckley returned the favor; when Kendall converted to Catholicism, Buckley was his sponsor.[12]

Kendall's relationship with Buckley was a stormy business, as Buckley himself acknowledged. "Willmoore Kendall, the finest teacher I knew at Yale, the most difficult human being I have ever known . . . he must not be on speaking terms with more than three people at any one time."[13]

It was Kendall who introduced Bill Buckley to another conservative leader, our former family friend Dr. Revilo Oliver, the brilliant linguist and virulent anti-Semite.

According to Carl T. Bogus's 2011 book, Buckley knew that "Oliver was the vilest sort of bigot. Oliver disparaged a wide assortment of ethnic groups, especially Jews, and did so in Buckley's presence and in correspondence with Buckley."[14] Those views did not disqualify Oliver from joining *National Review* as a regular contributor, and even after Buckley expelled Oliver from the magazine, the two remained personal friends.[15]

Buckley also cultivated a relationship with Robert Welch, and when Buckley started *National Review*, in 1955, he turned to conservative leaders for financial backing. "I was all for it," Welch wrote. "I gladly contributed my small pittance of a thousand dollars to the fund. . . . [A] year later, when Buckley's magazine had run out of money and was facing its first financial 'crisis,' I contributed another thousand dollars."[16] (That "pittance" would be about $15,000 today.)

In the fall of 1958, Buckley wrote to Robert Welch requesting a copy of the confidential manuscript Welch had written about President Eisenhower, the book subsequently published as *The Politician*. According to Welch, Buckley stated that he'd "very much appreciate being permitted to read a copy." Welch did send manuscript #58 to Buckley with a "strong explanatory letter" concerning the confidential nature of the book and stressing that it was "for his eyes only."[17]

Several months later after the Birch Society was organized, Buckley's mother joined and one of his sisters became a chapter leader in Hartford, Connecticut.[18] By 1959, Buckley, whom my parents called "Bill," was recognized as a Birch ally.

Beyond my parents and Welch, Buckley was respected by a large swath of the anti-Communist, small-government gang. Even Phoebe and Kent Courtney, the eclectic founders of the Conservative Society of America, embraced him.[19] The Courtneys were such Birch cheerleaders that they described their efforts as picking up "where the John Birch Society leaves off."[20] One of those efforts included seeding a new political party, the States' Rights Party, which, according to the Courtneys, would be powerful enough to control both Congress and the White House.[21]

In October of 1959, my parents attended a Conservative Society of America conference in Chicago that featured both Robert Welch and Bill Buckley as speakers. Along with these luminaries of the newly emerging Right, a who's who of the John Birch Society was on hand to applaud both speakers.[22]

During the meeting, my parents and other prominent Birchers talked privately with Buckley. After that, Mother and Dad were even more enthused about the prospects of a national conservative movement. "We'll all work together," Dad told our Birch chapter. "Bill [Buckley], Bob [Welch], and the Courtneys."

For a few years, it seemed like a match made in heaven: Buckley and the John Birch Society leading the energized Right. The bloom started to fade when Buckley realized that with "the JBS growing so rapidly, the right-wing upsurge in the country would take an ugly, even Fascist turn rather than leading toward the kind of conservatism *National Review* had promoted."[23] Analysts inside Buckley's organization predicted that "Goldwater would turn to the *fundamentalist right*," if he did not get the 1964 GOP nomination.

Buckley wanted Goldwater at the top of the GOP ticket, but he was concerned that the JBS could derail the whole plan by making the Republican Party look too radical for most voters. Buckley decided that it was time to criticize Welch's philosophy—while trying to avoid attacking JBS members. As one of Buckley's closest advisors said, "Some of the solidest conservatives in the country are members of the John Birch Society, and we should act in such a way as to alienate them no more than is strictly necessary."[24]

Buckley's first critiques focused squarely on Robert Welch. "I myself have never met a single member [JBS] who declared himself in agreement with certain of Mr. Welch's conclusions," Buckley wrote in *National Review* in 1961. "If our government is in the effective control of Communists, then the entire educational effort conducted by conservatives . . . is a sheer waste of time. . . . The point has come, if Mr. Welch is right, to leave the typewriter, the lectern, and the radio microphone, and look instead to one's rifles."[25]

This jab did not create a major breach between Buckley and the JBS. In fact, Welch wrote that "the article is both objectively fair and subjectively honorable."[26]

My father took a sanguine view of the Buckley article. "Bill wants Goldwater in the White House. The society wants Goldwater in the White House. We can live with Bill's criticism if it helps Barry," he explained to his conservative friends.

By late 1961, Bill Buckley realized that the Birch Society was inflicting real harm on the Republican Party. Carl Bogus wrote of the situation, "The John Birch Society had been effectively discredited to the public at large . . . but it had not been effectively discredited on the political right. Like a cancer, it was continuing to grow and threatening the life of the conservative movement."[27]

Buckley knew he had to do more to stop the Birchers. He wrote a six-page editorial, "The Question of Robert Welch," in which Welch was described as "the kiss of death" for conservatives. Even Barry Goldwater agreed completely with the Buckley article and suggested that Welch should resign from leadership of the Birch Society.[28]

From that point on, my parents and Robert Welch were at war with Bill Buckley. Welch claimed, "Mr. Buckley has been utterly and continuously unwilling to take his hands off our throat."[29]

My father put it differently: "Buckley's a goddamned turncoat."

William F. Buckley Jr. became the most influential right-wing thinker of his generation—"the golden boy of Conservatism"—and continued to be an influential American pundit until his death in 2008. His rejection of the JBS on intellectual grounds was a blow to Welch and to the national leadership.

Despite Buckley, however, the JBS continued to grow. By 1965, it was reported that the society had "eighty thousand or more members, a paid staff of 220, and annual revenues of $6 million [the equivalent of $39 million today]. It would also have its own publishing company [Western Islands] and operate 350 bookstores across the country. *American Opinion* magazine would boast a paid circulation of forty thousand."[30]

I understood that my parents were mad as hell at Bill Buckley, and I wasn't really surprised. After all, anyone attacking their precious Birch Society brought down their wrath. I was surprised, however, when they determined that the cause of Buckley's move to the dark side—the all-powerful, omnipresent, capital-letter *Left*—was due in large part to his choice of college.

"Yale poisoned him," my father said. "He even joined Skull and Bones."

"Skull and Bones?"

"The secret college club controlled by the conspiracy," Dad explained. "It's the training ground for Lefties, socialists, and other big-government types."[31]

"Isn't Buckley a conservative?"

"He is not. He's one of the boys," Dad insisted.

"Take a lesson from this," my mother added. "You have to resist liberal contamination."

My parents believed that even a man with a prodigious brain like Bill Buckley's couldn't resist the allure of the liberals at Yale. If the worst had happened to him, imagine how easily I could fall prey to the insidious evil peddled at left-wing colleges.

"That's why we insisted on UD," Mother added. "It will be your salvation."

My parents pushed me to give careful thought to my "course of study," as they called it. Since they'd already found the "correct" school for me, they had no qualms about picking my major—history and politics. Only engaged in such a rigorous study, they reasoned, could I beat down my liberal tendencies and align myself with them, the Constitution, and God Himself.

"UD has Willmoore Kendall. He's marvelous. Take his class," Mother said.

"Dr. Kendall was Buckley's teacher, and Revilo Oliver's good friend," I reminded Mother and Dad.

"Don't be snide," Mother said.

The first day of the second semester, I took a seat in Lynch Hall, our multipurpose auditorium and awaited the arrival of Willmoore Kendall, the university's most eccentric professor and head of the Politics and Economics Department.

Kendall had arrived at UD a year earlier after a tumultuous fifteen years at Yale. In addition to discovering and mentoring the young Bill Buckley there, Kendall had vexed the administration with his antics and his temper. One writer described Kendall as a "wild Yale don of extreme, eccentric and very abstract views who can get a discussion into the shouting stage faster than anybody I have ever known."[32] When Kendall left New Haven with a tenure buyout, the University of Dallas offered him the chance to build a department free from the liberal biases of the Ivy League.

On our campus, the new professor gained instant larger-than-life status. Some of the faculty, so I'd heard, shuddered at his escapades, but students—especially arrogant male ones—idolized him for his prowess with women, whiskey, and words.

It was clear early on that Kendall's love for debate extended primarily to the boys; girls were better off being seen and not heard. As one of my upper-class friends put it, "No matter what he says, don't argue. He likes his girls cute, not smart."

A couple minutes after class was scheduled to start, Dr. Willmoore Kendall strode down the aisle of the auditorium with an armful of papers. He wore a rumpled sport coat and jeans, which were not permitted on campus except on weekends, and never in class or chapel.

When Kendall reached the stage, he dropped his stuff on one of the front-row seats and reached inside his jacket for a smoke. He puffed on his cigarette and flicked ashes on the floor as he prowled across the front of the auditorium. A minute later, he leaned over one of the seats and pointed directly at me.

"And who is this?" he asked.

"I'm Claire Conner."

"Ah, the Birch baby. Let me make one thing clear: your father and his friends know nothing about *real* Communists. The Birch business is a waste of time."

I felt the blush blazing from my neck to my cheeks. Kendall paused and looked around the room. No one said a word.

Then, he turned back to me. "I'll be watching you, Miss Birch. If you have a brain in that head of yours, maybe we can make something of it. We'll just have to see."

Dr. Kendall called me "Miss Birch" for that entire semester.

After class, I tried to make sense of what had happened. But an hour later, I'd talked myself into a huge headache and an undeniable reality: as long as my dad was a Birch big shot, I would be the target of teasing and ribbing. It had been true in high school, and it was turning out to be true in college, even in a school as right-wing pure as the University of Dallas.

I never told my parents about Kendall's disdain for the JBS. I figured my father would have been angry with me for gloating. This was one secret I could keep.

Be that as it may, I did decide to take some definitive action of my own regarding Dr. Kendall. I grabbed my purse and my room key and tramped across campus to the student union, where I found my friend Socks sitting at a table playing bridge. This boy had two things I needed: an ID and a car. "I want a drink," I told him. "Got any ideas?"

Pizza and beer helped my attitude but did nothing to change my problem: Dr. Kendall did not like me. Ironically, my brother—as much a Birch baby as I was—escaped Kendall's needling. I couldn't figure out how that worked until I watched Kendall arrive at a party with his entourage of enthralled students in tow. At the front of the pack was my brother, laughing at every comment that tumbled out of Kendall's mouth, scurrying to refill his glass, and spouting as many Kendallisms as he could.

"The boys adore Dr. Kendall," I said to a friend.

"Yes, they do," she answered. "Just look at them, fawning over him. Aren't they jackasses?"

"For sure," I said. "Every last one of them."

"Dr. Kendall, too," she added.

"I know. He's the worst."

A few weeks into the semester, I realized how little I knew about political philosophy and the colonial period, a situation I attempted to remedy with diligent study. Plowing through *The Federalist Papers* proved to me that the founders of our country, so revered now, had fought like cats and dogs over the principles of our new government. It was a miracle, from my perspective, that we ever got a functioning federal structure at all.

Willmoore Kendall used his lectures to drive home one of his core ideas: the Constitution of the United States stood head and shoulders above the Declaration of Independence in importance. He passionately believed that the "all men are created equal" clause from the Declaration was never a defining idea in American governance. In fact, he went so far as to declare the whole business of individual rights and equality to be "false, liberal criteria."[33]

Kendall said the defining principle of the United States was "self-government by virtuous people deliberating under God."[34] Those virtuous souls were the ones who spoke in the first three words of the preamble, "We the People."

I'd read those words many times. In fact, I'd memorized the entire preamble and recited it as part of declamation exercises in grammar school and high school. Before 1964, I'd given the founders kudos for their wisdom in including all the people in the Constitution.

It was in Dr. Kendall's class that I bumped up against one of the realities of colonial America—"We the People" actually included only a small group of citizens, those who were white, male property owners over the age of majority, an age determined by each state legislature.[35]

According to the first census, in 1790, free women made up 40 percent of the population and free men under the age of sixteen were 20 percent.[36] Twenty percent of the people were slaves, but for purposes of electoral representation, each one was considered as 60 percent of a free human. Don't even look for information about Native Americans; no one bothered to count them at all.

Quick addition and subtraction proved that those lauded words, "We the People," really meant "We—the 20 percent or less—of the People."

"Guess what," I reminded myself. "You, your sisters, and your mother were not part of that 'We.' "

Kendall left little doubt that he would have preferred an America governed in the old colonial way. So what if slaves had finally been set free at the cost of a terrible civil war and women had fought 130 years to get the vote? Those good old days when noble white men of high moral principle and great wisdom ruled the country were, in his view, the golden era of the American republic.

In Kendall's political philosophy, demands for individual liberty and equality—including any expansion of voting rights—were radical and dangerous. Ultimately, he reasoned, the pressures of liberty and equality would transform our constitutional government into a totalitarian one.[37]

In a paper Kendall presented in 1964, he identified the civil rights movement as the greatest existential threat to America, arguing that it would precipitate a "constitutional crisis comparable to and graver than that which precipitated the Civil War."[38] The civil rights effort was a "rebellion" fanned by "a liberal propaganda machine and advanced by the Warren Court," he said. This rebellion would threaten the survival of the American political system unless immediate action was taken.

One action Kendall suggested was a change to—or repeal of—the Fourteenth Amendment of the Constitution. Granting citizenship and the right of due process to former slaves was just a bridge too far; absolute individual rights were not part of the constitutional bargain.[39]

I was no genius about politics, but I could see the obvious: federal civil rights legislation would secure the voting rights of African American citizens, a fact that the white boys who ran the South understood. Despite his elegant prose and complex reasoning, Dr. Kendall was just another disgruntled Confederate fretting over the prospect of black folks actually voting.

"The shock of it," I joked to friends. "First women get the vote. Now the Negroes. Where will it end?"

"When we're barefoot and pregnant, and the black folks are pickin' cotton," my friend Lee Ann said.

———

Willmoore Kendall's views on voting rights spread throughout the right wing. He'd already imprinted his ideas on his former student, Bill Buckley.

In an article in *Esquire* in 1961, Buckley described the idea that everyone was qualified to vote as "one of the great self-delusions of democracy." Buckley continued, "I don't have any theory worked out on who should vote, but let's say, as a hypothesis that fifty per cent of the people are qualified to vote—or seventy-five per cent. I don't know how you determine it."[40]

Not to be outdone, Robert Welch followed the Founding Fathers in calling for "some 'limitation on suffrage.'"[41] My parents were "all-in" on this limiting the vote idea. My father pontificated on the benefits of landowners only having the vote, while Mother thought that anyone who got anything from the government should sit out elections.[42]

In 1980, Paul Weyrich, a good friend of my parents, explained why he favored limiting the vote: "I don't want everyone to vote. As a matter of fact, our leverage in the elections quite candidly goes up as the voting populace goes down."[43]

Weyrich may not be a household name, but he was the architect of much of the infrastructure of today's right wing. Think the Heritage Foundation, a huge conservative think tank. Think "the Moral Majority," the movement that brought the evangelicals into the GOP. Think ALEC, the American Legislative Exchange Council, responsible for many of the voter-suppression bills that recently came to life in state legislatures across the country.[44]

In 2011, Republican-led legislatures introduced and passed scores of bills limiting access to the polls, a reasonable response, the GOP said, to the huge, ballooning problem of voter fraud. However, the Brennan Center for Justice, which studies voting issues, disputes those GOP conclusions: "It is more likely that an individual will be struck by lightning than that he will impersonate another voter at the polls."[45]

No matter, I'm sure that Bill Buckley, Willmoore Kendall, Robert Welch, Paul Weyrich, and my parents would cheer every effort to make it harder to vote. After all, too many of those lily-livered, bleeding-heart, damn-fool people were likely to vote for . . . liberals.

Chapter Sixteen

Carrying the Cross

The true fundamentalists in our midst, whether Catholics, Protestants or Jews, are the moral salt of the earth—of an increasingly savorless earth where such salt is like a stream of clear water in a desert.

—ROBERT WELCH, 1958[1]

In 1964, I was still a good Catholic girl. I knew my Baltimore Catechism, confessed my sins, and believed in the Pope as Christ's representative on earth and the infallible head of the Church. Every Sunday, I went to Mass. I never allowed myself an excuse—Sunday meant Mass and that was that.

Early in my college career, I discovered that many of my friends had a more flexible relationship with the Catholic Church. They were—*gasp*—liberal in their interpretation of rules and guiltless about sins. While I was towing the black-and-white moral line, I noticed that my friends were not only on a different path; they were also having a lot more fun than I was. "Time to learn their secrets," I told myself.

I was, of course, fighting the rules and wresting back some control over my own decisions, but, mostly, I wanted to be included in the partying, such as it was. When I was offered a choice between playing bridge in the student union and chugging beer at California Crossing, I was going for the beer. Soon I could say "shit" with appropriate inflection and conviction. I choked down whatever liquor concoctions were served, from the infamous "Purple Jesus" to cheap booze right out of a bottle. I smoked like a chimney but drew the line at a sweet weed called "Mary Jane." I parked with a date but refused to play the "baseball game" he described. I listened to raunchy jokes and tried to laugh at the punch line, even when I didn't really get it.

As much as possible, I talked smart and pretended to be cool.

No matter what else I tried, however, this good Catholic girl forced herself out of bed every Sunday morning and into the chapel for the ten thirty Mass. Not only were very few of my friends in the pews, but my brother Jay R. was also among the missing. "Do you even go to church?" I asked him.

"Sure," he answered. "I stay up all night, go to the seven o'clock Mass, and eat breakfast. I'm back in the sack before nine."

"Really?"

"Yeah, it's the fastest Mass in history. Twenty minutes—start to finish—sermon included. Everyone goes," he explained.

"Does it count?" I asked.

"Sure, as long as it has all the essential parts," Jay R. assured me.

The next weekend, I set my alarm for 6:45 Sunday morning. I brushed my teeth, threw a trench coat over my pajamas, and stumbled into the chapel. The place was packed. The service was just as Jay described. In less than thirty minutes, Father Maher said the complete Mass (in Latin), gave a sermon (a very short one), and led two hymns (one verse of each). At 7:30 a.m., I was in the cafeteria eating scrambled eggs, bacon, and toast. By 9 a.m., I was back in my bed for a Sunday nap.

I added the "fast Mass" to my "forget-this-happened-as-far-as-Mother-and-Dad-are-concerned" list, along with Dr. Cowan's view of John F. Kennedy, Willmoore Kendall's attack on the Birch Society, and all shenanigans having anything to do with my brother.

Three times a week, Father Thomas Cain entertained my theology class with his version of Australia's favorite folk tune, "Waltzing Matilda." Exactly why this kindly Dominican priest, who had been educated in Manila and Rome, whistled this song, I never knew. But it became his signature.[2]

Thanks to him, I learned the strange story of the Bush swagman (hobo) who drowned himself in the billabong (deep lake) rather than be arrested by the squatter (landowner) and three troopers (cops). All because of a stolen jumbuck (sheep) and a tucker bag named Matilda.

"Crazy business, those Australian folk songs," I said.

Thanks to Father Cain, I also figured out that theology as explained by Thomas Aquinas, the great Dominican teacher of the thirteenth century, would never be my strong suit.[3] While some of my brainiac friends debated how many angels could dance on the head of a pin, I laughed. "How many beers does it take to care?" I wondered.

What I did learn from Father Cain, however, went far beyond either Matildas or angels. He was the first teacher I had ever had who used the Bible as a textbook. Anyone who wanted to pass his class had better read it, starting with the Book of Genesis.

Of course, as a good Catholic girl, I already knew that God had created the world in six days and rested on the seventh. He had also made our first parents, Adam and Eve, and given them the Garden of Eden as their home.

Satan, taking the shape of a serpent, had tempted Eve to disobey God. She fell for the devil's snares, ate the forbidden apple, and, in turn, offered a bite to Adam, who also ate. The sinners were cast out of Eden, naked. Thus, sin—original sin—came into the world, bringing with it labor, suffering, and death.

"Crazy business, those talking snakes," I thought.

Before long, under Father Cain's tutelage, the Creation story took on a whole new meaning. My teacher called that "putting away the things of a child." In Genesis, Father Cain found two different Creation stories, each written by a different author with a very different style and for a different purpose. One emphasized God's transcendent power, bringing something out of nothing. The second showed God's intimate relationship with humans while pondering the questions of sin, free will, and punishment.[4]

I had been taught that Moses wrote the first five books of the Old Testament, taking dictation from God Himself, and now I had to reconsider. Father Cain offered no definitive answer to the questions raised by modern biblical study, but his lectures kept me reading and learning.

As summer approached, I actually looked forward to sharing my new interest in the Bible with my parents. "Mother would love Father Cain," I thought. "This is one safe dinner subject."

————

Shortly after my parents joined the Birch Society, Robert Welch introduced them to Alphonse Matt, the editor of the *Wanderer*, a weekly Catholic newspaper published in St. Paul, Minnesota. Matt, an engaging, persuasive fellow, convinced Mother and Dad that the forces driving the country to the far left were also pushing the Catholic Church in the same direction. In no time, Matt had enlisted my parents in a crusade to save the Church, a crusade they embraced with the same fervor they gave to the Birch Society.

In 1960, Mother became the research director for the Catholic Fact Research Association. I never knew anything about the association or her job, and I had no idea if she was a paid staff member, but every so often one of her articles appeared in the *Wanderer*. One article, written in January of 1964, was typical of Mother's work. In it, she accused the National Council of Catholic Women—the largest educational organization of laywomen in the country—of promoting the "liberal establishment's materialistic diagnoses and Socialistic remedies for the social, economic and political problems of Catholic Latin America."[5]

When my mother sent me a copy of her article, I skimmed it, stuffed it in my desk drawer, and forgot all about it. A few months later, my father's article "The Catholic Church and the John Birch Society" appeared in the spring issue of *Ramparts* magazine.[6] I read it and then shoved it in my desk. My parents had embraced a new religious activism, and these articles were my clues. But I did not connect the dots.

I came home from college in late May with a determination to avoid arguments about politics. Instead, I steered my parents to safe topics, like my theology class. One evening, as I described Father Cain, "Waltzing Matilda," and the biblical exegesis he presented, my parents said nothing. Mother tapped her pencil against the placemat. Dad's color was high and his lips thin. "Jay, I'll handle this one," my mother stated.

My mother, who'd never attended college, never taken a theology class, and never met Father Cain, proceeded to castigate my teacher's interpretation of Genesis. According to her, the Creation story was historically accurate in every detail. The author of the book, under divine guidance, had recorded the facts, which were handed down to us in the Scriptures and confirmed by the tradition of the Church.

"Your Father Cain must be under the sway of the 'Modernist' heresy," Mother declared.[7] "His interpretations are riddled with error. How can such a man be teaching at UD?"

"Mother, he's not just some teacher," I said. "He's a scholar whose opinions are valued by the students and the faculty at school. He even studied in Rome."

"I don't care. He is promulgating ideas that have been forbidden. The Pope himself has declared that Moses wrote the Pentateuch and that Genesis is literally true. You are forbidden to take another class from that priest. He's a liberal, and he's wrong."

After that conversation, I paid more attention to my parents' new "orthodox" Catholicism. It became apparent that they'd fused their Catholicism with their Birchism and created an anti-Communist, anti–big government, pro-business Jesus who gave men absolute dominion over the earth. This Jesus approved of "just war" and disapproved of "social justice."

Before I'd been home another week, I understood that my parents' ideas came directly from Robert Welch, who railed against the conversion of Christianity into "a so-called *social gospel*, that bypasses all questions of dogma with an indifference which is comfortable to both themselves and their parishioners; and which *social gospel* becomes in fact indistinguishable from advocacy of the welfare state by socialist politicians."[8] Welch went on to charge that "some [ministers] actually use their pulpits to preach outright Communism, often in very thin disguise if any, while having the hypocrisy as atheists to thank God in public for their progressive apostasy."

It became more and more difficult to see where Mother and Dad's politics stopped and their religion began. Or vice versa. Before long, there was no separation of church and state as long as the church was Christian and the state was, well, Christian too.

While my father maintained his Birch activities, my mother became the religious crusader in the family. For almost thirty years, she wrote and spoke in defense of "Holy Mother Church," while fighting anything and everything that carried the slightest tinge of liberal Catholicism. She was unstoppable.

Mother believed that the dangerous ideas were part of secular humanism, a new and awful religion that put "self" at the center of all and used terms like "consciousness-raising" and "empowerment."[9]

Mother traced humanism's many manifestations, including an unnamed liberal Catholic program for women that she called "a mass-indoctrination program." One proof of the evil of that program was this: it incorporated materials "connected with the Communist American Civil Liberties Union."[10] From the New Age movement of the 1970s, which she called "a dark and hostile agent," to the "spider's web" of the nuclear disarmament movement of the 1980s, Mother tackled any idea that deviated even one millimeter from what she called "orthodox" Catholicism.

Religious fervor prompted my parents to found and fund the Wanderer Forum Foundation in 1965. The foundation was a self-described "network of lay Catholics banded together to promote and defend Catholic teaching, and to infuse principles based on that teaching into the social consciousness of this nation."[11]

Though Dad was Birching and Mother was churching, there was very little difference between them. Both wanted to dramatically change the United States by shrinking the federal government, eliminating all programs of the New Deal, gutting regulation, getting out of the United Nations, impeaching Earl Warren, and halting civil rights legislation. It went, almost without saying, that a strong military—complete with an awesome nuclear arsenal—was an essential part of their fight.

Equally important, especially to my mother, was fighting the new (and totally awful, ungodly, and liberal) feminist movement. She wrote several critiques of feminism's impact on women religious. In her view, Catholic nuns had been corrupted by the "corrosive effects of the feminist mentality with its emphasis on 'self' that have invaded many Religious communities."[12] Like her friend Phyllis Schlafly, Mother believed that feminism was a "disease" and the cause of Eve's original sin. As Karen Armstrong explains in her book *The Battle for God*, "The women's liberation movement filled fundamentalist men and women alike with terror. . . . Ever since Eve disobeyed God and sought her own liberation, feminism had brought sin into the world and with it . . . all varieties of ugliness."[13]

No good Catholic woman could ever be a feminist or support the Equal Rights Amendment, being proposed in the 1970s. My mother, Phyllis Schlafly, and a host of other right-wing Christians saw the defeat of the ERA as an essential step to preserving the traditional role of women (inside the home) and stopping what they saw as the destruction of the family.[14]

My parents viewed their personal efforts as a small part of a much larger battle: the ultimate battle between good and evil, between God and Satan. When they succeeded—when evil was destroyed and God was on his throne— America would be restored to its rightful place, a nation dedicated to Christ under Christian law.

My parents visualized the United States of America as a Catholic country—one much like Spain under Franco. Their fundamentalist friends, however, looked to biblical law—with its six-hundred-plus Old Testament regulations—as the inspiration for their Christian nation.

———

The first proponent of a biblical legal system for America was Rousas John Rushdoony, the leader of the Christian Reconstructionist Movement, and a personal friend of Robert Welch. Rushdoony admired the Birch Society but never became a member. "Welch always saw things in terms of conspiracy," he explained, "and I always see things in terms of sin."[15]

In his magnum opus, *Institutes of Biblical Law*, published in 1973, Rushdoony described the Old Testament laws that would be the backbone of the new justice system in a Christian America, along with the punishments he envisioned for those who broke them. Criminals would be burned at the stake, stoned, and hanged, depending on their sins. The folks facing such punishment included gays, blasphemers, unchaste women, and incorrigible juvenile delinquents. Of course, doctors providing abortions and their patients would also be executed.[16]

Rushdoony realized that it would take work to bring his vision for America to fruition, and he saw home schooling as the way to "train up a generation of people who know that there is no religious neutrality, no neutral law, no neutral education, and no neutral civil government. Then they will get busy in constructing a Bible-based social, political and religious order which finally denies the religious liberty of the enemies of God."[17] It was Rushdoony who first urged Christians to take "dominion over the land as the Bible commanded them to do."[18]

The evangelical leader Francis Schaeffer was reading Rushdoony and teaching others about his work. Schaeffer, as much as anyone, spread the idea that the United States was founded as a Christian nation and Christian principles had to be central in the government. It's probably safe to say that Schaeffer was the catalyst for most of the fundamentalists who claimed to have been called by God to run for political office, usually as conservative Republicans.

According to writer Max Blumenthal, Schaeffer was also responsible for creating the myth that Christians were "victims of persecution at the hands of a tyrannical secular elite not unlike the Romans who dragged Christians before teams of lions 2,000 years before. . . . To defend their supposedly threatened rights, Schaeffer suggested that Christians at least consider righteous violence as a last recourse."[19]

My parents admired Francis Schaeffer and his son, Frank, who had taken up his dad's cause very publicly and very successfully as both a writer and a filmmaker. It was not uncommon for Mother to compare my behavior unfavorably to that of young Frank. "See how he honors his father, while you turn away from your parents," she said.

Years later, Frank Schaeffer would publicly denounce his father's movement. In his riveting memoir, *Crazy for God*, Frank wrote: "To our lasting discredit, Dad and I didn't go public with our real opinions of the religious-right leaders we were in bed with. . . . We were on an ego-stroking roll. We kept our mouths shut."[20]

For many years, until my early forties, I was a practicing Catholic, but to my parents, my church attendance alone was not enough. No matter what, I wasn't devout enough or penitent enough or obedient enough. My mother and father had a high bar for approval, one I could never quite reach.

It would take me a long time, but eventually, in painful steps, I would stop trying.

Chapter Seventeen

AuH$_2$O

Goldwater's doomed candidacy was the political awakening for millions of young Americans thrilled by his promise of a campaign that was a "choice not an echo." They did not go back to sleep when he lost. They would shift the tectonic plates of the two-party system . . . introduce the concept of ideology into American elections . . . and eventually elect a president.

— GLENN GARVIN[1]

Early in 1964, a lot of University of Dallas students fell in love, but not with each other or with academics or entertainment. The new campus heart-throb was an old man—fifty-three years old, to be exact—with gray hair, a receding hairline, black eyebrows, and a real ten-gallon hat. Our hero—Barry Goldwater, the Republican senator from Arizona—had his sights set high: he planned to become the next president of the United States.

When Goldwater announced his candidacy, he promised to take on two things college students hated: regimentation and authority. "I believe we must now make a choice in this land and not continue drifting endlessly down and down for a time when all of us, our lives, our property, our hopes, and even our prayers will become just cogs in a vast government machine," Goldwater said.[2]

I certainly didn't want to be another cog in the wheel, a prisoner of a huge, unwieldy federal bureaucracy. I objected to being shouldered with a huge tax burden because the government coddled those who were too lazy to work. Many of my friends felt the same way. After all, we were the hope of the nation; we were the future. As my brother put it, "We're free, white, and [almost] twenty-one."

Many of my friends—lovers of *Atlas Shrugged* and everything Ayn Rand—believed that the chains of collectivism had to be busted, once and for all. Failure to beat back the government tsunami would push great minds to follow John Galt—Rand's fictional hero—into hiding, leaving America to crumble under the weight of socialism.

Rand preached that selfishness was a virtue. In her interview with Mike Wallace, she defended her idea that self-sacrifice, or altruism, is actually evil. She went on to explain that "a person who is weak is beyond love."[3] According to Gregory Schneider, she believed that "caring about anyone beside yourself was evil."[4]

Her philosophy appealed to many young people who flocked to her speeches. One of her devotees, who became a member of her inner, inner circle—the "Collective"—was the young economist Alan Greenspan, who later became the chairman of the Federal Reserve.[5]

Personally, I couldn't abide Rand or her novel *Atlas Shrugged.* I started the over-500,000-word tome with every intention of reading all of it. When I realized that the book was both tedious and boring, I cut the process short. I turned to the last page: "He [John Galt] raised his hand and over the desolate earth. He traced in space the sign of the dollar."[6]

"That's enough of that," I told myself.

Though I wouldn't know it for decades, I had famous company in the hating–*Atlas Shrugged* department. In 2003, I watched Bill Buckley talking with Charlie Rose on PBS. Responding to a question about Ayn Rand, Buckley said, "*Atlas Shrugged* is the biggest-selling novel of all time. I had to flog myself to read it."[7]

Still, Rand lover or no, I had been well-schooled in the horrors of thought control and indoctrination. I could look at the calendar: 1984 was only twenty years away, and time was "a-wastin'."

For a lot of Americans, the presidential election of 1964 marked a critical juncture in our history. If Barry Goldwater did not win, freedom could not survive; our destruction under the boot of Communism would be inevitable.

———

I'd known about Barry Goldwater ever since my parents forced me to read *The Blue Book of the John Birch Society.* In it, Robert Welch praised "Barry" as a "friend, a great American, and someday, God willing, the president."[8] To Birch members, Goldwater was far more than the senator from Arizona—he was Our Senator.

In the run-up to the 1964 election, when sniping at the Birch Society became the favorite pastime of Republicans, Goldwater resisted joining the fray. "Every other person in Phoenix is a member of the John Birch Society," Goldwater explained. "I'm not talking about Commie-haunted apple pickers or cactus drunks; I'm talking about the highest caste of men of affairs."[9]

Eventually, confronted by the impossibility of becoming president while hugging the Birchers, Goldwater kind of, sort of distanced himself from the society and embraced Bill Buckley's more acceptable version of conservatism.[10]

My father didn't appreciate Goldwater's "sell-out," as he called it. He reminded everyone in hearing distance that "the JBS made Goldwater." Dad had a point.

In 1959, it was Clarence (Pat) Manion, my Dad's friend and a Birch council member, who had convinced Goldwater to write *The Conscience of a Conservative*. When Goldwater had complained that he wasn't a writer and "wouldn't know how to go about it," Manion hired a ghost writer—Brent Bozell, editor of *National Review* and Bill Buckley's brother-in-law.[11]

In an effort to guarantee that *The Conscience of a Conservative* would have a substantial readership, Manion committed to printing fifty thousand copies from his own press, Victor Publishing Company, in Shepherdsville, Kentucky. According to Rick Perlstein, the push to sell Goldwater's book went all the way to a JBS council meeting, where none other than Fred Koch, then a Wichita oil refiner, ordered 2,500 copies.[12]

By the end of June of 1960, *The Conscience of a Conservative* had sold over five hundred thousand copies. In college bookstores, it flew off the shelves.[13] Pundits were not surprised that college kids loved Goldwater's book. Perlstein explained: "Freedom, autonomy, authenticity: he [the student] has rarely read a writer who speaks so clearly about the things he worries about, who was so cavalier about authority, so *idealistic*."[14]

A young Patrick Buchanan put it a bit more bluntly: "*The Conscience of a Conservative* was our new testament. . . . For those of us wandering in the arid desert of Eisenhower Republicanism, it hit like a rifle shot."[15]

In the winter of 1964, while I wrestled with matters such as Willmoore Kendall, Greek tragedy, and Western civilization, Goldwater was focused on neutralizing the liberal wing of the GOP and its surrogate, Nelson Rockefeller. The New Hampshire primary in March was supposed to be Goldwater's first big win, but blunders and missteps created uncertainty. Some supporters wondered if Barry could deliver a winning message.

On *Meet the Press*, Goldwater was uncomfortable and gaffe-prone. During the half-hour program, he said he'd break the nuclear test-ban treaty and hinted that he'd let the Senate withdraw diplomatic recognition from the Soviets. On questions of disarmament, Goldwater said, "I don't think negotiations are possible. If you mean what you say, Mr. Khrushchev, put up or shut up—as we Western poker players say."[16]

The press was put off by these comments and began to paint Goldwater as a dangerous hawk. Many Americans were also concerned, but Goldwater's base—the far-right flank of the GOP—loved him. The right wing, which had been ignored in elections, relished the idea that they'd finally have a real conservative candidate, not a half-liberal, almost Democrat who just happened to be a Republican.

At the University of Dallas, politically savvy young conservatives cheered when Goldwater accused the Democrats of measuring "welfare by the number of votes it produces."[17] People were thrilled when their guy promised to eliminate poverty by getting government "off the backs of business." Goldwater sealed the deal with his college battalions by declaring that contributing to Social Security be made voluntary. After all, many of us thought we shouldn't be taxed for a program that would be broke long before we were old enough to collect our share.

College students weren't alone in their enthusiasm. Goldwater's positions resonated with the editor of the *Manchester Union Leader*, New Hampshire's most important paper, which offered an enthusiastic endorsement. In those days, when newspaper endorsements influenced elections, this was a big get. It was evident that Goldwater would win the New Hampshire primary and win big.

I was as positive as anyone. Then I went to the movies.

Dr. Strangelove, Or: How I Learned to Stop Worrying and Love the Bomb chronicled an insane general's delight in starting a thermonuclear war. Some of my friends blamed the media for equating Goldwater with General Jack D. Ripper, the cigar-chewing, lunatic in the Stanley Kubrick movie.

A month later, *Seven Days in May* outlined the rise to power of a militaristic senator from the Southwest who plots to overthrow the president rather than accept a nuclear disarmament treaty. General James Mattoon Scott sounded a lot like Goldwater.

I wouldn't swear to my skill at analyzing movies, but Goldwater did sound like a warmonger when he proposed adding more nukes to our arsenal. I worried that this man could start a nuclear crisis.

Beyond my concerns about nukes and war, I struggled with Goldwater's anti–civil rights position. He stood firmly on states' rights, a smokescreen designed to protect the interests of white folks in the Bible Belt.

On the other hand, I couldn't stand Lyndon Johnson. He personified the worst of horse-trading and back-room dealing, the stuff that gave Washington a bad reputation. No doubt about it: compared to Johnson, Goldwater looked good.

Making a decision was, for me, academic. I could enjoy all the political bantering and assessment without actually doing the deed. I would only be nineteen years old on November 3, 1964, two years from that magic age of majority.

Still, I was disappointed when Goldwater lost the New Hampshire primary to Henry Cabot Lodge, our ambassador to Vietnam. It was a humiliating to lose by twelve points to a man who was not even in the country. Worse, Lodge was a write-in candidate.[18] In response to the embarrassing loss, Goldwater said, "I goofed up somewhere."

Even Bill Buckley—who'd supported the Goldwater movement since 1960—began to have doubts about the candidate. In his personal papers, Buckley referred to Goldwater as a man "who, after all, did not really have his heart in the campaign, and was not as well qualified to run, or serve, as (fill in the new hero)."[19] Apparently, many Americans shared Buckley's reservations. After New Hampshire, national Gallup polls recorded the senator's approval rating as a dismal 14 percent.

The rank-and-file Goldwater supporters hung their heads. Little did we know that an ace political strategist, Clif White, had spent the last four years gaming out paths to Goldwater's victory. White had figured what most politicos missed: the majority of convention delegates—those folks in funny hats shaking noisemakers and dancing in the aisles—came from non-primary states, states that picked their convention delegates at their state conventions.

In those days, the party nominee actually was chosen at the convention, and primaries were not held in every state. In 1964, thirty-one states held no statewide primary. White homed in on those places and made sure that the delegates chosen from those states were committed to Goldwater or strongly leaning in his direction.[20]

Though his boss lost fourteen New Hampshire delegates, White lined up dozens of others from Southern, non-primary states.[21]

In this election, Dixie mattered. Goldwater's Senate vote against the 1964 Civil Rights Act made him the go-to candidate for angry whites, many of whom renounced their lifelong Democratic ties and became Republicans. One conspicuous defection was the staunch, bombastic Democrat from South Carolina, Senator Strom Thurmond.[22] Ironically, while Thurmond was railing against integration, he was also supporting Essie Mae Washington-Williams, the daughter he had fathered with his family's African American maid.[23] No one breathed a word of the scandal for thirty-nine years, however, and the 1964 primary season rolled on.

Goldwater struggled to break away from the GOP pack. He was seen as a weak front-runner, a situation attributed to "disarray" in the Republican

Party. Even after Goldwater pulled in more than 50 percent of the Illinois vote, *Time* downplayed the result, emphasizing that "200,000 Republicans who voted for a gubernatorial candidate did not bother about the presidential primary."[24]

Goldwater's win in Texas, with 75 percent of the votes cast, was described as "low-key and lackluster."[25] Goldwater had a different perspective on the primaries. As he waited for the results of the California primary, he said, "I don't worry about it. We take what comes. We've done the best we can."[26]

The best he could do was good enough. Goldwater squeaked through the California primary with a slim fifty-nine-thousand-vote margin and headed into the convention with almost enough votes to win. Everyone who had worked for him crossed their fingers, said their prayers, and waited.

In the middle of July, I camped out in front of the television in the basement of my parents' home to watch the convention. After all the ups and downs of the primary season, after all the hand-wringing and in-fighting, Goldwater captured the nomination on the very first ballot. On the last day of the convention, Richard Nixon, Goldwater's arch-nemesis, introduced the Republican nominee as "Mr. Conservative and Mr. Republican," adding, "And here is the man who, after the greatest campaign in history, will be Mr. President."[27]

I wasn't sure about that "greatest campaign" business or the "Mr. President" part, but my parents were grinning from ear to ear as they heard those words. I guess they thought the inauguration of President Barry Goldwater was inevitable.

A few minutes later, after the convention band had played "The Battle Hymn of the Republic" and San Francisco's Cow Palace was deluged with red, white, and blue balloons, Goldwater addressed the crowd. "Our people have followed false prophets," he said. "We must and we shall return to proven ways—not because they are old but because they are true."[28]

Then Goldwater returned to the standard conservative words: freedom and liberty with dashes of honesty, destiny, and vision thrown in for good measure. Finally, he worked up to his climax: "I would remind you that extremism in the defense of liberty is . . . no . . . vice." The place went wild with cheering. It lasted a long time.

When Goldwater finished speaking, the far right wing was ecstatic. The rest of the GOP, who'd expected Goldwater to make nice with the moderates, was horrified. The 1964 election was under way.

The next morning, my father left an AuH_2O button on my desk with a handful of Goldwater pamphlets and instructions to put them in the neighbors' mailboxes. I was officially marching in the Goldwater army. I continued in the Chicago contingent until late in August. Then, it was back to Dallas, where the pro-Goldwater forces at my school were big and bold.

For Goldwater's supporters, his campaign slogan said it all: "In your heart, you know he's right." Unfortunately, the country seemed to lean toward a more satirical version of it: "In your guts, you know he's nuts."[29]

In early September, after a summer of "can he, will he?" I came face-to-face with the fact that Barry couldn't and he wouldn't. I knew—in my heart—that the blizzard of pamphlets and phone calls, radio spots and contributions would make no difference to his cause. The final nail in Goldwater's political coffin was a one-minute television ad that was only shown one time.[30]

This ad, tagged "Daisy," began with a toddler standing in a field pulling the petals from a daisy. She counted: "1 . . . 2 . . . 3 . . . 4 . . . 5 . . . 7 . . . 6 . . . 6 . . . 8 . . . 9 . . . 9 . . ." Then a deep adult voice picked up the count from 9 and counted down to 0, followed by an explosion, a stream of smoke, and a mushroom cloud. "We must either love each other or we must die," President Johnson said, followed by a reminder to vote on November 3. "The stakes are too high for you to stay home."

Another Johnson ad, also shown just one time, cemented the image of Goldwater as a "bomb-dropper." Goldwater's campaign manager admitted that he lost sleep trying to figure a way to "lick" that image. No commercial or ad could change the perception that Goldwater was dangerous. Americans had made up their minds. "Barry Goldwater scared them."[31]

There was one bright spot in the Goldwater campaign: "Its grassroots army of almost 4 million activists had mobilized. Campaign workers personally contacted more than 12 million households by mid-October, 4 million more than the Democrats."[32]

A week before Election Day, Ronald Reagan, movie star, host of *General Electric Theater*, and new Republican convert, added his voice in support of Goldwater. His speech, "A Time for Choosing," which Reagan had been giving in venues all over the country for several years, put Reagan's velvet voice and speaking prowess on display for the entire country.[33]

"History will record with the greatest astonishment that those who had the most to lose did the least to prevent its happening," Reagan said. "I think it's time we ask ourselves if we still know the freedoms that were intended for us by the Founding Fathers."[34] He concluded, "You and I have a rendezvous with destiny. We will preserve for our children this, the last best hope of man on Earth, or we will sentence them to take the last step into a thousand years of darkness."

Americans cheered Reagan. "A flood of telephone calls and contributions followed the telecast, testifying to Reagan's appeal."[35] No matter, over 43 million Americans raced to the polls to vote for LBJ. Barry Goldwater got 38 percent of the popular vote, carried only six states, and received fifty-two Electoral College votes.[36] It was a shellacking.

I sat through the election results in stunned silence. My guy had gone down in flames, and I didn't even get to vote for him. Dejected University of Dallas students bemoaned the plight of conservatives.

"It'll be a cold day in hell before another conservative is nominated," one friend said.

"Never mind that," I answered. "The whole right wing is kaput. My parents and the Birchers just became ancient history."

Good grief. Were we ever wrong.

———

On November 4, 1964, Republicans across the country woke up with hangovers no amount of coffee or aspirin would cure. The worst electoral rout in thirty-plus years provoked reams of analysis. Much of it focused on the impact the Goldwater debacle would have on the GOP in general and the conservative movement in particular.

James Reston, writing in the *New York Times*, stated what appeared, at the time, to be obvious: "Barry Goldwater not only lost the Presidential election yesterday but the conservative cause as well. He has wrecked his party for a long time to come."[37] The *Dallas Morning News* had a similar take: "Democrats Rout GOP." *Life* described Johnson's win as "The Mighty Landslide," and inside, Theodore White's article spoke of "Republican Wreckage—Now What?"[38] *Time* magazine believed that "the conservative cause whose championship Goldwater assumed suffered a crippling setback" and "Barry Goldwater and his type of conservatism have had their moment in the sun."[39]

For months, the pundits dissected and catalogued, opined and bloviated. One of the conclusions reached by almost everyone was simple: the GOP had to embrace moderation.[40] "A defiant conservative," as Reston of the *Times* described Goldwater, could not win a national election.

These political junkies gave passing thought to the five states Goldwater grabbed, states that really heralded the beginning of a major political reorganization. In Mississippi, he had won over 80 percent of the vote, followed closely by Alabama with 70 percent. He also won in South Carolina, Louisiana, and Georgia. Folks noted these wins but didn't understand the impact. "Dixie's defection to conservatism" was a "one-shot affair," according to the *Washington Post.*[41]

Looking at today's solid-red South, it's hard to ignore the inroads made by Goldwater, consolidated by Richard Nixon, and locked down by Ronald Reagan. These days, a Democratic win in the South is as improbable as a hurricane in North Dakota.

Barry Goldwater took some of the blame for the electoral disaster, saying he was "sorry I didn't do better," but he insisted that it was the GOP moderates who killed his chances.[42] Those folks, he believed, "have no difference at all with Democratic concepts." He summed up his analysis with this broadside, "I wasn't *dishonest* enough in this campaign to win."

In his biography of Barry Goldwater, Robert Alan Goldberg writes: "Those who fought the odds that year [1964] . . . wear specials badges of identity and honor. They stand apart as the founding generation that in defeat marked future victory."[43] Others have said that Goldwater really won the 1964 election but that it took until Reagan to count the votes. I don't know if either of those statements is one hundred percent true, but I do know how Robert Welch and the John Birch Society looked at the election.

Welch believed that the Americans who voted for Goldwater were "desperate and almost dying to have, a crusade against the collectivist menace, or against the frightening moral decline . . . or against both."[44] The forty-two million who voted for LBJ, however, were "voting for the repeal of the Declaration of Independence" and "scrapping the United States Constitution entirely, as an absurd and useless antique; and for replacing it with whatever modernistic pieces of legislative furniture might appeal to the taste of the Supreme Court."[45]

Welch berated the "good people who have voted for steps which . . . will wipe out the value of all of their savings, their life insurance policies, their bonds and mortgages, and will redistribute wealth from the industrious and frugal into the hands of the shiftless."[46]

Over the course of eight pages of election analysis, Welch called Social Security a "gigantic embezzlement" and reminded his readers that "*while food, shelter and clothing are necessities for an individual in a civilized community, the guarantee that he will always have them is not.*"[47] (Emphasis mine.)

He also described the views of the Democrats this way: "We protect ourselves from being murdered by committing suicide; or, more specifically, that we prevent the Kremlin's agents from making us Communist slaves by beating them to it."[48]

Though Welch took to task the forty-two million Americans who voted for LBJ, many pundits laid the election debacle at the feet of the extremists, including the Birchers. Be that as it may, the society bragged that the Goldwater loss had generated big membership gains.

According to Welch, by December of 1964, the JBS had formed 274 new chapters.[49] Across the country, a newly energized JBS ran a big ad campaign, "Now Will You Join the John Birch Society?" Apparently thousands of people were saying, "Yes."

Chapter Eighteen

Something's Happening Here

Robin Williams—irreverent, talented, crazy Robin Williams—once said, "If you remember the sixties, you weren't there."[1] I laughed. I also had to admit that I missed a whole bunch of stuff that defined the 1960s as "the sixties." I didn't do Woodstock or experience a California love-in. I was nowhere near the riots in Watts or the shootings at Kent State. Love beads and muumuus were as close as I got to the hippies. I never smoked a joint, dropped acid, or snorted cocaine. As one of my friends said, "Your 'hip' gene is missing."

While the cool cats were stoned and "Hell no, we won't go" echoed on college campuses, I was safe in my little bubble, reading and studying. I was no genius, but before the decade ended, I thought it would be defined by three assassinations (two Kennedys and one King), racial strife, and the war in Vietnam.

Ronald Reagan, the GOP's newest star, was gung-ho for the war. "We should declare war on North Vietnam," he said in October of 1965.[2] "It is silly talking about how many years we will have to spend in the jungles of Vietnam when we could pave the whole country and put parking stripes on it, and still be home by Christmas." The prowar folks, echoing Reagan, shouted, "Give Us Joy, Bomb Hanoi."[3]

Reagan never got his wish about the war declaration, but he got the war he wanted. The year 1966 dawned with 215,000 Americans serving in Vietnam. By December the number had climbed to 389,000. Eventually, 540,000 men would be serving in Southeast Asia.[4]

As the war escalated, boys my age explored every possible way to avoid the draft. The lucky ones landed critical-skills deferments. Others sought out doctors who would declare them unfit for duty. When all else failed, some fled to Canada. The draft dodgers had plenty of reasons to find ways out of military service. In 1968, 15,000 young Americans came home in body bags. Their average age was twenty.[5]

For young Americans like me, the Vietnam War was a disaster, a heartbreaking, gut-wrenching one. I believe we saw the truth of it long before the "grown-ups" did.

By early 1968, President Johnson woke up to reality: his presidency had been shattered by the war. Despite landmark civil rights legislation and the Great Society social-safety-net policies, Vietnam was his Waterloo.[6] The Tet Offensive—considered by many historians to have marked the turning point in the Vietnam War—ended Johnson's political career.[7] On March 31, 1968, knowing he could not win reelection, Johnson announced, "I shall not seek and I will not accept the nomination of my party for another term as your president."[8]

Four days later, Dr. Martin Luther King was killed by a sniper. Then, on June 5, Robert Kennedy, a front-runner for the Democratic presidential nomination, was gunned down in Los Angeles. To put it mildly, the country was in chaos.

When I think about those times, I believe Robin Williams took the easy way out. It really was easier to be stoned and forget than to be sober and remember.

The chaos of the '60s played out in my personal life, too.

Two days after Barry Goldwater suffered defeat at the hands of Lyndon Johnson newspapers across the country were analyzing, evaluating, and editorializing about the meaning of the results. It wasn't enough that Goldwater had lost; everybody with an opinion had to weigh in on some aspect of the election. Even the Russians offered their congratulations to President Johnson, along with some platitudes about "consolidating universal peace."[9]

The *Chicago Tribune* bemoaned the election results: "It is apparent that socialism is on the march. The people want pie and they do not reckon tomorrow's costs as long as they have the illusion of tasting it now."[10] Ironically, my parents wouldn't read that editorial for three days. They had to wait until the U.S. Postal Service delivered the *Trib* to their new address: Arlington Street, Marshfield, Wisconsin.

When I thought about my upcoming Christmas vacation, I had to remind myself that I would never sleep another night in my Sioux Avenue bedroom or meet my friends for a pizza at Lou's. No, the Conners now lived in a town with a population of thirteen thousand.

"There are more cows than people," my brother Jay R. told me.

"That is not comforting," I answered him.

"Look on the bright side, sister of mine," he added. "In this state, we are old enough to drink beer."

Great, I lived in a place with cows, beer, and a whole lot of nothing else. And just to add to the fun, winter was so damn cold that a person could freeze to death. After a few weeks in Wisconsin, I pressed my dad to explain how we'd landed in that place. It was, in my opinion, a long way to fall.

After lunch at Julie's, a local tavern Dad frequented, he lit a cigarette, sipped his martini, and explained what had happened.

"The Birch attacks escalated and our business slipped. More and more customers disappeared. Finally, Lou and Ray [Dad's business partners] demanded that I quit the JBS. Of course, I refused. Then, they called a corporate meeting and voted their shares—66 percent—against me. I had to settle for the deal they offered."

"What was the deal?" I asked.

"They took control of Conroth, including our factories and all the other business interests. I got this little furniture factory right here. They forgot to tell me that no one ever looked at the books; the company had never made a dime."

"What are you going to do?" I asked.

"I've borrowed everything I can, even against my life insurance policies. Now I'm trying to keep the wolf from the door," my father said.

"What does that mean, exactly?"

"I'm trying to keep from going broke," Dad said.

That night I thought about my parents and the situation they faced in Marshfield. I felt sorry for them, and I worried for their future. At the same time, I made a personal decision. "I'll never live here," I said. "Never, ever, and that's final."

Such an absolute, cast-in-stone, nonnegotiable promise was, as the saying goes, made to be broken. But that day, I had total confidence in my pledge. I had one good reason for that confidence: I'd met a boy, a handsome, tall, smart fraternity boy who went to Southern Methodist University, the crown jewel of Dallas's colleges.

SMU was known all over the Southwest as the stomping grounds of Peruna, the school's mustang mascot, and the home of 96 Guys and a Doll, the awesome marching band. Thanks to a blind date, arranged by my friend Lee Ann, I was introduced to everything UD didn't have. "I'm finally going to college," I told my friends after a few months. Suddenly, I had the best of all worlds: I studied at UD and played at SMU. The arrangement was just dandy.

Like me, my new boyfriend was a Midwest transplant, and like me, he had no plans to return to his roots. He was already working at Texas Instruments in an engineering school work-study program. Upon graduation, he'd be working full-time on a secret project for the Department of Defense, a job that guaranteed a critical-skills deferment. With it, he'd never see the jungles of Southeast Asia or the alleys of Saigon.

"Thank God," I said. "He can serve Uncle Sam from an assembly line in Richardson."

———

GOP members used the months after the election to fight among themselves. The *Chicago Tribune* blamed "party [Republican] leaders who sulked in their tents" and the "ideological split . . . that dragged down Goldwater's popular vote and undoubtedly cost him many states."[11]

The fighting and fussing didn't affect the John Birch Society; they went on the offense. In newspapers across the country, a slick fifteen-page insert appeared that painted the JBS as the real American patriots the country longed for. Heaping praise on Robert Welch, Birch founder, the ad quoted *National Review*, "There is no question that he has stirred the slumbering spirit of patriotism in thousands of Americans, roused them from lethargy, and changed their apathy into a deep desire to first learn the facts about communism and then implement that knowledge with effective and responsible action."[12]

Bill Buckley probably didn't like the reference, but the Birch ad had an impact. In July of 1965, Ben Bagdikian, writing in the *New York Times*, acknowledged the effectiveness of Birch efforts to turn Goldwater's loss into their gain. "Tightest and shrewdest of all ultra operations is the John Birch Society, which claims to have inherited 30 per cent of the Goldwater activists in Los Angeles County," a number around 3,500 people.[13]

Much of the credit for the JBS success has to go to John Rousselot, a former congressman from California who served as the society's national PR director. Rousselot developed and implemented the new Birch advertising, including a coast-to-coast weekly radio message, *The Birch Reports*. He found the key to Birch success and conservative electoral success in one place—the Southern states. Turning that region Republican was Rousselot's goal.[14]

According to Donald Critchlow, "Republicans were eager to move the party to the political center and reestablish it as a party of moderation."[15] But many conservatives pushed back against the desire to purge the Far Right from the party's ranks. Their rising star, Ronald Reagan, said, "We don't intend to turn the Republican Party over to the traitors in the battle that just ended."

Robert Welch added fuel to this GOP civil war when he published his annual assessment of the level of Communist control in the United States. In the 1965 "Scoreboard" issue of the Birch Society magazine, *American Opinion*, Welch concluded that the United States was "60–80 percent Communist dominated."[16]

This assessment pushed Bill Buckley and *National Review* to take action. In the October 19, 1965, issue, they devoted twenty pages to pillorying the JBS, accusing it of harming the anti-Communist cause. Buckley used the example of the Birch position on the Vietnam War to prove his point: "The President of the United States is engaged in anti-Communist action in Southeast Asia, and for that reason is under great pressure from the American Left. But he is also, astoundingly, under pressure from a segment of the American Right which has been taught by Mr. Robert Welch that apparently anti-Communist action undertaken by the government of the United States cannot really be anti-Communist for the reason that our Government is controlled by Communists."[17]

Here's a simpler translation of Buckley's criticism. According to the JBS, our government is almost totally controlled by the Communists. Obviously, those Communists would design our foreign policy to help the Communists, not harm them. Therefore, the Vietnam War can't be hurting the Communists; it has to be helping them.

Buckley had it right; that was exactly why the JBS opposed the Vietnam War.

Robert Welch explained it like this: "There [is] less chance of this Administration conducting an honest war in Vietnam, for honestly anti-Communist purposes, than there is of Khrushchev being elected President of the United States Chamber of Commerce." Welch continued, "The Communists . . . create a left wing demand that the U.S. pull out of Vietnam and fool the American people into thinking that we are serving some purpose, other than exactly what the Communists want. Naturally the Communists have been doing everything to advance the theme that it is our patriot and humanitarian duty to 'stand firm' in Vietnam."[18]

One historian portrayed the Birch position on the war this way: "Welch's neo-isolationist posture on Vietnam . . . earned him the most vociferous ire of the conservative movement leaders. In a convoluted, conspiratorial interpretation of events, Welch saw the war as a carefully managed fraud, designed to convince the U.S. public of President Johnson's anti-communist goals."[19]

The JBS position on the war cost them. Many folks who had supported the society abandoned the cause. In 1965, the California Fact-Finding Subcommittee on Un-American Activities reversed its previously positive view of the society, declaring that it "has attracted a lunatic fringe that is now assuming serious proportions" and "had been beset by an influx of emotionally unstable people."[20]

———

For the next two years, Mother made sure that I was in the loop on all things Birch. Every time we talked, she urged me to step up and make the Birch cause my own. "You're an adult now," she told me. "It's time to act like one."

She faithfully forwarded the Birch bulletins to me—I'd never given the society my Texas address—and every month, she underlined passages and added comments. It didn't take me long to flip through the pages and then toss the thing. When Mother would ask if I'd completed the Birch agenda for the month, I'd cross my fingers and say, "Just like always."

I congratulated myself on the ruse. "I'm here and they're there," I told myself.

The day after Christmas in 1966, on a bitter cold day in Marshfield, I married my college sweetheart. Our future looked bright: all we had to do was get back to Dallas, set up our little duplex on Anita Street, and discover what being married was all about.

"You've landed that most important of all degrees," my friends teased. "The MRS."

"Yes, I'm a real Texas girl now," I bragged.

For a couple of years, I dodged Birch politics. In our house, most of the stuff my mother sent ended up in the garbage while *Time*, *Life*, and *Newsweek* lived in our magazine rack. I thought of myself as a conservative, though not a John Bircher; but politics was not my priority. I was more interested in "fun and games," as my mother would say.

Then in 1968, I became the focus of my parents' full-court political press. Their goal was a simple one: they wanted me to support George Wallace for president. *Time* quoted Wallace as saying, "We're going to shake the eyeteeth of the liberals of both national parties," adding, "By liberal, he means anything left of the far, far right."[21]

No wonder my parents were Wallace all the way.

My mother and father forgot one thing in their campaign to get my vote for Wallace—I despised the bombastic little man from Alabama and the racist ideas he peddled. As much as I wanted to appease my parents, on this issue I dug in my heels. "I will never vote for Wallace," I told them.

Wallace's campaign did nothing to change my mind. I was appalled when he explained his plan to stop the race riots and war protests to a *Life* reporter: "Bam! Bam! Bam! Shoot 'em dead on the spot! Bam!"[22]

Six weeks later, the magazine interviewed Wallace campaign staffers and supporters in Indiana. "He will bring tranquility," one woman said. "He will put everyone in *their* place—the colored, the students, the people on welfare, anyone who's causing so much trouble."[23] In the same article, another Wallace fan, said, "The only difference between the races is that the majority of blacks are bad, and with the whites it is only the minority."

Time followed Wallace to Pittsburgh, where he roused a standing-room-only crowd of two thousand at a "Stand Up for America" rally. In the audience, the reporter spotted "well-dressed men sporting John Birch Society pins. At one point, an enthusiast shouted, 'Wallace is a new Messiah!'"[24]

Though Wallace's position on civil rights disturbed me, his position on the Vietnam War scared me. When he was asked about the idea of withdrawing from the growing quagmire in Southeast Asia, he took a whole different tack from that of most other politicians. "I think we've got to pour it on," he said.[25] To prove the point, Wallace selected as his running mate retired general Curtis LeMay, a hawk's hawk who believed that the most efficient way to win the war would be to use nuclear weapons. "Bomb 'em back to the Stone Age," was LeMay's victory strategy.[26]

My father loved the general even more than he loved the governor. "The general understands. If it takes a nuke, it takes a nuke," Dad said to me.

At first blush, my father's prowar position appeared to be a complete switch from the antiwar position that the JBS had previously taken. But understanding the shift actually was easy. In my father's mind, and in the minds of the rest of the JBS, the current administration was pro-Communist, which made their Vietnam War pro-Communist too. A Wallace administration would be absolutely anti-Communist, thus making *their* Vietnam War absolutely anti-Communist.

During the 1968 election, Robert Welch never took a position on the war or the candidates. In fact, in the November JBS bulletin, Welch went out of his way to defend his neutrality in the campaign, insisting that "nothing is going to be changed basically by this election." He went on to describe what would happen if Wallace were to be elected: "The drive to thwart everything [Wallace] tries to do to expose the Communists and to halt their advance will be 'out of this world.' It will produce incredibly foul and determined efforts to smear him into the outstanding exhibit of a frustrated, futile, and angry man."[27]

Conversely, according to Welch, a Nixon election would have this effect: "The only thing between us and the final catastrophe of subjugation, which the Communist influences that surround [Nixon] will seek to achieve, is also the increasingly vocal and determined opposition of an increasingly informed and aroused public opinion." As Welch's readers knew, those "informed and aroused" folks had to come from the JBS. No one else "has the slightest chance of doing the job," he added.[28]

I suspected that Welch and the Birchers were putting everything they had into the Wallace campaign, but I had no proof until I read the 1996 book *The Politics of Rage*, by Dan Carter. "Beginning in 1965, Robert Welch had used Selma's [Alabama] sheriff, Jim Clark, as a go-between to pass along the names of key Birchers across the nation anxious to help George Wallace," Carter wrote. "In state after state outside the South, dedicated Birchers stepped into the organizational void in the 1968 campaign; they dominated the Wallace movement in nearly a dozen states from Maine to California."[29]

As Election Day approached, my parents pushed harder for Wallace. They called me every day or two with the same message: "This is your first vote for president. Make it count."

I did. On November 5, 1968, I cast my first vote as an adult American. After weighing the only two candidates I considered sane—Richard Nixon and Hubert Humphrey—I voted for Nixon. I don't remember the exact reason I decided on him, but it had something to do with what I called the "Democratic boredom factor."

When Mother called late in the day, she got right to the point. "Did you vote, dear?" she asked.

"I did, Mother," I answered.

"Did you follow your parents' direction and vote for Wallace?" she continued.

"I listened," I said.

Apparently, she was satisfied. "Phew," I thought. "That's over for another four years."

In late December of 1968, my husband and I made the trek to Marshfield, Wisconsin, to celebrate the New Year with my family. As a special present, Mother Nature sent us a blast of Arctic air that plunged the thermostat to an incredible forty degrees below zero. My little brother described it as "colder than a witch's tit" and no one even raised an eyebrow. Over dinner at the country club, my husband proposed a toast: "Happy New Year. We can all climb in the refrigerator right now and be seventy degrees warmer."

In the morning, while I huddled in front of a heating vent with a cup of coffee, my dad and my husband ventured out to take a "little look" at the factory. I knew about the challenges Dad faced in running the place, beginning with too many bills and too few customers. I wished my father well, but the business had been on a downward spiral long before he'd taken over, and nothing seemed to be changing the trajectory. As far as I was concerned, his best move was to pray for a jackpot in the next Irish Sweepstakes.

Little did I know, but my father had already set his eyes on the "jackpot" he needed—a trained industrial engineer with production experience, someone just like the man I had married. Before I could mount a strong counterargument, my dad and my husband had made a bargain: he'd run the plant for three to five years as long as Dad didn't interfere with his management decisions.

Knowing my dad as well as I did, I was doubtful about the "noninterference" agreement. But the two men shook hands and that, as they say, was that. A few months later, I found myself in a tiny apartment in Marshfield with a six-month-old infant and a husband who dashed out the door at 5 a.m. and returned twelve to fourteen hours later.

"This will only last three years," I reminded myself and him.

My husband corrected me. "Five," he said. "At the outside."

Chapter Nineteen

A Good Man Is Hard to Find

This party is a distillation of the John Birch Society, the Christian Crusade and the Minutemen. We're revolutionaries. . . . We'll have constitutional government in this country and if we don't get it through the ballot box, we'll get it in the streets.

—DEL MYERS, AMERICAN INDEPENDENT PARTY OFFICIAL[1]

I was still unpacking boxes and organizing the kitchen in our Marshfield apartment when my mother arrived with a stack of "material" and a summons to the next John Birch Society meeting.

"We have a core of loyal John Birchers," she said, "all eager to meet you."

I brewed tea for both of us and joined her at the table. "Mother," I said, "I'm not going to be a reliable member, with the baby and all."

"Bring him. He can sleep upstairs."

"Not this time," I told her. "But we'll see about next month."

"Your father and I will expect you," she said.

Before she left, I promised to read the new Birch bulletin cover to cover. "Small price to get out of the meeting," I told myself as I thumbed through the pages.

Over the first fifteen pages, Robert Welch focused on the new appointments to President Nixon's staff while insisting that he had "no wish to rock the 'unity' boat before it leaves the station."[2] But wishes aside, Welch lit into Henry Kissinger, the president's national security advisor, for his "vigorous anti-anti-Communist leanings" and his three degrees from Harvard, "the alma mater of subversion." Welch then teed off on Daniel Moynihan, head of the Council on Urban Affairs, for "applying socialist measures to give the Negroes economic equality."[3] Before long, Welch was in one of his frenzies about catastrophe lurking on the horizon if Americans didn't wake up soon. "Must we wait to become aware of what is happening only when thousands of our daughters and sisters and sweethearts are herded together in some huge enclosure and subjected to several days of repeated rape by occupying Communist troops?" he wrote.[4]

"Same old, same old," I thought. "Welch has not changed a whit."

A few pages later, Welch introduced the newest Birch ad hoc committee: MOTOREDE. The name, shorthand for the Movement to Restore Decency, was dedicated to stopping the "growing indecency in American life," evidenced by the breakdown of "modesty, of cleanliness, of good manners, of good taste, of moderation in appetites, of restraint in behavior, of morality and tradition, and of all those attitudes which distinguish civilized man from pre-pastoral aborigines."[5]

Robert Welch identified the first step to any revival as opposition to the "filthy Communist plot" of sex education in the public schools. He insisted that sex education class included "instruction on sexual methods followed by encouragement to experiment and practice."[6] "It is not unusual," he wrote, "for a high school teacher to ask his students (boys and girls together, ages fifteen to eighteen) to tell the class about, or write themes about . . . kissing, masturbation, light petting, fondling breasts or genitals, sexual intercourse . . . and *sexual activities with an animal*."

I laughed. "Sex with Fido? What the hell?"

MOTOREDE joined the other ad hoc committees of the John Birch Society: Get US Out!, TACT (Truth About Civil Turmoil), TRAIN (To Restore American Independence Now), and SYLP (Support Your Local Police).

My mother eagerly took up MOTOREDE and looked to me to partner with her. "Do it for your son," she urged me one day while we sat at the kitchen table and I held my newborn. "What kind of world will he inherit if the sex peddlers win?" There I sat while my fifty-six-year-old mother talked about sex and perversion, quite the change for a woman who'd taught me about the "birds and the bees" by leaving a pamphlet on my pillow.

I tried to end the conversation by pointing out that lax morals were common in many civilizations throughout history, but Mother would have none of it. She was positive that 1969 marked the summit in the history of sexual sinning. In her mind, for the first time, children were learning how to have sex in school. And, adding insult to injury, teenage boys and girls were being taught how to use condoms, behind their parents' backs.

"You need to listen to your Mother, young lady," she admonished me. "Morality is under attack, from all sides, and the Communists are behind it."

As she lectured, I remembered the fierce textbook warrior in 1959. There she was, marching to the principal's office in her hat and gloves, the click-click of her three-inch pumps echoing on the tile floor. I remembered how my classmates whispered, "She's here, again." I remembered how I groaned and turned away.

I knew that she'd be just as formidable in her new fight. In fact, she was giddy when she described her confrontation with the principal of the local Catholic high school. "It was wild," she told me. "Just like Chicago."

———

Given the tsunami of terrible, awful, no-good, very bad events that dominated the news, I gave little thought to mother's crusade against sex education. It was the war in Vietnam that held my attention.

In April of 1969, the United States had reached peak troop strength of 543,400. Six years later, when the last American was evacuated from the roof of our embassy in Saigon, more than 58,000 Americans had come home in body bags.[7] The intervening years were hell.

When the My Lai massacre was leaked to the press in late 1969, eighteen months after the incident occurred, I struggled to understand what was happening in the jungles of Nam. I was appalled that William Calley Jr. and his C Company had murdered over three hundred unarmed Vietnamese civilians, including women and children, in a horrific execution-style sweep.[8] I saw the *Life* photographs of My Lai, and I knew America had abdicated its role as the "good guys."[9] I wanted every American home from the hellhole called Nam, and I wanted the My Lai killers in jail for the rest of their lives.

Many Americans, however, still believed in the war, a reality I confronted almost every time I turned on the Marshfield radio station. Several times a day, Barry Sadler roused the audience with his 1966 "Ballad of the Green Berets."[10] While Sadler cheered for the military's most elite killing squad and prayed that his son would join their ranks, I held my baby son and shuddered at the thought of him registering for the draft.

The chasm between Barry Sadler and me was repeated day after day, all across the country. One writer put it like this, "Clearly, there were two Americas, Left versus Right."[11] Even a cursory peek at the 1972 presidential campaign proved the point. On the Left, the Democrats pasted together a coalition of labor, antiwar protestors, hippies, feminists, and African Americans with a smattering of druggies and draft dodgers thrown in for good measure. All of these discordant personalities led the Republicans to label the Democrats as the party of "acid, abortion, and amnesty."[12] In contrast, many Christians, with their demure wives and respectful children, raced into the arms of the GOP along with anti–civil rights Southerners, anti-Communists, and America-love-it-or-leave-it patriots.[13]

I realized how deep the partisan rift had become when a wheelchair-bound Vietnam vet, Ron Kovic, was insulted and attacked by pro-Nixon Republicans at the GOP convention in Miami. "I gave three-quarters of my body for America," Kovic said to a reporter covering the convention. "And what do I get? Spit in the face... I sat in my chair still shaking and began to cry."[14]

In the John Birch Society, the Vietnam War dilemma was still unresolved. On the one hand, the Birchers loved the idea of a strong military under the direction of a strong anti-Communist government, which they did not see happening in the Johnson or Nixon administrations. In addition, America had entered the Vietnam War without a formal declaration from the Congress. Thus, for many Birchers, the incursion into Southeast Asia was unconstitutional.

Despite that, my parents and the leadership in Belmont, Massachusetts, would have supported the war if the American military had been given the go-ahead to bomb Hanoi with nukes, if necessary. They wanted a decisive victory, no matter how it was achieved.

Robert Welch wrote about the failure to achieve victory in Vietnam as having "the stench of deliberate and blatant treason so strong, in the very top circles of our national life, that real patriotism is being downgraded and replaced by the same doubts, confusion and despair which are eroding all other American virtues that once were commonplace."[15]

Welch spoke for my parents and every other right-winger I'd ever met. They wanted real patriots who fought for American virtues without counting the cost. Anyone, like me, who doubted the cause was a scaredy-cat and a traitor.

Despite our huge differences about the war and civil rights, my parents were determined to drag me back into the Birch fold. Whenever conversation veered toward these issues, tensions rose. My father yelled and swore just like he always had, but now I pushed back. My father only yelled and swore louder. As for my husband, who had come from a family where table talk was about the Chicago Cubs or the latest doings at the American Legion Post, the uproar at Conner family dinners was not to his liking. He counseled me to keep my mouth shut. I tried—I really did—but my silence riled my parents even more.

Mother attacked. "You're half-baked. How can you be such a milquetoast in this critical moment in history?"

In 1971, I was invited to my parents' home to meet one of their favorite young Birchers, a forty-one-year-old ex-Marine who'd used his powerful voice to stop a vicious knife attack. Despite the fact that the victim died, the man was lauded as a hero. Before long, he had joined the Birch Society, won election to the California State Senate, and then the Congress. He became the youngest man to serve on the John Birch Society National Council, where he met my father. The two became good friends.

"He's the society's rising star," Dad said.

My mother hailed him as a "staunch traditional Catholic" and "a man among men."

I'd never met a congressman before, so I made sure I was at my parents' home right on time. In the living room, my father was engaged in conversation with a dark-haired, mustached fellow who looked up at me and broke into a huge grin. "Claire," my father said, "meet Congressman John Schmitz."[16]

When I asked John why he'd joined the Birch Society, he said, tongue in cheek, "To get the middle-of-the-road vote in Orange County."[17] That answer was John's standard response—to me, to my parents, to the press. Over dinner, John charmed me with stories of his wife, Mary, and their seven children. I remember him talking about three, three, and one: three boys, three girls, and one boy. He called his oldest girl "Cake," and I had the impression that she was his favorite. Before long, I realized that John's youngest son, Philip, and my little daughter (she'd arrived in April of 1970) had been born one month apart.[18] By the time the evening ended, I quite liked the man. "He's an honest man and a good dad," I told myself.

A few months later, Congressman Schmitz caused a ruckus when he said, "I have no objection to President Nixon going to China. I just object to his coming back."[19] Apparently, the voters in his district did not appreciate these remarks, especially since Nixon's San Clemente home was in Schmitz's congressional district, and by the time the smoke cleared, John was out, beaten in the Republican primary by a Nixon-loving challenger.

Schmitz's defeat stunned the Birch leadership. Robert Welch himself, in a long letter to Schmitz, decried the failure of the congressman to fly the Birch flag aggressively enough during the campaign. This failure, Welch wrote, explained why Schmitz had lost: "Birch membership is emerging as almost the one criterion on which the public can count for certainty that any 'Conservative' candidate really is a Conservative."[20]

Welch saw Schmitz's congressional primary in apocalyptical terms. Richard Nixon would use the Republican Party to take "our country and our people into a one-world Communist tyranny," he claimed.[21] In addition, Welch said, "the Insiders still hope and intend to have the formal framework [for that one-world government] . . . established by 1976."[22] The four-year time horizon made Schmitz's loss devastating; he would be unable to use legislative power to slow the Communist advance.

A lot of folks, my father included, couldn't make sense of the apparent missteps in Schmitz's campaign. After all, he'd won five elections and each time he'd touted his Birch membership as proof of his true conservative convictions. This time, though, his Birch affiliation had been ignored. Welch thought that Schmitz's campaign was out of character for the candidate and had lost "all trace of its educational flavor, or purpose."[23]

My father agreed. "What in the hell happened to John?" he asked.

Two months later, in a stranger-than-fiction twist, Schmitz got a chance to redeem himself. When George Wallace's party—the American Independent Party—gathered for its national convention in Louisville, Kentucky, the nineteen hundred delegates were leaderless: Wallace was still gravely ill from an assassination attempt that had nearly killed him.[24] Someone had to step up and lead the party.

Wallace had blasted into the 1972 Democratic presidential primary contests with his usual bombast. But in this cycle, he painted himself as a moderate and insisted that he no longer favored racial segregation. He did, however, vehemently oppose busing students around their districts to achieve racial balance. Busing was hated almost everywhere, and Wallace's message found a ready audience.[25] In Florida, Wallace captured 42 percent of the total vote and notched victory in every county.[26] Based on the first months of the primary season, it was clear that Wallace was still a force in U.S. politics. Then Arthur Bremer pumped six bullets into him.[27]

The delegates to what was now known as the American Party couldn't accept their hero's fate. Despite the injuries plaguing Wallace, they planned to draft him as their candidate. Finally, the governor put the whole idea to rest when he addressed the party delegates from his bed. "I have two open places still draining" and "another big pocket of infection," Wallace told his fans.[28] Those words ended the Draft Wallace idea. The American Party had to find another candidate to carry its law-and-order, voluntary-school-prayer, anti-busing, anti–women's-liberation banner.

My mother called me the second she heard the news. "John Schmitz was nominated."

"For what?"

"For president," she answered.

"President of what?"

"Don't be a ninny," she said. "President of the United States."[29]

I had no use for George Wallace or his party, but in 1972, I became an American Party activist anyway. That time, and for the only time in my life, I knew—not knew of, not knew about, I knew—the man at the top of the ticket. For me, knowing changed everything. I convinced myself that it wasn't necessary to agree with everything he said in order to help him. Within a couple of weeks, my home became the hub for the Schmitz campaign.

One day, my father called me over to talk about the campaign. When I arrived at his house, Dad was in the living room with a man I'd never met before. The fellow was short, at least an inch shorter than me, and hefty, which is a polite way to say he outweighed me by at least 125 pounds. By the way he fiddled with the collar of his shirt and wriggled in his suit coat, I guessed that those were his "Sunday" clothes.

The man was Thomas Stockheimer, the American Party's candidate for the 70th Wisconsin Assembly District. Stockheimer presented himself as a spokesman for the little guy who'd been so downtrodden by the oppressive government. He hated Wisconsin's high taxes—a position he shared with almost everyone in the Badger State. His approach to fixing the problem was simple—he proposed slashing state government and ending the legislature's power to raise taxes. My father gave Tom his full-throated endorsement. From that point on, I not only worked for Schmitz; I worked for Stockheimer, too.

At first, I thought Tom was just another really conservative guy. But as the campaign wore on, I realized that Stockheimer spoke more like an anarchist than a small-government guy. He supported local militias and preached against taxes. He loved guns, not just for hunting but for carrying around everywhere. And he had a mile-wide mean streak coupled with a hair-trigger temper.

I went to my parents with my concerns. "Stop being melodramatic," Mother said. "Tom's a little rough around the edges, but he's a good man."

My father had a similar response. "Stockheimer appeals to farmers; he speaks their language. Stop being such a snob."

I quickly learned that a political campaign is all about phone calls, knocking on doors, raising money, and advertising. Our little, upstart American Party campaign faced another challenge: we had to make the case that a third-party vote was not a vote wasted. The only way to accomplish that was to talk, face-to-face, with as many voters as possible. Over the next months, I found out for myself how many streets, avenues, roads, and lanes were in Marshfield, a town of over thirteen thousand. I rang doorbells on nearly every one of them.

John Schmitz might have been running for president on another planet for all the press he generated. Shortly before the election, *Time* reported that he "has sued the three TV networks for $20 million in damages because their failure to cover him, he claims, has prevented him from getting campaign contributions."[30]

Despite his inability to break through to the masses of voters, John was entertaining. From his campaign slogan—"When you're out of Schmitz, you're out of gear" ("When you're out of Schlitz, you're out of beer" was a major advertising campaign at the time)—to his classic one-liners, he kept his small audiences laughing. "There is nothing wrong with the Catholic Church that a good inquisition wouldn't cure" was one of his favorites.[31]

Long before Election Day, I realized there was a zero chance of Schmitz getting even one Electoral College vote. On November 7, 1972, Nixon was reelected in a landslide. John Schmitz, as I expected, did not win a single state or a single Electoral College vote. The American Party, which had garnered over nine million votes four years earlier, had shrunk to a million-vote party. In Wood County, Wisconsin, we grabbed over 6 percent of the vote, a good result, all things considered.

A gloomy group spent election evening at the home of Marshfield's former mayor. We tried to ease our pain with liberal doses of brandy and beer while we waited for the final vote tallies. Even though the national race was called early on, it took several hours to finalize the local contests. It was after ten before our local radio station, WDLB, gave the final Assembly District 70 results.

I breathed a huge sigh of relief when Stockheimer turned out to be the big loser, receiving just a hair over one thousand votes. Eight percent of voters had pulled the lever for Tom, and I was *not* one of them.[32]

As the after-defeat party progressed, I could hear a ruckus punctuated by strong words and loud voices. I moved to the source of the noise and found Tom Stockheimer holding a mini-rally in the kitchen. It was immediately clear that Tom and his supporters were not taking defeat gracefully. The dozen or more people circling him were furious with the liberal establishment and its embrace of integration, big government, and high taxes.

Someone called for a "pure white race" and "putting Negroes back in their rightful places." Others insisted that the ultimate enemy was not the black man but the Jews, who "controlled the banking system and the money supply." The crowd was positive it was those same Jews who had caused interest-rate spikes and created inflation—two things killing the family farm.

The crowd was eager to "take back the country." Real Americans, they said, had to arm themselves—to the teeth—and prepare to fight tyranny. All of this anger, hatred, and fear came with a gigantic dose of the Bible and the flag. Over the clamor, Tom shouted his final rallying cry: "It's time for the Posse to ride, and I'm the man to lead it!"

I had no idea what that last statement meant, but after the months I'd endured with this man, I was in no mood to listen to another of his over-the-top rants. Ignoring the little voice inside my head that told me to shut up and go home, I jumped into the fray. "Tom, you're a bigot and a fool," I said.

Stockheimer responded by attacking me as a disgrace to my parents and a traitor to America. Before he was finished, I was declared unfit to be in the same room with real patriots. I looked around that circle, at folks I'd worked with over the last three months and waited for someone, anyone, to jump to my defense. No one did.

That night I slept fitfully and dreamed of guns and shouting.

The next day, I told my parents about the confrontation. To my shock, they defended Stockheimer and criticized me for starting the argument. "You missed the whole point," Mother told me. "The federal government is the reason for all of this, not Stockheimer."

My father agreed. "Big government is the culprit here, not Tom."

In my parents' view, all the issues of the campaign—civil rights, busing, gun control, taxes—were the result of big, intrusive government. Stockheimer and his friends were simply standing up for their rights as Americans.

I want to believe that my parents had no idea what Stockheimer was really up to: recruiting members for the Posse Comitatus, a group of militant anti-government folks who spread the idea that the troubles in the heartland, especially for farmers, were part of bigger international events. Author James Ridgeway, who has documented the rise of white supremacist groups in the United States, wrote about Posse beliefs: "Whites are the true descendants of the lost tribes of Israel and Jews, blacks and other minorities have sprung from Satan and are subhuman. Jewish bankers . . . are at the heart of the conspiracy against the Midwestern farmers."[33] That election year of 1972, Stockheimer was also organizing his "Little People's Tax Advisory Committee," described by Daniel Levitas in *The Terrorist Next Door* as "a protest group that he [Stockheimer] quickly transformed into a launching pad for the Posse Comitatus."[34]

Over the next ten years, my parents would have plenty of reasons to rethink their support of Thomas Stockheimer, but the day after the 1972 election, they were still fans. "Tom and his friends may not be as refined as you'd like, but they are making an effort," my mother told me. "What are you doing?"

"I'll tell you exactly what I'm doing. I'm quitting," I said. "I will not help you with another election or another Birch project, period." I pulled on my coat and huffed to the door.

"Remember this," my father shouted after me. "You worked for a good and honorable man in John Schmitz. Nothing else matters."

———

I believed my parents. John Schmitz was nothing like Stockheimer. After the disastrous election, John returned to his old teaching position at Santa Ana College. I was glad he'd have a job until he found a path back into politics.

Almost everyone in the right wing wanted John back as soon as possible, and they made it clear by giving Schmitz a slew of awards. National groups with really pro-American names couldn't do enough for him: We the People, the Congress of Freedom, and the Freedom Foundation all named Schmitz either Congressman of the Year or Man of the Year. Schmitz even landed the George Washington Medal from the National Economic Council.[35] For these folks, he was the whole package: right-wing principles and "family values" personified. Now he just needed to win another election.

In the middle of August 1973, John and Mary Schmitz hosted the neighborhood for a barbeque and swimming party at their new home in Corona del Mar, California. Sometime in the afternoon, eleven-year-old Mary Kay—John's "Cake"—was left alone to watch her brother. No one ever knew exactly what happened, but three-year-old Philip was discovered on the bottom of the pool, drowned.[36]

When my father told me the news, I was sick for John and his family. I worried for poor Mary Kay and the terrible reality that she'd have to carry: her little brother had died while she was babysitting. I hoped no one blamed her for the tragedy.

Some days after the boy's death, I asked my father how John and his family were holding up. "They're fine," Dad said. "John continues to teach while he plans a return to politics."

"They are remarkable people," Mother added. "True models of Catholic life."

Late in 1974, several cartons of John Schmitz's memoir, *Stranger in the Arena: The Anatomy of an Amoral Decade, 1964–1974*, arrived at my parents' home.[37] The preface was penned by one of their favorite conservative Catholics, Brent Bozell, president of the Society for the Christian Commonwealth and ghostwriter of Barry Goldwater's *Conscience of a Conservative*.[38]

"Brent framed the issue so well," Mother said as she turned to the first page of the book. "Listen to this. 'I salute this man [Schmitz] for his understanding of the duty to which God is calling America's Christians . . . the essentially apostolic mission of making America Christian. Schmitz finished his years in public office a better man than when he entered it—the opposite of what usually happens.' "[39]

In 1978, Schmitz returned to politics as a California state senator, determined to carry the John Birch Society message of small government, lower taxes, and family values to Sacramento. During his term in office, however, John's behavior became increasingly erratic. No one knew why, but he seemed to be a gaffe machine, saying on one occasion, "A good military coup might be the best we could hope for if President Reagan's policies are not successful."[40] After abortion-rights hearings in the committee he chaired, his office issued a press release titled "Senator Schmitz and His Committee Survive Attack of the Bulldykes" and describing witnesses as "imported lesbians from anti-male and pro-abortion queer groups in San Francisco and other centers of decadence."[41] The fallout from these outrageous comments rumbled all the way to the Birch headquarters in Belmont.

In early 1982, John Schmitz was removed from the JBS National Council.[42] When I asked my father about the situation, he refused to give me any details. "John expressed opinions contrary to the views of the Society," was all he'd say.

On a warm August evening in 1982, while my husband was golfing and the kids were sleeping, I relaxed with the current issue of *Time*. In a short article, "Fouling Up," the name Schmitz jumped off the page along with a shocking revelation: John actually had two families. In addition to his wife, Mary, and their six (living) children, he had two children with his mistress, Carla Stuckle. All of this had come to light when Stuckle's thirteen-month-old, John George, was taken by his mother to the emergency room with some signs of possible physical abuse. During a court hearing to determine protective custody, Stuckle acknowledged the father of the baby as John George Schmitz.[43]

The next day, I pestered Dad for information, figuring that the inner circle of the John Birch Society would know a lot more about this than *Time* did, but my father was silent. He never spoke about John Schmitz or his family again, even as the sordid Schmitz scandals continued.

Beyond the hypocrisy and the lies, beyond the secret life and the other family, there was this: after his second family became public, neither Schmitz nor his wife did a thing to help the children borne by his mistress. Schmitz admitted to being the father of Carla Stuckle's babies, John George and Eugenia, but he refused to pay child support. The courts eventually ordered him to pay $275 per month, but it's not clear whether a dime was ever paid.[44]

In 1994, when Carla Stuckle died from complications of diabetes, her children were eleven and twelve years old. John Schmitz refused to take custody of them, and the children ended up living with Jeane Dixon, the famous psychic, who was a friend of the Schmitz family. A few years later, when Dixon died, the children became wards of the state.[45]

"So much for the pro-life, pro-family, Catholic paragon," I thought, musing that if I never heard the name Schmitz again, it would be too soon.

Several years later, a thirty-five-year-old sixth-grade teacher and mother of four was arrested for the rape of a thirteen-year-old student. It took me a while to realize that the woman the press identified as Mary Kay Letourneau was the all-grown-up "Cake" Schmitz, John's favorite daughter.[46] Letourneau went to prison, where she gave birth to her victim's baby.

On January 10, 2001, while Letourneau was still serving her term, John Schmitz died at the Naval Medical Center in Bethesda, Maryland, surrounded by his family. He was buried with full military honors at Arlington National Cemetery.[47] The website dedicated to his memory describes Schmitz this way: "He strove to be a devout Roman Catholic and a modern day Renaissance man."[48]

The words on Schmitz's website sounded so much like those that John wrote in his memoir. On the last page, after 314 pages chockful of morality and public-policy ideas to save our country, Schmitz explained what he would do after leaving Congress: "I shall be working for . . . an affirmation of Eternal Truth, Eternal Right and Eternal Being, timeless but ever new whose regenerative power is an undying echo and unsullied reflection of the Resurrection of Our Lord and Saviour Jesus Christ."[49]

On first reading, those words made me mad. I could have gone on quite a rant about the hypocrisy and the lies and the deception. But then I felt something different, something personal: regret. I had to admit that I'd bought what John Schmitz was selling because he was friendly and funny—and because I wanted my parents to accept me as a good daughter.

Worse, I had tried to pawn off John Schmitz and Tom Stockheimer on Marshfield as conservatives with good ideas for the country. All the while, I knew that Schmitz was a John Bircher and Stockheimer was something even more sinister. I had to live with that.

In an effort to make amends, I promised myself that I would never embark on another political crusade, adding the phrase "anytime soon," just in case. One of my friends laughed when I told her. "You will," she said. "It's in your blood."

I thought about that conversation many times, especially after I found myself leading another crusade. Sometimes I looked in the mirror and wondered, "Am I just like my parents?"

"No, no," I told myself. Even when I was pretty sure that the answer was . . . yes.

Chapter Twenty

One Woman's Heart

I am outraged that [the abortion issue] is viewed from the perspective of the woman—a femme-centric perspective that condones the self-indulgent conduct of the woman who was damn careless in the first place.

— DICK ARMEY, FORMER U.S. HOUSE
MAJORITY LEADER (R-TEXAS)[1]

Just a few weeks after John Schmitz was crushed in the 1972 elections, I jumped into my new crusade. My decision to go full-bore seemed hasty and impetuous to my friends, but I had had a toe in this fight for five years, ever since I'd married my college sweetheart.

Only a couple of months after our wedding, I found out that I was pregnant. It was a shock, but we accepted reality and turned to our friends for moral support. For the most part, the men toasted my husband's virility with lots of beer and hilarity, and I tried to get as much information as possible from the women I knew who'd had babies. I was surprised that they knew little more than I did about the whole process. Their main suggestion was to "trust Dr. Nabors."

Dr. Tom Nabors, *the* Catholic obstetrician on the north side of Dallas, where we were living, assured me that I was healthy. He offered a few guidelines for my pregnancy: smoking—okay, drinking—okay, weight gain—no more than twenty pounds. At the end of the first visit, he patted me on the arm and sent me home to rest. "Don't worry," he said. "I'll take care of everything."

A month later, I complained about my violent morning sickness. "It'll be over soon," my doctor told me. "You're three months along now and we can relax." He calculated my due date as early October—give or take—and sent me home. That evening, I was too tired to eat supper. I crawled into bed while it was still light and I instantly fell asleep.

Out of a foggy gray haze, something big and heavy slammed down on my belly. I could hear myself whining while I twisted and turned to get away from the pain. A voice called out to me. "Wake up," it said. "Wake up now."

I awoke, sweating and terrified. The dream slowly faded until I knew I was in my own bed and I was safe. Next to me, my husband snored quietly while I pulled the blanket around my shoulders and relaxed into my pillow.

Ten minutes later, unable to fall back to sleep, I realized how wet and sticky I felt—like I'd rolled in warm maple syrup. Slowly, I got out of bed and tiptoed down the hall to the bathroom. Under the glare of the overhead light, I saw that blood had soaked the lower half of my nightgown. I grabbed a washcloth, wet it, and started wiping my legs. Almost immediately, blood covered my hand and dripped onto the floor.

"Oh God," I prayed. "Help me. Help my baby."

My husband, who must have heard me get up, poked his head in. He took one look at the blood, pressed a towel between my legs, replaced my gown with a clean one, and wrapped me in a blanket. In just a few minutes, we were racing through the Dallas night toward Methodist Hospital.

For the next hour, the emergency-room staff tried to slow the bleeding. After a lot of stabs, a nurse finally found a usable vein and got an IV going. Someone else drew blood for the lab while an aide brought ice chips for me to suck. Over all the comings and goings, I could hear the interns who examined me huddled at the back of the room whispering.

"Where's Dr. Nabors?" I asked.

"On vacation," one man said. "The doctor covering for him will be here soon. Try to get some rest now."

For some time, I drifted in and out of consciousness until a voice pulled me back to reality. "I'm Dr. McCarty. I'm going to take care of you and your baby." This new doc poked, prodded, and pushed forever, it seemed, before he announced, "You haven't lost the baby."

The doctor proceeded to talk about things I didn't understand, things I'd never heard of before that night: dilatation and curettage, cervix and placenta, spontaneous miscarriages, and trimesters. Today, young mothers pore over pregnancy guides and websites, but in 1967, there were few resources available. One, *Pregnancy and Birth* by Alan Guttmacher and Anthony Ravielli, was not recommended to me.[2] Dr. Guttmacher favored contraception—an absolute no-no for Catholic women—and his book would never be suggested by a Catholic doctor. I know this is hard to believe, but in the world of pregnancy and childbirth education, 1967 was still the dark ages.

So, while this young doctor explained and educated, I focused on five words: you . . . haven't . . . lost . . . the . . . baby. That was all I heard and all I wanted to hear. My attention homed in on the little being clinging to life inside me. I rubbed my belly and willed my unborn child to live. "Your momma loves you," I said.

Nothing around me broke my concentration until I heard Dr. McCarty say, "While I'm struggling to save your baby, there are women paying doctors to kill theirs. And no one says a word."

"I don't understand," I said, suddenly alert.

"These women don't want to be pregnant, so their doctors do procedures to end their pregnancies," my doctor explained. "It's happening all over, maybe even in one of the ORs in this hospital tonight."

"I've never heard of that. What happens to the babies?" I asked.

"They're cut into pieces and thrown in the trash."

"I could never do that," I swore. "Never."

Early in the morning, I was sent home with strict orders to stay in bed for the next five days. By then, if all went according to plan, the danger of miscarriage would have passed. My brother volunteered to stay with me during the day so I wouldn't be tempted to sneak out of bed to answer the door or fix lunch. Luckily, Jay R. turned out to be an eager helper and a terrific one-man entertainment committee.

By day three, the bleeding had slowed to a trickle and I ventured out of bed long enough to take a shower. Later, however, I awakened from an afternoon nap with severe cramping. After what seemed like forever, I passed a mass of tissue and blood, which I carefully gathered in a towel. Tears poured down my cheeks while I said the words of Catholic baptism—*I baptize you, in the name of the Father, the Son, and the Holy Ghost*—words reserved for a priest, except in an emergency. I carried the towel with the remains of my baby to the hospital.

After a D & C, Dr. McCarty pronounced me young and healthy. "You'll have other babies," he told me.

"I don't want other babies," I said. "I want this baby."

Later, when I called my mother, she echoed the doctor. "You'll have other babies."

"I don't want other babies," I repeated. "I want this baby."

"Don't be so emotional," Mother said. "Offer up your suffering to Our Lord."

Like so many women who've miscarried, I grieved alone. I held the memory of that tiny being in my heart, and I believed I had sent a new saint to Paradise. While I mourned the life I'd lost, I nursed my outrage toward those women who deliberately killed their babies. "Wrong, wrong, wrong," I said. "Absolutely wrong."

In September of 1969, my first son was born. He was the most wonderful creature I'd ever seen and absolutely perfect. Before I left Dallas for Wisconsin, I had my last appointment with Dr. McCarty. Much of our conversation is lost to me now, but I do remember his alarm about the movement to legalize abortion. "All loyal Catholics will have to do their part to stop abortion. That includes you, Claire."

Dr. McCarty was at the forefront of the early anti-abortion movement, then an almost totally Roman Catholic movement. As Roy White, the executive director of the National Right to Life Committee, said, "The only reason we have a pro-life movement in this country is because of the Catholic people and the Catholic Church."[3] The anti-abortion position of the Church was so absolute that there were calls for the excommunication of Justice William Brennan, the only Catholic on the Supreme Court, when he sided with the majority in *Roe v. Wade*.[4]

———

In 1971, when I was pregnant with my third baby, my mother gave me a copy of *A Child Is Born* by Lennart Nilsson, the best-selling book chronicling life before birth.[5] For the first time, the world inside my womb became visible to me. The little beings captured in those amazing images seemed almost otherworldly with their transparent skin, delicate bones, and paper-thin eyelids. Each one floated in a water world, secreted away until it was big enough and strong enough to live outside the womb. In one photo, the tiny one sucked its thumb, an image that brought me to tears.[6] I remembered how my son had found his thumb just after he was born, and I knew he'd been sucking away in my womb for months.

When I was tired, uncomfortable, and sick of being pregnant, I turned to Nilsson's book. The photos reminded me that my body had built a perfect nursery for my baby. Tired, uncomfortable, and sick of being pregnant was a small price to pay for that precious life.

The feminist movement talked about a woman's absolute right to control her body, but I couldn't get my head or my heart around that idea. The photographs proved, beyond a reasonable doubt, that though my baby was, for a short time, living in me, *it was not me*.

Many years later, I learned that most of the fetuses Nilsson photographed had been removed from their mothers' wombs. As Sandra Matthews and Laura Wexler say in their book *Pregnant Pictures*, "They were *dead* embryos."[7] I would have put it differently: those little ones had been aborted.

The Roman Catholic Church teaches that human life begins at conception, the instant when the sperm and the egg unite and God infuses a soul into that new being. To destroy that life is the most terrible sin, one punishable by eternal damnation.[8] Most Catholics don't know, however, that the Church has not always taken that position. In fact, for several centuries, the Church taught that the soul arrived in the body long after conception. St. Thomas Aquinas, the greatest Catholic theologian, claimed that the male embryo became human at forty days. Pity the poor female embryo; she didn't become human for eighty. But after all, according to Aquinas, the female came from a defective seed.[9]

When this topic had come up in my theology class, back at the University of Dallas, the boys thought it was hilarious. For me, it was nonsense. But, gender wars aside, Aquinas's teaching was Church law for hundreds of years.

By the fifteenth century, the Church had refined her position: The developing fetus had no absolute value in its own right. It could be killed, without sin, in order to save a mother's life as long as the death of the fetus was not the doctor's first intention. Welcome to the Catholic principle of the "double effect."[10] By the middle of the nineteenth century, however, no abortions were ever permitted in any circumstances. Even in the worst-case scenario, a good Catholic doctor stood aside while both mother and baby died.[11]

In the twentieth century, the Church returned to the "double effect" doctrine permitting a doctor to remove an ectopic pregnancy as long as he didn't intend to kill the embryo inside. Unfortunately, the same compassion did not extend to those other hard cases: rape and incest. For Catholic doctors, it was never permitted to perform an abortion for a girl who had been raped, even by her own father.[12]

At the time, these twists and turns meant little to me. The Church said that abortion was wrong because it killed a human baby; I agreed. The feminists claimed that a woman's right to control her body was more important; I didn't agree. But until late in 1972, I wasn't about to "make a federal case about it," as we used to say.

Then I met Dr. Charles E. Rice, professor of law at Notre Dame Law School and a friend of my parents. By the time I sat across the table from Charlie—he insisted I call him Charlie—I'd read his book *The Vanishing Right to Live* in which he reviewed the Catholic positions on the "life issues."[13] Given his strict views—no contraception or abortion ever—I was surprised to meet a man who was only fourteen years older than me.

During dinner, Charlie delivered a passionate argument against abortion—punctuated with a vivid description of a vacuum machine ripping the developing baby out of the womb and turning it to mush. That evening I lost my appetite and my neutrality.

The next day, I called a group of Catholic men and women I knew and invited them to my home. Together we launched an anti-abortion committee aligned with Wisconsin Citizens Concerned for the Unborn, the organization that would become the Wisconsin Right to Life Committee.

On January 22, 1973, the same day that former president Lyndon Johnson died, the Supreme Court of the United States handed down the *Roe v. Wade* decision. The sweeping decision, supported by a 7–2 majority, removed all restriction on abortion in the first trimester and hampered the right of states to limit abortion in the second. Justice Blackmun, in writing for the majority, declared that only after the fetus was developed enough to survive on "his" own—usually during the seventh month—"may a state regulate and even proscribe abortion except where it is necessary . . . for the preservation or health of the mother."[14]

While feminists celebrated, I girded for war. It would take a national movement to overturn *Roe*, and I intended to be part of it.

A couple of weeks after *Roe*, I had coffee with Linda, the friend who had warned me about a new crusade. "I won't say I told you so," she said.

"This is different," I fired back. "I have to do this."

Unfortunately, Linda and I found ourselves at loggerheads over the issue, and our friendship became the first casualty of my fifteen-year anti-abortion battle.

In early July of 1975, my husband and I packed our three kids in our van and drove to Whitewater, Wisconsin, for the holiday weekend. I was excited to be out of town for a few days to enjoy time with our dearest college friends, Nancy and Bob, the very same "Socks" I'd met on my first day in Dallas.

As usual, we stayed with our friends in their Whitewater home, but in a nod to my pregnancy, we planned fewer activities. I'd been having a rough go with daylong bouts of morning sickness. I kept telling myself that I'd be better in another week, or another two weeks, or another month. But I was nearly at the end of the first trimester, and I still felt no better.

On the Fourth, while Nancy and I were strolling through the kiddie section of the Milwaukee Zoo, I started to gag. In the restroom, I realized I was not only vomiting; I was bleeding. I didn't want to ruin the holiday, so we rented a wheelchair. I enjoyed the penguins and the elephants from the four-wheeler while the other three adults kept track of the kids. No easy task with eight to watch: three of ours and five of Nancy and Bob's. When we got back to Whitewater, I was banished to bed, where I was treated to "room service" and uninterrupted naps. After two days, the bleeding slowed and then stopped. "All I needed was a mini-vacation," I told my husband. "I'm fine now."

Back at home in Marshfield, we'd just unpacked the car when the bleeding started again. My husband rushed me to the hospital where my doctor determined that I hadn't lost the baby. I was sent home for three days of complete bed rest. "After that, we'll have to see," the doctor said.

I kept the windows in the bedroom open so I could hear the kids playing in the yard below. Squeals and shouting drifted in on every puff of breeze and I realized the three kids had filled squirt guns and were racing around soaking each other. While I eavesdropped, I dreamed of hearing our new baby laugh with her brothers and sister. (I was so sure this child was a girl that I'd already named her Emily.)

After three days, the bleeding stopped and I was cleared to return to normal life. My freedom lasted about an hour before a new rush of blood sent me right back to bed. After that emergency, I was in bed for two months, waiting.

Every morning, I worried that the new day would bring cramps, labor, and death for little Emily. Every night, I worried that my baby would slip away while I was dreaming. I kept a baby blanket, a small vial of holy water, and a prayer book under the bed, just in case. Next to these things, I had a small overnight bag packed. If I had to be rushed to the hospital, I was ready.

In the middle of September, on my husband's thirty-third birthday, the bleeding stopped, completely. By the next day, I knew that the crisis had passed. I wanted to hug my children and throw in a load of laundry. I wanted to crank the stereo and dance to We Five. I wanted to bake cookies and clean out the refrigerator, but I was afraid to do anything until my doctor gave me the thumbs-up.

"I'm cautiously optimistic," he said after examining me. "But you've bled for a prolonged period of time. I've ordered more tests, just to be on the safe side." He handed me the name of a specialist in Madison, 145 miles away, who would get me in for amniocentesis before I was too far past the twenty-week limit. "We don't do it here," he said. "Catholic hospital and all."

"What?" I asked.

"Amniocentesis will tell us if there are anomalies," he answered. "You could still terminate."

From someplace far, far away, I heard myself roar, "No, I will never abort this baby."

"Don't you want to know?" he asked.

"Why? I've been in bed for months saving this baby. I could never kill her, no matter what."

My doctor never mentioned Madison or termination again. At night, when I worried, I put my hands over my belly and prayed. "You're safe, Emily. Nothing will happen, now. Nothing."

Four months later, I delivered a tiny baby boy. He was so little and so fragile that I could only hold him a minute before he was whisked off to the preemie nursery.

"He's perfect," my husband said through his tears. "But, we can't call him Emily anymore, can we?"

———

Before *Roe*, the anti-abortion movement had no political clout and no organizational umbrella. It was a collection of local, unaligned groups like the one I headed in Marshfield. That changed immediately after *Roe* when pro-life activists gathered in Detroit and organized the National Right to Life Committee. The new group selected Marjory Mecklenburg, a Methodist, as its first chairman.

Abortion foes understood that the movement would make little headway until it found support beyond Roman Catholics. In 1976, Francis Schaeffer, the most prominent evangelical Christian in the country, proclaimed abortion to be "the final leg in Western civilization's death march."[15] That statement from his popular book *How Should We Then Live?*, coupled with the three-part film of the same title, helped "cultivate a new generation of shock troops for the coming culture war."[16]

Later, Schaeffer's son, Frank, said, "My father and I were amongst the first to start telling American evangelicals that God wanted them involved in the political process. It was the *Roe v. Wade* decision that gave Dad . . . and me our platform."[17]

Schaeffer explained, so perfectly, how he felt about abortion and, to a large extent, how most of us in the movement felt. "Abortion became *the* evangelical [in my case, read: Catholic] issue. . . . The anger we stirred up at the grass roots was not feigned but heartfelt. And at first it was not about partisan politics. It had everything to do with genuine horror at the procedure of abortion. The reaction was emotional, humane and sincere. It also was deliberately co-opted by the Republican Party."[18]

The Schaeffers empowered other leaders who shaped, defined, and controlled the pro-life movement: James Dobson, Jerry Falwell, and Pat Robertson. I first heard of Dobson through his hugely popular (and, in my mind, awful) book *Dare to Discipline*. It was my pleasure to deposit the book in the garbage only a few hours after my mother gave it to me. Spanking children as young as eighteen months old was simply not going to happen in my house.

Evangelical preacher Jerry Falwell built his "Moral Majority" into a political juggernaut, while Pat Robertson built an empire selling salvation on TV's *700 Club*. Together, these folks and a few idea men like Paul Weyrich and Ralph Reed created the "religious right." Of it, Frank Schaeffer wrote, "The new religious right was all about religiously motivated 'morality,' which it used for nakedly political purposes."[19]

Only a few months after my son Kevin was born, I went full-steam ahead into the pro-life movement. I used the story of my pregnancy to illustrate the importance of stopping the abortion juggernaut. I believed that the Court had made a terrible mistake, but for me, pro-life went beyond abortion. The issue was always about baby and mother—before birth and after. I felt strongly that the government—federal, state, and local—had obligations to mothers and children, including food, shelter, child care, and education. I expected all pro-lifers, regardless of political party, to agree with me.

In the summer of 1976, my parents offered the first clue that I might be wrong.

"You can't stop abortion with government programs," Mother said.

"Government is never a solution," Dad added. "Private charity is always the answer."

I rolled my eyes and pushed back, but Mother and Dad dug in. They brought out the latest John Birch Society bulletin, a special edition to honor America's Bicentennial. In it, Robert Welch surveyed the highlights of American history, focusing on those aspects that the right-wingers favored: freedom and tiny government.

Of the early twentieth century, Welch wrote, "There was still plenty of poverty in many areas, of course, but it was a *healthy kind of poverty*, where every man took for granted that relief from dire want was entirely his own problem and responsibility . . . even *the poverty was offset by the enormous blessing of freedom*."[20]

"So," I said to Mother, "you want women and their newborn babies to enjoy that same healthy kind of poverty, free from interference by the government?"

"There you go with those bleeding-heart liberal tendencies," she answered me.

"Government never fixes anything," Dad added. "It can only destroy freedom."

Before long, I'd have to consider that a whole lot of Republicans who were pro-life to their core agreed with my parents and Robert Welch.

That fall, pro-lifers scored their first major legislative victory, the Hyde Amendment, which prohibited all federal funding of abortion, primarily affecting the Medicaid program.[21] Women's groups and other advocacy groups howled about the impact of the new rules on poor women, but I couldn't hear them. As far as I was concerned, every life snatched from the grasp of the abortionists was my personal victory.

It was years before I could even acknowledge that those pro-choice organizations had a valid point: poor women were denied abortions while their rich sisters could always find a doctor to "help" them. Poor women went to the back alley. Rich women went away for a "rest."[22]

Over the next ten years, my activism took me from leader of my local anti-abortion group to state board member of Wisconsin Right to Life. I spoke in high schools, churches, and colleges across the state, led pro-life demonstrations, and wrote scores of letters. I debated members of the National Organization for Women, gave interviews to local papers, and testified in favor of pro-life legislation at the capitol in Madison.

Within a few years, the pro-life movement had fashioned itself into a one-issue constituency. No one cared about candidates' positions on other issues—abortion was the litmus test. It didn't matter if candidates believed in closing day-care centers or cutting food stamps, as long as they supported the Human Life Constitutional Amendment. No one blinked if candidates supported war at the expense of domestic programs to help the needy, as long as they supported the Hyde Amendment. It didn't matter if candidates wanted to cut Medicaid for poor children, as long as they believed that a zygote was a human being.

I started to have my doubts, doubts that pushed me to think outside the pro-life box. My first jolt came over the question of abortions for rape and incest, exceptions pro-lifers had opposed. We called those abortions "the hard cases."

In every speech I gave, I argued that one act of violence (the rape or the incest) doesn't justify a second (the abortion). I leaned on the authority of Dr. Charles Rice, who wrote: "To legalize abortion in pregnancies caused by rape would affect an infinitesimal number of cases. . . . In any event, the rape issue is an emotional lure used by those who seek a general relaxation of the abortion laws."[23]

I shared the conclusions of Dr. John Willke, the chairman of the National Right to Life Committee, who held that the "psychic trauma of assault rape" made pregnancy unlikely. In his first book, *Handbook on Abortion*, Willke described a study of 3,500 cases of rape in the Minneapolis–St. Paul area that revealed "zero cases of pregnancy."[24] In several subsequent books and in his public speeches, Willke calculated that fewer than three hundred pregnancies per year resulted from rape.[25]

I was shocked to discover that these so-called experts were wrong. The actual number of pregnancies resulting from rape is closer to twenty-five thousand per year.[26]

I'd learned in the pro-life movement that the abortion of "defective" children is considered a form of "eugenic engineering" that would "open the way to the systematic elimination of defective or 'inferior' people as a matter of government policy."[27] Then I read the stories of mothers and fathers who faced an excruciating choice when their unborn babies were diagnosed with terrible fetal anomalies. I read heartbreaking reports of pregnant women battling cancer who had to decide either to abort and continue their chemotherapy or to go untreated and hope they survived the pregnancy.

Pro-lifers couldn't admit that their "100% pro-life" congressmen and senators slashed medical services for the poor, leaving tens of thousands of women without access to prenatal care. And we could never tell the inconvenient truth that cuts to federal nutrition programs took food out of the mouths of women and their babies.

Pro-lifers have never been able to admit that Planned Parenthood, the ultimate bogeyman, did more than abort babies. Millions of women rely on their local PP clinic for cancer screening, contraceptives, and treatment for sexually transmitted diseases. And I've yet to run into a real pro-life advocate who accepts that, according to its latest annual report, less than 4 percent of Planned Parenthood money goes to abortion services. By law, those dollars must be kept absolutely separate from government money.

Pro-lifers do know that every year in the United States almost 1.3 million women have abortions. What I don't hear from them is the fact that this is an awful choice for most of those women. Many of them do it alone, without the help of their parents or the support of the man who fathered the baby. I finally realized that these women are not evil or stupid or lazy. These women are terrified. For a hundred reasons, they feel that they cannot carry their pregnancy to term.

This number—1.3 million—has remained almost constant, both before and since *Roe*. So, all the yelling, protesting, debating, legislating, and posturing ignores this reality: we are no closer to helping these women than we were forty years ago.

Realizing that politicians were using the "pro-life" label to advance a right-wing agenda broke my heart, but I had to face the truth. I no longer fit in the movement I'd help build.

Chapter Twenty-one

Bang the Drum Slowly

On January 20, 1981, Ronald Reagan, former Democrat turned conservative messiah, became the fortieth president of the United States. He had trounced President Carter in the Electoral College, grabbing 90 percent of the votes, after racking up an impressive win in the popular vote total.[1] It was a landslide, with some pundits even dubbing it the "Reagan Revolution."[2] Political scientists who lived to analyze and dissect elections characterized the Gipper's winning coalition as the Old Right, New Right, Dixiecrats, Christian Right, and Americanists—a patchwork of conservatives melded into the new GOP.[3]

For my parents, the win was personal, a vindication of everything they'd preached for the last twenty-five years. When the new president said, "Government is not the solution to our problem; government is the problem," Mother and Dad were over the moon.[4] Finally, there was a real conservative at 1600 Pennsylvania Avenue.

My parents had reason to gloat: some of their closest friends and associates had helped build the Reagan majority. Front and center was Paul Weyrich, architect of the New Right. Weyrich had come up with the term "Moral Majority" and convinced the preacher Jerry Falwell to use it to describe evangelical activists.[5] Mother also recognized the success of Senators Jesse Helms and Strom Thurmond, who had turned the South into GOP country, while Phyllis Schlafly was busy firing up her contingent of housewives. Mother's newspaper, the *Wanderer*, got into the act by activating the conservative wing of Roman Catholics.[6] Of course, their greatest salute was for Robert Welch, who had unleashed the power of the John Birch Society.

"It's glorious," Mother said. "Finally, Christians are in power, and your parents were in on the ground floor."

"You, however, have turned your back on your parents and your country," Dad said to me. "I demand to know how you voted."

"I thought we still had a secret ballot," I answered.

"Don't be a smart aleck, young lady," Mother fired back. "We know you voted for Carter."

I shrugged, provoking both of them even more.

"You're a goddamn lib!" my father shouted. "I give up on you."

My father may have given up, but he never let up. Almost every time we were together, he pushed, argued, cajoled, and threatened. Mother, ever vigilant about "fixing" me, joined in. They were determined to pull me from the grip of godless liberalism and remake me as a good right-wing, pro-Reagan, Christian Republican. For my parents, my pro-life work was not redemptive. Because I failed to adhere 100 percent to their agenda, I was forever a hopeless liberal no-goodnik.

In a nod toward appeasement, I promised to keep an open mind about the new president. But beyond his devotion to Nancy and his love for Jelly Bellies, I couldn't find anything I liked about the man. When he railed against the homeless on national television, I stopped looking. "You can't help those who simply will not be helped," our president declared on *Good Morning America*. "One problem that we've had, even in the best of times, is people who are sleeping on the grates, the homeless who are homeless, you might say, by choice."[7]

Right up to the end of his second term, Reagan continued to insist that his policies had nothing to do with the increase in homelessness or, for that matter, in the increase in joblessness. Steven Roberts, writing in the *New York Times*, wrote of the president's views, "Mr. Reagan, who frequently insists that his policies have caused few economic hardships, repeated a suggestion he has made before that jobless workers are unemployed by their own choice."[8]

In my little town of Marshfield, Wisconsin, Reagan's policies forced drastic cutbacks in residential mental health programs. Suddenly, there were men and women pushing their possessions in Shopko shopping carts and huddling in doorways to sleep. It was evident that these folks needed help, and the Reagan Revolution guaranteed that they wouldn't have any, at least not from government.

Just like my parents, the good Christian in the White House hated any government program targeting people in need. Mother, Dad, and Ronald Reagan imagined a utopia where the poor and the sick would be taken care of by a magical combination of private charity and benevolent business. The fact that their scheme was fiction made no difference.

According to William Kleinknecht, in his book *The Man Who Sold the World*, President Reagan believed that "sustaining the poor and healing the sick should be the responsibility of private interests, not the government," and he set out to make that happen.[9] His first round of budget cuts for social programs amounted to more than $128 billion, an amount that was supposed to be made up by increased private-sector philanthropy.

Private giving did increase under Reagan, but not enough to close the gap, not even close to that. Even more alarming, though, was that much of the private giving was going to support universities, museums, and the arts, and not to help the needy. "In fact," noted Kleinknecht, "the amount of money donated for health and human services actually declined in Reagan's first term."[10]

To many observers, the Reagan administration "made a mockery of the promises to reduce government waste while preserving programs for the 'truly needy.'"[11] I fell into that group. As I watched the Department of Housing and Urban Development scandals, the Iran-Contra mess, and the Savings and Loan debacle unfold, I came to believe that Reagan was a phony, in every way. He proved what P.J. O'Rourke, the libertarian satirist, said, "Republicans are the party that says government doesn't work, and then they get elected and prove it."[12]

No matter what I thought, my mother and my father were no more likely to budge from their vision than Ronald Reagan was. After all, the president was the same guy who'd explained to a *Time* reporter back in 1976 that "fascism was really the basis for the New Deal."[13]

A few months after President Reagan left office, Anthony Lewis, writing in the *New York Times*, described his legacy: "The intangible cost of the Reagan years . . . are the costs of hostility to the role of government, of indulgence toward private greed, of insensitivity to the needs of the weak in our society."[14]

Despite the negative impact of Reagan's policies, the man passed into GOP mythology, where he took his place as the high priest of conservatives. For me, however, he personified the worst in right-wingers and their policies.

The Reagan victory sent the right wing into a dance of joy. Even the John Birch Society joined in the celebration. In January of 1981, Robert Welch highlighted the "very encouraging developments on the political front," while tipping his hat to JBS members who "proved conclusively that an informed and energetic few can make a whale of a difference."[15]

Later on in the same bulletin, JBS staff member William Guidry exhorted members to stay vigilant: "Mr. Reagan has suggested the Department of Energy and the recently instituted Department of Education as likely targets of expulsion. Senator Orrin Hatch of Utah, soon to be chairman of the Senate Labor Committee, has set his sights on the Equal Employment Opportunity Commission by vowing a senatorial assault on the institutionalized racism known as 'affirmative action.'" JBS members were encouraged to write to senators and congressmen to urge "that legislative action against these and other regulatory monstrosities be initiated as soon as possible."[16]

By July, though, the wave of euphoria had vanished, and the JBS was up in arms, no pun intended, about the Reagan administration's decision to sell arms to China as part of the effort to push back against Soviet expansion. Robert Welch attacked this policy as inconsistent with the "repeated pronouncements of opposition to communism that, in large part anyway, helped to put the new administration in office."[17]

The Chinese arms sale was not the only foreign policy move of Reagan's that alarmed the JBS. His administration forgave millions of dollars in Polish debt, a move described by Birchers as "bailing out the dictators with our tax money."[18] That same month, Reagan shored up support for President Jose Duarte's government in El Salvador, which the JBS referred to as "a decidedly Leftist creation of the Carter Administration."[19] And after Reagan's famous "Tear Down This Wall" speech, given in front of Berlin's Brandenburg Gate, the JBS continued to point out the "chasm between Mr. Reagan's words and his actions."[20]

On the domestic front, the president's tax policy also raised red flags. In an open letter to Reagan in August of 1982, the JBS wrote, "Something is wrong. . . . You campaigned strongly in 1980 for a three-year, thirty percent tax cut, and in 1981 you used your influence with Congress to get that cut approved. But, with your approval, Congress may soon impose a tax hike of $99 billion on an economically battered public, the *largest single tax increase in American history!* Why, Mr. President, why?"[21]

These tax hikes were necessitated by the huge deficits run up in Reagan's first years, deficits from the economic policy dubbed "Reaganomics." Sara Diamond described Reagan's plan as supply-side economics with a new twist—"a benefit for the rich is a benefit for all."[22] "Reaganomics" worked so well that the wealthiest folks prospered mightily. For the rest of America, though, the economy sputtered, government revenue plummeted, and unemployment spiked.

My father complained loudly and often about the bad economy, blaming the government for creating inflation and reducing the value of the dollar. This downturn was sharp enough that my husband took a salary cut. I guessed that my father did too.

The John Birch Society was hit hard by the economic pinch when donors who'd previously provided generous support shut their wallets. In April of 1982, Welch penned an urgent appeal to Birchers for $5 million to shore up the empty coffers and provide resources to fund new growth. He concluded his appeal for money with an ominous warning. "Your editor feels a solemn duty to tell you that unless there soon is a very marked change in the total course that our Government has been following since 1932, we have in my opinion only from five to about ten years more before we shall be living as enslaved serfs under the rule of Communist Commissars."[23]

In December, the society admitted that there had been a steady decline in membership, resulting in a precipitous drop in bulletins mailed—twelve thousand fewer per month—according to numbers reported to the postal service.[24]

In the middle of 1982, Robert Welch retired with the title chairman emeritus. My father called it "being kicked upstairs." The council named a new president, Dr. Larry P. McDonald.

McDonald sported the middle name Patton (he was the cousin of the famous World War II general), along with the title of congressman in front of his name and MD after it. It surprised me that McDonald was a Democrat—from Georgia—and that he had accepted the Birch position while still serving in Congress.[25]

In September of 1983, only six months after McDonald took the Birch helm, the congressman boarded Korean Air flight 007, bound for Seoul. He was part of a congressional delegation commemorating the thirtieth anniversary of the U.S.-Korea mutual-defense treaty. Without warning, the plane disappeared from radar over the island of Sakhalin, a Soviet military base. It took seventeen hours to confirm that the flight had strayed over Soviet territory and been blasted out of the sky by a Russian missile. All 269 persons aboard were presumed dead.[26]

McDonald's wife, Kathryn, declared that her husband had been the victim of "an act of deliberate assassination" and insisted that it was no accident that "the leading anti-Communist in the American Government had been shot down."[27]

At McDonald's funeral, an emotional Jerry Falwell delivered the eulogy, comparing McDonald to the biblical Samson, "a victim, a prisoner of a society moving to the left. But he never moved with it."[28] My parents agreed wholeheartedly with Jerry Falwell, and my father often said, "Larry was a martyr for the cause." And my mother would point out, "The Commies killed him because he knew too much, just like Joe McCarthy."

Alan Stang, who had been McDonald's chief of staff and was a longtime Birch associate, insisted, as had McDonald's wife, that McDonald had been singled out for capture because he was "the most dangerous enemy the Communists had."[29] Building on Stang's supposition, the Far Right constructed a new theory of Larry McDonald's fate: Instead of being shot down, the plane had actually survived the missile hit and landed safely on Sakhalin, the Soviet island north of Japan. McDonald had been taken prisoner by the Communists and subjected to continuous torture and abuse.[30] That belief persists; even today the JBS continues to push for a federal investigation into the "real" circumstances of McDonald's death.

The sudden death of the young Birch Society president created a leadership vacuum. I wasn't privy to the behind-the-scenes machinations, but I could see the stress and the worry on my father's face as the National Council tried to figure out the next step. When Robert Welch died, at age eighty-six, a year after McDonald's death, Dad became more and more paranoid and hostile. "The Commies are on the move," he said. "This is the endgame."

The JBS tried to stabilize the organization with the appointment of Birch staffer A. Clifford Barker to the presidency. Just a few years later, Barker was removed and the presidency passed to another Birch staffer, Charles Amour. All of this commotion at the top of the organization had very severe consequences, consequences that eventually did become public. A *Chicago Tribune* article in 1986 pointed out that the society had a $9 million deficit and faced an increasingly hostile internal battle on the question of "how much to criticize President Reagan."[31]

The internal clashes impacted everyone in the organization and led to the resignations of a number of prominent members, including Robert Welch's widow, who'd been a loyal, behind-the-scenes Bircher since 1958.

John McManus, the society's chief spokesperson, admitted to the *Chicago Tribune* that membership had dropped to several tens of thousands and not more than fifty thousand.[32] When asked why the JBS was shedding members, McManus attributed the lack of growth to "a decline of morals in the country and because of the news media which has labeled society members as paranoids and lunatics."[33]

Given all of this turmoil, I tried to give my dad plenty of latitude. But my efforts to avoid fighting failed; my father just couldn't stop fussing with me, and I couldn't stop pushing back. My husband try to help me understand what was happening: "Your dad is hurting. He's old, and he's lost his edge. He resents everyone who reminds him of that. He argues for the sake of arguing."

My husband was able to separate my father's tirades from the man himself. I wished I had the same perspective, but when my father attacked me, he always made it personal. He knew just where to hit and just how to do it.

During one absurd shouting match over the right to bear arms, my father insisted that the Second Amendment permitted individual ownership of any weapon, even submachine guns and rocket launchers. After that, I declared my home off limits for any political conversations with my parents, forever. Of course, as often happens, I was the one who broke my own rule.

———

The ring interrupted my preparations. I glanced at the clock, grabbed the phone, and tucked it between my chin and shoulder. I had only a minute to chat; my parents were arriving in an hour, and I was still mixing potato salad and slicing berries.

"Father Don here," my friend on the other end said. "I'm worried."

"Why? What's wrong?" I asked.

"I heard a rumor that you're becoming a Lutheran."

"I didn't become anything." I laughed. "I'm going to Good Shepherd Lutheran once in a while, that's all."

"I know, but what happens when your folks hear the same stuff I heard?"

"They won't."

"They will," he said. "You know how it goes in this town. Someone will say something to your mom while she's at Karau's or the hairdresser. Then what?"

"I have to think about this."

"Please do," he said. "And tell them soon. I don't want you to be blind-sided."

Over several years, Father Don had become my friend and confidant. When the priest sex-abuse scandal engulfed the Church, Don shared my shock and disgust. I felt free to rant to him about the Pope and the bishops protecting predators because I knew he shared my anger. When I could no longer be a Catholic, I explained my reasons to him. Friend that he was, he didn't try to change my mind.

Because I trusted him, I usually listened to his advice. But on July 4, 1990, I thought he was worrying too much about my parents finding out that I'd left the Church. I was sure I had time to plan how to tell them. "It can wait until another time," I said to myself.

The afternoon was peaceful; no raised voices, no arguments. After dinner, while I was loading the dishwasher, my parents, my husband, and my oldest son joined me in the kitchen. The chatter stopped abruptly when my father said: "Claire, I'm asking you a question." He grabbed my arm and pushed me back against the cabinet. Before I realized what was happening, he had raised his hand. "Did you leave the Church?" he hissed as he leaned closer toward me.

I didn't answer.

"You are an absolute disgrace," my father shouted. He tightened his hand into a fist and pulled it back. I knew he was going to punch, hard.

"Leave my mother alone!" my son cried as he lurched toward his grandfather. "Don't you dare touch her."

"This is none of your business!" my father yelled back at him.

I found my voice. "Stop! Stop now!" I shouted. "You will not hit me. Not now, not ever."

My father pulled his arm back. For a few seconds, there was not a single sound in the room. Then I spoke. "You have to leave my house, now," I said. "You are no longer welcome here."

Shortly after the Independence Day uproar, my father was admitted to the hospital with a bad attack of "indigestion." Ten days later, after a diagnosis of pancreatitis, he was released with orders to follow a strict diet and a box of syringes loaded with pain meds. As 1990 turned into 1991 and then to 1992, Dad didn't go to the office very often; he spent most days in his recliner with a heating pad on his belly. My mother cooked him bland food, gave him his pain shots, and dispensed handfuls of prescribed medicines and over-the-counter supplements.

In the 1970s, my parents had become part of the Laetrile movement, a naturally healing approach to cancer. After reading several articles written by Birchers they knew and respected, Mother and Dad were convinced that cancer was caused by dietary deficiencies. Luckily, Mother Natured had offered the cure—Laetrile, a substance that occurred naturally in the pits of apricots.[34] The FDA found no value in Laetrile and cracked down on the folks making money from selling the quack medicine.

My parents were outraged and joined the new Committee for Free Choice in Medicine, which fought for the use of Laetrile.[35] A number of prominent Birchers were involved in the committee, including Dr. Larry McDonald, who worked as the committee's legislative advisor. Before his death, McDonald had prescribed Laetrile to his own patients in his urology practice back home in Atlanta.[36]

In addition to Laetrile, Mother bought nearly every vitamin ever marketed. The inventory was so great that it filled an entire kitchen cabinet and a shelf in the refrigerator. Every morning, Mother sorted out Dad's pills—and hers—into glass saucers. I'm sure they each swallowed upwards of sixty pills a day.

After the July debacle at our home, my husband encouraged me to make peace with my father. I tried to do just that, but my mother rebuffed every effort I made to see Dad. "You'll upset your father," she said. "You always do."

———

In early June 1992, my husband and I were summoned to my parents' house. We arrived early in the evening to find Dad freshly showered, shaved, and settled in his chair. He asked a few perfunctory questions about work and our kids, but he wasn't really interested in the answers. After a couple of minutes, he got to the point.

"In the morning, I'm checking into the hospital for surgery," he said. "I'm sick of being sick and nothing is really helping anymore. Your mother and I agree this is the best decision."

This "best decision" was to remove his pancreas, gallbladder, spleen, and part of the stomach, a radical operation with the innocent-sounding name of the Whipple Procedure. Dad believed that this surgery would end his indigestion and his pancreatitis attacks.

"Your father will be home in less than three weeks with a very positive prognosis," my mother claimed.

"What exactly is the diagnosis?" my husband asked.

"Persistent digestive-tract problems," Mother said.

Dad said, "My pancreas is on the fritz."

After the surgery, my father spent three weeks in the intensive-care unit. He wasn't improving; he was just staying alive. The doctors finally confirmed that he had pancreatic cancer, which had spread all through his body. I knew he wouldn't live long.

Most afternoons, I sat with him in the hospital. Sometimes I read to him. Sometimes I just sat quietly and watched him sleep. One day, while I paged through a magazine, a small, raspy voice called me. "Claire," my father asked, "am I dying?"

I took his hand very carefully so I wouldn't hurt him or dislodge one of his IVs. I put my lips close to his ear, so he'd hear me. "Dad," I said, slowly, "you are not dying today." I paused for a second and then added, "But I will sit next to you and tell you when it's time. I promise."

My father smiled a little, relaxed, and drifted back into a half-alive, half-dead sleep.

A week later, the doctors who been treating him announced the obvious: there was nothing more to be done. Dad was dying. We could either take him home or move him to hospice.

"Absolutely no," Mother said, rejecting both alternatives. "I will not kill him. I want him in intensive care, and I want everything possible to be done to keep him alive. That's final."

It took a kindly priest—my friend Father Don—to change Mother's mind. He was able to convince her that prolonging Dad's life was contrary to God's will. "We have to let God be God," he said.

That dear man sat with Mother when she signed the transfer papers. He walked beside her as Dad's bed was wheeled to the hospice ward. He waited while the hospice staff removed my father's feeding tube, bathed him, shampooed his hair, and shaved his beard. When he was dressed in his own pajamas and tucked into a clean bed, Father Don said the last rites, the Catholic sacrament for the dying. After that, I looked in on my father; for the first time in weeks, he was resting peacefully.

That evening, our family gathered to say our good-byes. My brothers had come with stories to share, while my sisters had planned personal blessings to help Dad on his way. I had a poem and a prayer tucked in my pocket.

My mother, however, had her own plans; she would allow no talking about Dad and no talking to Dad. All she wanted was the Rosary. "We're here to pray for your father's immortal soul," she said. "That's all."

Finally, after we'd prayed the entire Rosary—five decades plus the "Glory Be" three times—Mother dropped her beads into her purse, touched her husband's hand, and walked out the door. In turn, each of my brothers and sisters said their farewells to Dad and left the room.

When everyone had gone, I closed the door, pulled a chair next to the bed, and took my father's hand. His eyes were closed. I could feel his weak breath on my face. I leaned close.

"Dad, it's Claire," I said. "A while ago, I promised that I'd tell you when you were dying. Tonight I'm keeping that promise." I choked back my tears and continued. "Your body is tired. You fought the good fight for a long time and it's time to let go."

Sometime later, the night nurse stopped in to check on me. "Go home and rest," she said. "I'll call if anything changes."

I kissed my father's cheek and whispered to him, "Good night, my dear dad. I love you."

Two hours later, my father slipped from his disease-ravaged body and went home.

The *Wanderer* eulogized my father, saying, "Jay provided the kind of thoughtful and principled leadership that enabled the Wanderer Forum Foundation to maintain a steady course throughout these years of crisis within the Church in America . . . his outstanding example as a faithful Catholic and a quietly effective leader will remain an inspiration for those who knew him."[37] The John Birch Society offered their condolences in the August 1992 bulletin, acknowledging Dad for thirty-two years of service on the National Council, honoring him for his "many contributions to the Americanist cause."[38]

Mother saved these memorials, along with the cards and letters she received after Dad's death. The most cherished message came from an old friend who wrote, "It must have been nice, and now very comforting, to have been married for so many years to a good man." The friend never signed the card.

Chapter Twenty-two

Attention Must Be Paid

It soon became evident that the killers were Americans, born in the USA and bred on resentments circulating wildly in the terror zone where gun nuts met militias.
— LEONARD ZESKIND ON THE OKLAHOMA CITY BOMBING[1]

Several days after my father's funeral, I relaxed in the family room with an old issue of *Time* and a tall glass of iced tea. I was bone tired after all the activity. That two-week-old magazine offered a good excuse to sit back and do almost nothing, at least for a little while.

I turned pages, paying almost no attention to the stories until I hit "White & Wrong," a report about Ku Klux Klan recruiting in, of all places, Janesville, Wisconsin.[2] "The KKK in Wisconsin," I said, right out loud. "What the hell?"

The Klan had erected a huge cross, soaked in kerosene, in the middle of Janesville's most popular public park. Demonstrators threw mud, rocks, and their anger at the Klan but couldn't get through the police barricade. The fellow who organized the whole thing, one Thom Robb, loved the uproar. "I couldn't have bought this advertising for a million bucks," he crowed.

A Klan wizard, Robb promulgated the idea of building a high-tech operation that would crank out articulate Klansmen and use modern advertising to enhance the organization's image. As Robb described it, he was "selling white pride, white power."[3] *Time* had combed through Robb's life and discovered that his right-wing roots stretched back to the extremist political tracts favored by his mother. While in high school, Robb had joined the John Birch Society and at some later point had picked up the KKK banner instead.

When I read that white pride and power junk, Revilo Oliver, my father's old JBS friend, came to mind. Though I'd tried to erase all memory of that hate-filled man, I learned later that he'd made quite a name for himself in the vilest segment of the radical Right, where he had a following among white supremacists and skinheads.

At the same time that the KKK was organizing in Wisconsin, the still-active and ever-obnoxious Revilo was busy writing and speaking in every venue that would have him. In one of his pamphlets he suggested that true democracy could be achieved in the United States by "deporting, vaporizing, or otherwise disposing of the swarms of Jews, Congoids, Mongoloids, and mongrels that now infest our territory and are becoming ever more numerous and audacious in their unappeasable hatred of us."[4]

I pushed Revilo out of my mind, grabbed my car keys, and drove over to see my mother.

A few days after Dad's death, Mother had returned to her self-appointed task of defeating the ever-present, ever-growing conspiracy, whether it was the Communists or the one-world government folks. Most days, she hid away in her little office, reading and writing. I understood that her work was essential for her; without it, she'd be shattered by grief. She believed that my father lived in the work they'd always done together. In pressing on, she honored him.

I honored him by looking after her, as I'd promised. So, at least once a week, I coaxed her out of the office long enough to share a pot of tea and some conversation. I tried to steer our discussions away from religion or politics, but Mother had little interest in anything else. I knew when she said, "This is a very serious situation, dear," that I'd be hearing about another nefarious scheme perpetrated by the scoundrels in Washington.

———

As far as I could tell, my mother and father had disapproved of every United States president since Herbert Hoover. Even Ronald Reagan, the conservative messiah, had fallen into disgrace for his embrace of amnesty for immigrants and his support for the United Nations' Genocide Treaty. Making matters worse, Reagan had provided aid to the Soviets, raised taxes, and run up huge federal deficits. All of these policies proved that Ronald Reagan was really a liberal.

My parents called Reagan the "actor/President," echoing what the JBS had written: "The actor/President who solidified his anti-Communist credentials with forensic fusillades against the 'evil empire' is now sharing top billing with Mikhail Gorbachev in an entirely new production promoting Communist goals."[5]

My parents were convinced that Reagan was the latest traitor to encourage "Merger Mania," the plan to merge the United States and the USSR and "lead all nations into an all-powerful world government." As John McManus, the new JBS president and a longtime friend of my parents, said, "Anyone with half a brain should see . . . a determination to tear the U.S. down with socialism and build the USSR up with Western aid. The result is that the two nations will become virtually indistinguishable and can be comfortably merged."[6]

As far as my parents and the rest of the JBS were concerned, President George H. W. Bush was perfectly suited to expand on the socialist policies Reagan had initiated. Bush had deep ties to the "Insiders," secret internationalists bent on merging the United States and Russia into a New World Order. Bush had been a member of both the Council on Foreign Relations and the Trilateral Commission, two of the key organizations in that Insiders web. He'd also been a member of the Skull and Bones Society while at Yale, the organization that many Birchers labeled a "recruiting ground for the international banking clique, the CIA, and politics."[7]

My parents and their right-wing friends had been worrying about the Insiders and their New World Order for decades, but the words of President George H. W. Bush on September 11, 1990, created a new level of concern. In a television address announcing the deployment of troops into Kuwait to beat back the invasion of Saddam Hussein's Iraqi forces, the president said, "The crisis in the Persian Gulf, as grave as it is, also offers a rare opportunity to move toward an historic period of cooperation. Out of these troubled times . . . *a new world order* [emphasis mine] can emerge: a new era—freer from the threat of terror, stronger in the pursuit of justice, and more secure in the quest for peace."[8]

According to my parents and the JBS, Bush's speech signaled the beginning of the conspiracy's final assault on the United States. For Mother and Dad and conspiracy fighters everywhere, the time had come to mobilize. War against the government was coming.

I was used to this New World Order stuff, but I was not prepared for the immensity of the rage when William Jefferson Clinton was sworn into office in January of 1993.

—————

My mother became fixated on Clinton and his "Insider" credentials. She reminded me, many times, that he was a member of the Council on Foreign Relations and the Trilateral Commission. Adding to the evidence against the president, Clinton had studied in Merry Olde Socialized England at Oxford University. And, most damning of all, Clinton was a Rhodes scholar.[9]

In addition to those strikes against him, Clinton was, according to the acting president of the JBS, a morally degenerate draft dodger who actively courted the homosexual vote, smoked dope, and married Hillary Rodham, a revolutionary in her own right.[10]

When our new president said, "There is nothing wrong with America that cannot be cured by what is right with America," I heard a positive vision for my country.[11] My mother heard a one-world socialist who would bring an end to America as we knew it and install a dictatorship controlled by the United Nations.

When the new president pushed for health-care reform, Mother was convinced that Clinton was moving quickly to reinvent the United States as a totalitarian state. "He's a socialist," she said. "He and that awful wife of his are pushing us to socialized medicine."

One afternoon while I sipped tea with Mother, she was particularly agitated by an article in the latest John Birch Society bulletin. "Look at this," she said. "Jack wrote it and he knows how serious the situation is."

Mother's friend "Jack" was John McManus, the president of the JBS. McManus had taken over in 1991, but he and my dad had known each other since 1966, when Jack joined the staff as a New England coordinator. One of the first decisions Jack made after becoming president was to move the national headquarters of the JBS from Belmont, Massachusetts, to Appleton, Wisconsin, the birthplace of Senator Joseph McCarthy. (As of 2012, McManus has been the JBS president for twenty-one years, making him the longest-serving executive of the society since Robert Welch.)[12]

McManus's article, "It All Fits!," traced the initiatives of the Clinton administration that were part of the plan to create a "new world order to replace the sovereignty of nations and the freedom of individuals."[13] Discussing everything from the mission in Somalia to the North American Free Trade Agreement, McManus built the case that Clinton was promoting a New World Order with every part of his agenda. If the JBS failed to get the message out, McManus guaranteed that the "looming new world order with all of its horrors will control the future."[14]

"Clinton is the worst president ever," Mother said.

"Maybe Clinton isn't evil," I suggested. "Maybe he's just a Democrat."

"Young lady, you ought to listen more closely to your mother," she responded. "If you read more, instead of focusing on fun and games, you'd understand how serious this situation is. Let me remind you that you and your children are at risk."

"You've been expecting this New World Order for thirty-six years," I reminded her. "Why is this time any different?"

"You're hopeless," she said in disgust. "If you don't understand the conspiracy by now, you never will."

The fear and anger on the right intensified when President Clinton pushed for the Brady Bill, the long-delayed legislation that increased the waiting period for handgun purchases and banned assault weapons.[15] The Brady Bill became, without exaggeration, the Far Right's call to arms. For the more intellectual right-wingers, like my mother, the weapons of choice were typewriters, pamphlets, and petitions. The more militant types took to the woods for combat training with their AK-47s and Glocks.[16] Most of the guys who tromped through the mud in camouflage and practiced target shooting were weekend warriors. Among them, however, was a hard-core group of revolutionaries who studied sabotage and explosives with an eye toward fomenting a race war.[17]

Like true believers everywhere, these men had their own sacred text, *The Turner Diaries*.[18] The book, published in 1978, was written by William Pierce under the name Andrew Macdonald. Pierce, an early member of the John Birch Society turned neo-Nazi, got the idea of using fiction to spread his white-supremacist ideas from his dear friend and mentor, Dr. Revilo Oliver.[19]

This grisly, violent, hate-filled story depicts America in 1991 as a police state where guns have been banned and government policies are enforced by roving bands of "Afros," a derogatory term for African Americans. The main character, diarist Earl Turner, joins an underground movement that is planning and eventually executes terrorist attacks across the country in hopes of starting the "Great Revolution." When Turner's cell is ordered to blow up FBI headquarters, the conspirators build a homemade bomb using fertilizer, fuel oil, and a delivery truck. Turner records in great detail the "recipe" for the bomb and specific directions for assembling the device.[20]

The explosion is devastating, killing over seven hundred people and mangling many more. No pangs of conscience prick the perpetrators, however. One minute before the explosion, they contact the *Washington Post* with this message: "We are now settling the score with your pals in the politics police. Soon we'll settle the score with you and all other traitors. White America shall live!"[21]

The book continues for another 150 pages describing the "Great Revolution" that purges the United States of all Jews and non-whites. One chapter details the "Day of the Rope," when the revolution had purged Los Angeles of all Jews, non-whites, and Latinos and began systematic executions of those in the remaining population. In the book, tens of thousands of white women who "defiled their race by marrying or living with Blacks, with Jews, or with other non-white males" are hanged from "tens of thousands of lampposts, power poles, and trees."[22]

The Turner Diaries might have remained underground, passed from extremist to extremist, if Trooper Charles Hanger hadn't pulled over a yellow Mercury Marquis, without tags, on Interstate 35 a few miles from Perry, Oklahoma. It was 10:20 a.m. on April 19, 1995—ninety minutes after an explosion tore through the Alfred P. Murrah Federal Building sixty miles away. Trooper Hanger had no idea that he'd just detained Timothy McVeigh, the Oklahoma City bomber. In McVeigh's car, investigators would find excerpts from *The Turner Diaries*.[23]

Sixty minutes before McVeigh was arrested, I stood in front of the television staring at the mangled shell of what had been, until 9:02 a.m., a federal office building. Minutes before the bomb blast, hundreds of people had come to this building to do what they did every day: go to work. Some had dropped off their babies at the second-floor day-care center before going upstairs to their offices. Others, everyday Oklahomans, had come to apply for Social Security benefits. Without warning, the building fell down on them.

America's Kids day-care center was destroyed, killing nineteen little ones. One firefighter, Chris Fields, wearing helmet number five, emerged from the building carrying the limp, blood-covered body of Baylee Almon. Little Baylee had turned one the day before.[24]

While rescue crews combed the wreckage for survivors, everyone wanted to know who had done this terrible thing. Almost immediately, an all-points bulletin was issued for "two men of Middle Eastern appearance with dark hair and beards."[25]

The media brought out a parade of "experts" with a deep understanding of Islamic terrorism. One particularly popular fellow was Steven Emerson, the filmmaker who had produced the 1994 documentary *Terrorists Among Us: Jihad in America* for PBS. A few hours after the Oklahoma City bombing, Emerson confirmed on television that "federal law enforcement officials were investigating the possibility that Islamic groups were involved."[26] He went on to explain that the bomb that caused the explosion was "NOT the same type of bomb that has been traditionally used by other terrorist groups in the United States other than the Islamic ones."

No one doubted Emerson. He had infiltrated meetings of radical Arab Americans, including one held several years before the bombing—also in Oklahoma City. He had intimate knowledge of the "Blind Sheikh," Omar

Abdel-Rahman, and of his terrorist friends who had bombed the World Trade Center in New York City two years earlier. He knew a call for jihad when he heard it.[27]

I went to bed that night convinced that a gang of turbaned Islamic terrorists had opened another front in their war against America. Oddly enough, I found the conclusion comforting—we had an enemy "over there." Our mighty military would eventually identify and capture the bad guys.

The next day, while the media prognostications continued, an FBI crew sifted through the rubble of the Murrah building looking for clues. Somehow, out of the mess that had been a building, one of the crew uncovered the rear axle of a truck with its identification number still visible. This clue led them to a body shop in Junction City, Kansas, where the Ryder truck had been rented. With the help of shop employees, a police sketch artist constructed the face of the man who rented that truck.[28]

Everyone expecting a dark-haired, dark-skinned, Semitic man with a beard had to be shocked when John Doe No. 1 turned out to be a young white man with a military crew cut and piercing eyes.[29] At a local motel, the Dreamland, a desk clerk was able to put a name to that face. Timothy McVeigh had signed the register on April 14 and had checked out the morning of April 18—presumably to drive 270 miles south in time to destroy his target in Oklahoma City.[30]

The FBI traced its prime suspect to the Perry, Oklahoma, jail where McVeigh was awaiting a bond hearing on the charge of driving an unlicensed vehicle. Oklahoma authorities had discovered that the man had no criminal record and no outstanding warrants, but they were unable to determine if McVeigh owned the car he'd been driving or why he was carrying a loaded Glock in a shoulder holster. Nonetheless, he was going to be released after posting a $500 bond. Luckily, the presiding judge was running late that day. McVeigh was still locked up when the FBI called.[31]

Over the weekend, authorities continued to search for two other suspects in the bombing case, men they dubbed John Doe No. 2 and John Doe No. 3. No one knew exactly who these men were, but the clues indicated that they were part of a network of underground citizens' militia groups that preached a schizophrenic kind of patriotism. These folks loathed the federal government, loved their own twisted interpretation of the Constitution, and embraced the idea of sovereign citizens—persons legally outside the reach of government rules, regulations, and taxes based on a "sovereign" declaration.[32]

While many people were scratching their heads trying to grasp that the Oklahoma terrorists were born in the USA, I was unnerved. I felt like I knew these men. They were duplicates of Thomas Stockheimer, the local gun-loving, government-hating loudmouth who'd called me names twenty-three years earlier.

After Stockheimer lost his 1972 race for the Wisconsin legislature, he gave up on electoral politics. He embraced the Posse Comitatus, a radical underground movement that urged resistance against the federal government and encouraged massive tax protests. According to its organizing guide, *The Posse Blue Book*—yes, the same title given to the Birch bible—the plan was to get a Posse up and running in every county in the United States.[33]

The Posse specialized in fire and brimstone directed toward its most hated enemy, the IRS. "Get ready for a declaration of war!" Posse leader Bill Gale said. "And if you don't have a gun, bring some rope! Because there's going to be one tax collector removed from office!"[34]

Tom Stockheimer took Gale literally. In 1974, he and several friends lured the local IRS agent, Fred Chicken, out to a farm, tied him up, punched, and threatened him. When Stockheimer was sentenced to prison, he jumped bail and fled the state. Before he ran, Stockheimer recruited one of his friends to assume Posse leadership.[35]

The new leader, a nasty fellow named James Wickstrom, used Posse members to disrupt meetings of the state legislature and harass local law-enforcement officers. One of their tactics was posting handbills in grocery stores, on public bulletin boards, and on light posts and fences all around Central Wisconsin. One of these posters carried the headline "It's time for old-fashioned American Justice" and a sketch of a corpse swinging from the tree. The text read: "The White Anglo/Saxon Posse's [*sic*] across this Christian Republic await for the opportunity to clear up America of which the Jews and their 'lackey' jerks called politicians have made a *GARBAGE DUMP.*"[36]

While Wickstrom encouraged the haters, Thomas Stockheimer spent the late 1980s and early 1990s expanding his criminal activities. As Daniel Levitas explained in *The Terrorist Next Door*, "[Stockheimer] and eight associates were charged with mail fraud and conspiracy for selling bogus Posse money orders." One of Stockheimer's customers was the second Oklahoma City bomber, Terry Nichols."[37]

———

By Sunday, I was beginning to grasp that Oklahoma City was a revenge killing. Timothy McVeigh and many other radical right-wingers had nursed a deep grudge against the federal government since the attacks on the Branch Davidians in Waco, Texas, on April 19, 1993.[38]

Like most Americans, I knew that the federal government had evidence of sexual abuse, child abuse, and the stockpiling of illegal weapons on the isolated compound ruled by David Koresh. When he refused to allow authorities to search the place, the feds and the cult members became locked in a fifty-one-day standoff.[39]

Then in April, fire had engulfed the compound, killing seventy-four people. Twenty-four were children.[40] I was heartsick. I couldn't understand how the situation had reached such a violent conclusion.

For right-wingers, Waco proved that the federal government had gone to war against its own citizens. They tried to justify Oklahoma City as an appropriate response to the Waco attack. I tried to make sense of the senseless, but I didn't have forever to ponder. My mother was coming for dinner, and I had a chicken to roast and the table to set.

For several months, I had avoided confrontations with my mother by focusing on safe subjects like her grandchildren, the weather, and family gossip about cousins, aunts, and uncles. Anytime she started a rant about politics, I tried to bite my tongue and say nothing. Sometimes I actually succeeded.

That evening I was about to congratulate myself on a trouble-free visit when Mother brought up the Oklahoma City bombing. "It's a tragedy," she said.

"I totally agree," I offered. "It is hard to believe an American, an Army vet—"

Mother interrupted me in mid-sentence. "He had his reasons."

"What are you talking about? What reasons?"

Mother put down her cup and looked right at me. "Waco," she said.

"Waco? The Branch Davidians two years ago?"

"Yes," Mother said. "The government killed lots of innocent women and children in that attack."

"So, McVeigh blows up a building in Oklahoma City and kills babies in the day-care center. Are you crazy?"

"I'm not crazy at all. Timothy McVeigh was defending the rest of us from the government," Mother said.

"Nineteen babies died," I reminded her.

"That happens in war," she said.

I stared at my mother. Her chin was set; her eyes, steely; her lips, stretched thin. She was determined, fierce, and unmovable. I realized that no amount of arguing would change her mind. She'd decided that the federal government was the enemy and terrorists like Timothy McVeigh were the good guys.

When Mother finished her tea and her lemon meringue pie, I brought her trench coat from the closet and helped her slip it on. She knotted the belt and wrapped a silk scarf around her head. My husband took her arm, helped her into the car, and drove her home. He returned a few minutes later while I was in the kitchen loading the dishwasher. He dropped his arm around my shoulder and hugged me.

"She doesn't know what she's saying," he said.

"Yes, she really does," I answered.

That day I gave up on my mother.

Chapter Twenty-three

Hell in a Handbasket

The knock on the door surprised me, but I was more surprised to see my mother on the porch, a white box in her arms. For the last few months, we had not seen each other very often, except for the must-do family things like Mother's Day and my youngest son's high school graduation. Otherwise, we confined our communication to weekly phone calls. By unspoken agreement, we skirted every topic even remotely controversial, which left us with the weather and the weather.

These chats never took long. Mother usually begged off after a few minutes. She always had some big project pulling her back to the desk. I didn't ask for details; short conversations suited me too. I just assumed she was writing something to do with Catholicism, most likely full of reverence for the Pope, who'd captured Mother's heart in 1978 when he appeared in a window in St. Peter's Basilica and called out his chosen name: John Paul II.[1] Mother believed that this Polish prelate was God's own anti-Communist, who would smash the last remnants of the Soviet empire, renew the Catholic Church, and bring millions of fallen-away Catholics back to their faith. She prayed that I would be one of those millions.

My mother would never grasp my profound disappointment with this Pope, who had claimed to love children while he denied reality: thousands of Catholic priests had sexually abused children. For me, no amount of piety or charisma could square that circle.

"Are you ever coming back to the Church?" Mother had asked me shortly after Dad's funeral. "I saw you didn't take Communion."

"Let's not fuss about this," I told her.

"If you die outside of the Church," she warned me, "you'll burn in hell."

In late June of 1995, while Mother stood in the open doorway, I flashed back to that "burn in hell" moment. "Stick to the weather," I reminded myself as I invited her in for tea.

"I have no time. I just wanted to drop this off."

"Thanks," I said. "What is it?"

"The Conner genealogy. Someday you might be interested." With that, she handed me the box and turned toward her car.

"Wait," I called. "Just a minute."

Mother stopped in the driveway and looked at me. "Now you can join the DAR," she said, adding, "Not that you care."

A few minutes later, I settled myself at the kitchen table and opened the box. Inside, on a carefully folded nest of tissue paper, sat a green-leather scrapbook and several manila folders. I pushed the folders aside and opened the book. The first page, titled "The Conner Family," featured a quote from Pope John Paul II about the family as a "community of generations."[2]

On the next pages, Mother had recorded the earliest known branches of the Conner family, documenting the names and birth and death dates of everyone she found. She outlined the line from Philippe du Trieux and his wife, Susanna, who married in Holland in 1621 and came to America in 1624. Five generations later, Jacob Truax married Rebecca Stillwell. That couple had a son, Stillwell Truax, who grew up to be an officer in the Continental army.

My mother had spent hundreds of hours piecing together my father's family tree. She had verified her findings with pages of old documents that she'd unearthed—birth certificates, death certificates, land grants, and Sons of the American Revolution applications. Her painstaking work proved the lineal, bloodline descent from a Revolutionary War patriot required to join the Daughters of the American Revolution.

Ironically, Mother—descended from German and Irish families who came to America a hundred years after the revolution—could not win entrance to that storied organization of arch-Americans. Her family had stayed too long in Europe.

As I put the book back in its box, I noticed one of the folders I had set aside. In a white envelope were old newspaper clippings, worn and yellowed. I carefully unfolded pages of "War-time Easter Parade" from the April 5, 1942, issue of the *Rocky Mountain News*.[3] At first glance, I couldn't understand why Mother had saved this clipping; certainly she could have cared less about the "well-dressed matrons" photographed in their spring ensembles.

I started to refold the brittle paper when I noticed a photo of a beautiful, young woman seated at the end of a sofa. The caption described the smiling woman as someone who "prefers a sophisticated type of frock for those *little dinners.*"

"Holy crap," I thought. "Sexy frocks and intimate dinners . . . Hello, Mother."

I promised myself that I'd find out about those days—before babies and rabid right-wingery. Unfortunately, by the time I started asking, my mother had no idea what I was talking about.

In February of 1996, I slathered myself with sunscreen, pulled on a cover-up and hat, and headed to the beach. It was early, but it was Cancun, so I ordered a golden margarita and settled down for a day of doing nothing and resting afterward.

Three thousand miles north, my frail eighty-two-year-old mother pulled on her winter coat, tied a wool scarf around her head, and headed out for her weekly hair appointment. She parked her Oldsmobile in the lot behind the beauty salon and inched her way along the slick black-top toward the door. Suddenly, a gust of wind picked up all 115 pounds of her and dropped her on the ground. Unable to get up, she lay in the cold, praying for someone to find her.

By the time I got home from Mexico, Mother's hip had been pinned back into place and she was recovering at St. Joseph's Hospital. She had enough spunk to complain about the food and the proposals for her care when she was discharged. Every day she said the same thing, "I am not going to the nursing home, period. I'll take care of myself in my own house."

Her doctor patiently explained, several times, how critical the next phase of recovery was for her. Sensing that he was not getting through, he took a more direct approach. "You will never walk again without physical therapy," he told her. "You'll be a crippled old lady, and the next fall will kill you."

Mother paled at this prediction. "I'll go for the therapy," she conceded. "But don't expect me to stay long."

Four months later, after a lot of hard work on the part of the rehab staff and Mother herself, she was cleared to go home, with the caveat that she have some help. "My daughter is available," she told the nurses. "I won't need anyone else."

It took me only a day or so to realize what "being available" meant. On Mother's command, I was expected to tie her shoes, run errands, pick up groceries, and get her to the clinic for seemingly endless appointments. I was her go-to-gal for all her needs, and not unexpectedly, I also became her political punching bag. I kept reminding myself to "shut up and talk about the weather," while Mother wanted to talk about President Clinton.

Even though I'd lived through her rants against Presidents Eisenhower, Kennedy, Johnson, and Carter, I was unprepared for her obsession with the Clintons. She ranted about Vincent Foster and Hillarycare.[4] At one point, she started calling the First Couple "the liar and the lesbian."[5]

I knew, from the way Mother said "lesbian"—with a snarl—that it was intended as the ultimate insult. Hillary was not a real woman, Mother thought; she was a pervert. Her view came directly out of the Catholic catechism, in which homosexual acts were described as "depraved" and "intrinsically disordered."[6]

Proving that the apple doesn't fall far from the tree, I had believed the very same things about gay people—years before I had any idea about any kind of sex. As a teenager, I heard whispers about "queers" and "limp wrists," and started to figure out that men were doing things together that were dirty. In my Psych 101 class, I learned that domineering mothers turned their sons into men who loved other men.[7]

It took me a long time, but by the time I was forty, I'd changed. I discarded Freud in favor of genetics as the determinant of sexual orientation. And surprise, I discovered that I had gay friends.

Then, while Mother was telling anyone who'd listen that Hillary Clinton was a lesbian, my third child came out.

"I'm gay," Brian told me. "I wanted you to know."

I needed to say the right thing. I wanted to offer comfort and understanding, but I wasn't sure how to say what was in my heart without somehow diminishing what was in his.

I know seemed arrogant and thoughtless. *I love you* seemed like a closing statement. I decided to wait. If Brian had more to say, I would let him say it.

"I've known I was different for a long time," Brian continued. "Since I was six or seven, I think. But I didn't know how I was different or what it meant. When I figured it out, I was too terrified to tell anyone."

"Look at you now, Bri," I said. "You are strong and honest and good. I'm proud of you, and I'm proud to be your mother."

And I was proud. That dear boy of mine had tried for years to figure out who he was and where he was going. His dad and I had suspected for some time that his sexual orientation was the reason. As parents, we so wanted to take away his pain, but we both knew that this struggle was his. All we could do was love him and trust that he'd find his way.

That day on the phone when my twenty-five-year-old son revealed his secret, he pushed open the closet door for himself and for his dad and me too. From that moment on, gay had a face.

When I told friends and family, many of them were surprised that Bri came out over the phone. They miss the point, I think. The circumstances of "coming out" are unimportant. What is important is that my son stood tall for who he is, and in that process, he became a man.

Less than a year after Brian came out, another young gay man—Matthew

Shepard—was pistol-whipped, tortured, and tied to a fence post outside Laramie, Wyoming. Eighteen hours later, two bicyclists noticed the body. They assumed, at first, that they were looking at a scarecrow.[8]

Matthew Shepard died five days later without ever regaining consciousness.

At his funeral, a group of protestors from the Westboro Baptist Church, based in Topeka, Kansas, appeared carrying signs declaring "No Tears for Queers" and "Fag Matt in Hell."[9]

After Matthew Shepard's murder, I began to pay attention to who was leading the hate-the-gay parade. I discovered, not surprisingly, that the right wing, the leadership of the Roman Catholic Church, and evangelical Christians were up to their eyeballs in homophobic nastiness.[10]

Author Michelle Goldberg examined the right wing's anti-gay politics and concluded, "For the right, gays are living signifiers of decadence and corruption. They're seen as both repulsive and tempting, their mere existence sparking some deep primordial panic among much of straight America. A great many of the anxieties stalking the country—fears about social dysfunction, family breakdown, cultural decay, and decreasing status—have been projected onto homosexuals and their ostensible 'agenda.'"[11]

The John Birch Society, which had been in the anti-gay business since its fight against AIDS education in the mid-1980s, took great exception to President Clinton's move to lift the ban on gays in the military. JBS president John McManus wrote that senior military men had told him that a "serious undermining of morale, discipline and good order" would result if the homosexual ban were lifted.[12] Clinton, who had taken "unusual pains to avoid serving" in Vietnam, could not understand that attitude, McManus contended. He went on to insist that since "half of our nation's cases of venereal diseases are found among homosexuals, the likelihood that military personnel would become incapacitated with syphilis and related diseases would raise significantly. Then there's the problem of AIDS." McManus finished with a brash flourish of moralism: "Is there to be any moral code for this nation? If homosexuality received an official acceptance, won't it and all its consequences spread?"

Jerry Falwell, who'd made his mark as the head of the Moral Majority, used the Clinton administration to revitalize his brand. In one of his fundraising letters, he wrote, "Has American lost its vision of being . . . ONE NATION UNDER GOD? Are we about to become a hedonistic nation of unrestrained homosexuality, abortion, immorality and lawlessness?" and, "We are only days away from seeing the U.S. military infiltrated with gay men and lesbians."[13] He even hinted that "churches would be forced to hire a quota of homosexuals."

My parents agreed with the JBS and Jerry Falwell. They were like so many in the right wing, folks described by Jean Hardisty in her book *Mobilizing Resentment* who believed that homosexuality "should be met with alarm and loathing and that the gains made by the gay rights movement were a threat to 'family values.'"[14]

If I hadn't already renounced all ties with the Right, the crusade to keep my son from enjoying basic civil rights would have done it. As it was, their views pushed me further and further left.

By 1997, Mother was convinced that the Clinton White House was about to surrender the United States to either Red China or the United Nations.[15] The scheme, a pet project of the New World Order conspiracy, was so close to completion that only one remedy was available to save the country: impeachment.

I guessed that Mother's new political crusade was a John Birch Society operation, orchestrated from the new national headquarters in Appleton, Wisconsin. A quick peek at the materials on her kitchen table confirmed my suspicion: the Birch Society had its own National Impeach Clinton Action Committee, selling "Impeachment Packets" and twelve-by-twenty-five-foot billboards reading "Impeach Clinton Now!" for $125.[16]

If Mother had been healthier, I'm sure she would have made the trip to Marietta, Georgia, in March of 1998 for the National Town Hall Meeting on Impeachment, organized by some previously unknown grassroots group called Citizens for Honest Government and their Birch Society allies.[17]

One reporter described the Georgia rally as "a multifaceted far-right strategy to hobble the Clinton presidency."[18] Among the speakers who took up the impeachment banner that day were Catherine McDonald, widow of Congressman Larry McDonald—the John Birch Society president who'd been killed in the Korean Air disaster fifteen years earlier—and John McManus, the current JBS leader.[19]

Republican Bob Barr of Georgia, who had been elected to the congressional seat previously held by McDonald, claimed that Clinton had committed treason by soliciting campaign money from China "in exchange for transferring military and computer technologies. The congressman cited "classified information" that he had seen but could not discuss as proof of his charges.[20]

The prospect of impeaching the president was a big shot in the arm for the Birch Society, a welcome respite from the irrelevance it had suffered through the Reagan administration. No one had needed a far-right, populist insurgency when the president himself was a far-right populist. A Democrat in the White House, however, offered new opportunities to recruit a new generation of Birchers and Birch wannabes.[21]

The society reinvigorated its summer youth camps, where kids were treated to a week of conspiracy classes and flag waving as an "antidote to left wing disinformation from public schools."[22] One fun activity was the so-called Night Patrol, in which a roving band of camp counselors wearing swords and headgear stormed into campers' cabins. According to the director of the Los Angeles camp, the patrol was intended to instill resentment against excessive police power.[23] Young patriots could also buy T-shirts, which included one that read: "I hate what Clinton and his gang of anti-gunner, gays and liberals are doing to America."

That slogan summed up the Birch view of the president. Whether they were Birch campers or Birch leaders, William Jefferson Clinton was public enemy number one.

That summer of 1996, a thousand kids also learned about the powerful "Insiders" working to create a totalitarian, atheistic world government and the Marxists who planned to send millions of Mexicans across the border— each one charged with killing ten Americans.[24]

That same summer, my mother had become a one-woman anti-Clinton committee. Every day she pounded out letters to newspapers, members of Congress, and a raft of folks she called her contacts castigating the president for anything and everything. And the harder she worked, the better she felt. I swear, the process of getting Clinton impeached added years to her life.

On December 11, 1998, when the House Judiciary Committee approved Articles of Impeachment against the president, Mother was as giddy as a schoolgirl.[25] "We did it," she said to me. "It's a grand day."

Several days later, the *Washington Post* acknowledged that the John Birch Society, along with Robert L. Barley of the *Wall Street Journal* and Congressman Bob Barr, had created the groundswell of support among Republicans for impeachment. "Together, their success is a demonstration of how a determined and ideologically committed group can change the course of history," Thomas Edsall wrote.[26]

After Clinton's acquittal by the Senate, the Birchers insisted that Republicans had blocked the crucial material needed to find the president guilty. It was another proof that the conspiracy pulled the strings: clearly the GOP and the Democrats were one and the same. David Shippers, investigative counsel for the House Judiciary Committee, said as much in *American Opinion*, the Birch Society magazine. The Senate Republicans, he wrote, had not just tried to rig the case but had "rigged it. It was rigged to make it impossible for us to win."[27] According to Shippers, one senator was completely clear about the situation: "I don't care if you have proof that [Clinton] raped a woman, stood up and shot her dead, you are not going to get 67 votes."[28]

———

Before the impeachment trial in January of 1999, Mother was euphoric about the new power of the right wing. Afterward, she was depressed, almost despondent. "That's it," she told me. "Any day the conspiracy will take over, and no one will lift a finger to stop them."

At first, I thought she'd break out of her funk and jump into a new cause. But as the months dragged on, she remained detached and depressed. I wondered if something else was happening. One day, after the bank called me about errors in her accounts, I spent an afternoon untangling the money messes and trying to make sense of her check register and bills.

Mother argued with everything I suggested until I lost my temper. "Don't call me anymore," I said. "Take care of this mess yourself."

I looked across the kitchen table at my little old mother and realized she was crying. "I can't," she admitted. "I can't see the numbers anymore."

Several trips to the eye doctor confirmed what she had dreaded: her early-stage macular degeneration had advanced, and now she had glaucoma. I held her hand while the doctor delivered the worst possible prognosis— before long Mother would be blind. She needed help beyond what I could provide, so I hired a trained caregiver who came three days a week. Almost immediately, my mother complained about cold tea, hard eggs, and burned toast. She hollered that the shower was too hot and fussed when it was too cold. The "maid," as she insisted on referring to her helper, could not get Mother's girdle on or adjust her back brace.

Several women quit without explanation. One, who was kind enough to warn me that she was leaving, explained the situation. "Working for the queen is impossible," she said. I understood exactly what she meant.

———

Mother had to move to an assisted-living facility, a reality she finally accepted after my brother Jay R. and my sister Mary championed the idea. The new arrangement took a mountain of pressure off of me. One of the staff workers at the new place put it like this: "We'll take care *of* her so you can care *about* her."

Mother refused to participate in any of the structured activities, declaring it all "fun and games for senile old ladies," but at least she was safe and received regular meals, showers, and meds. Her eyesight deteriorated and her hearing failed, and she seemed to lose track of things all the time, but compared to a lot of the residents, she was stable.

Over the next year, I began to notice how many things she didn't "know" anymore, like my name and the names of her grandchildren, but she was an ace at fooling the doctors. After all, how many women nearing ninety could name the first five American presidents and recite the Preamble to the Constitution? Mother was so convincing that no one bothered to ask her what year it was, where she lived, or her deceased husband's name. "She's sharp as a tack," one doctor told me. "No Alzheimer's."

I knew he was wrong.

Two weeks before the 2000 presidential election, I arrived in Tampa to visit my sister and take a much-needed vacation. As I stepped out of the airport terminal into the delicious warmth of Florida, I twirled and giggled. "I don't want to live here in the summer," I told Janet. "But in November, it's Florida forever."

A couple of days later, as we basked in the joy of French roast coffee and the *New York Times*, I complained about the presidential election. "I can hardly wait for this thing to be over," I said. "It has gone on and on and on."

I'd voted absentee—for Al Gore and Joe Lieberman—before leaving Wisconsin, but my decision was more of a "no" to nominee George W. Bush rather than a "yes" to Vice President Gore. As far as I was concerned, anything would be better than a Texas Republican selling himself as a "compassionate conservative."[29]

"We're still suffering from Reagan's compassion," I said.

"I'm voting Gore," my sister said. "But his whole campaign has been as dull as dirt."

"You are right about that," I said. "But I'll take a professor, even a boring one, over a cowboy any day."

Two weeks later, eight hours after Janet and I had settled on a sofa to watch the election returns, neither one of us was laughing. The network reporting of vote tallies and projections for state winners had devolved into chaos. Ultimately it all came down to Florida, Florida, Florida, just as Tim Russert predicted.[30] We went to bed expecting the whole mess to be sorted out in the morning.

But instead of clarity, we had thirty-six days of "hanging chads," recounts, and court challenges. It took the Supreme Court to award those twenty-six contested electoral votes through a tangled process of three competing lawsuits.[31] In the end, George Bush became the forty-third president of the United Sates, and Al Gore walked away with a moral victory: he'd actually received more popular votes than Bush—543,816 more to be exact.[32]

Bush was inaugurated president on January 21, 2001, promising to "advance my convictions with civility, to pursue the public interest with courage, to speak for greater justice and compassion, to call for responsibility and try to live it as well."[33]

Protestors, the largest since the swearing in of Richard Nixon in 1973, lined the inaugural parade route. Some shouted, "Hey, hey, ho, ho, that son of a Bush has got to go." Others waved posters reading "Hail to the thief" and "Selected not elected."[34]

Things improved for President Bush, First Lady Laura Bush, and Vice President Dick Cheney as they moved through their eight formal balls, funded by $40 million from the Presidential Inaugural Committee. Much later, America learned that a lot of that cash had come from big corporations that did business, or wanted to do business, with the federal government.

President Bush was everything I didn't want in the White House, and I breathed a sigh of relief when he seemed to favor clearing brush on his Crawford ranch over any legislative agenda. He did, of course, sign first-day executive orders undoing as many Clinton-era policies as possible without going through the Congress, and he got a slew of right-wingers, many from his dad's administration, confirmed for various federal posts.

For the JBS, the new Bush administration proved that little separated the two political parties. As Birch president John McManus wrote, "Rhetoric aside, each has labored for many years to bring our nation into a New World Order. This long-standing goal of the Insiders calls for building an all-powerful United Nations with total authority over a weakened United States and for fastening big-government socialistic programs on the American people."[35] According to McManus, Bush was cementing his place in that Insiders' club by filling his administration with those very Insiders, especially members of the Council on Foreign Relations, an influential think tank "used to promote the destruction of U.S. sovereignty."[36] Among the CFR members in Bush's inner circle were Condoleezza Rice (national security advisor), Donald Rumsfeld (secretary of defense), Paul Wolfowitz (deputy secretary of defense), Colin Powell (secretary of state), and George Tenet (CIA director).[37]

By far, the most influential and dangerous of all the Insiders had to be the vice president, Dick Cheney, a man who filled the role of Bush's "primary mentor." Cheney had actually outlined his agenda for U.S. foreign policy in a number of position papers spanning the period from the early 1990s through the Bush era. Writing in *Harper's* in 2002, David Armstrong described that agenda as a plan "for the United States to rule the world. . . . It calls for dominion over friends and enemies alike. It says not that the United States must be more powerful, or most powerful, but that it must be absolutely powerful."[38]

The JBS agreed with David Armstrong that Cheney had written his war plan and implemented it when the United States invaded Iraq in 2003. They had one area of disagreement, however. Armstrong thought Cheney's goal was absolute U.S. power. For the Birch Society, the objective was more sinister: "Mr. Bush and his team of Insider strategists (Dick Cheney and others) have ignored their solemn oath to uphold the Constitution while committing America's military might to UN-authorized conflicts. The planned transfer of U.S. armed forces to the world body's control continues to unfold."[39]

Once Bush and Cheney choreographed the invasion of Iraq, the JBS escalated its critiques of the war, calling it "President Bush's plan to make Iraq into the U.S. of the Middle East," while pointing out the seemingly endless glitches, mistakes, and disasters of the ongoing conflict.[40]

Of course, none of these plans were known when our leaders gathered on September 14, 2001, for the National Day of Prayer and Remembrance in Washington's National Cathedral.[41] Like millions of Americans, I watched as the church filled with row after row of decorated military officers, influential politicians, former presidents and first ladies, and leaders of every major religion.

That day my heart was broken and afraid. Those leaders, strong and resolute, were our hope, my hope. That day I was no Democrat. I was no liberal critic of the GOP. I had put away my politics. On September 14, 2001, I was an American, period.

I had no idea that the terrorist attacks three days earlier would usher in a decade of war and crush the American economy. I had no clue that my country would redefine torture as "enhanced interrogation" and use waterboarding to try to get information from detainees. I wouldn't have imagined that my country would cover up the abuses of prisoners in Iraq.[42] I would never have believed that our policies would make Iraq a prime recruiting area for more extreme terrorists while our president declared "Mission Accomplished."[43]

I could not know that in seven years, millions of people would be unemployed, the American economy would be in free fall, and George W. Bush would become America's most unpopular politician.[44] And I never would have guessed, not in a hundred years, that the John Birch Society would be as critical of President Bush and the fiasco in Iraq as I was.

All of this was future shock.

On September 14, 2001, like millions of Americans, I wrapped myself in the flag and wept as the Navy's Sea Chanters sang "The Battle Hymn of the Republic."

"We're coming for you," I said. "Whoever you are."

Chapter Twenty-four
Bedtime Story

The pundits like to say that 9/11 brought Americans together. Whatever our creed, whatever our race or politics, when the Twin Towers fell, America was reborn. Out of the rubble of horrific tragedy and unbearable loss, we'd rise again—a nation united in common purpose. That day was the crucible in which we were purified.

I thought of my mother on the Day of Prayer and Remembrance, and I promised to find a new way with her. Perhaps, maybe, just maybe, 9/11 could bring us together.

It took only a few days to realize that Mother had a very different view of it than I did. She'd already identified the true enemies of America, the dark forces at the heart of our suffering. The horror in New York was, first and foremost, the work of a righteous God exacting awesome retribution for the sins of homosexuality, abortion, contraception, and perversions rivaling those of Sodom and Gomorrah.

I was sure Mother didn't actually watch the *700 Club*, but she sounded a lot like Jerry Falwell when he appeared on that show on September 13. "God continues to lift the curtain and allow the enemies of America to give us probably what we deserve," he said, naming the pagans and the abortionists and the feminists and the gays and the lesbians "who have tried to secularize America—I point the finger in their face and say, *you helped this happen.*"[1]

Pat Robertson, the forever host of that show, agreed: "It happened because people are evil. It also happened because God is lifting His protection from this nation, and we must pray and ask Him for revival so that once again we will be His people, the planting of His righteousness, so that He will come to our defense and protect us as a nation."[2]

In addition to seeing the attacks as God's punishment on a sinful nation, Mother accepted the John Birch Society interpretation, as outlined in the October 22 issue of the *New American*, the Birch bimonthly magazine (previously *American Opinion*). In a forty-four-page special report, various writers argued that the totalitarians who led the United Nations hoped "to use the terrorist threat and other crises to build their new world order."[3]

In one article, "The UN Is NOT Your Friend," William Norman Grigg wrote, "UN Headquarters in New York City would be more accurately called Terror Central," and, "The UN long ago defined itself as an ally of terrorism and an enemy of the American way of life. . . . But that will not prevent . . . advocates of world government from seeking to exploit public fear and outrage over global terrorism in their effort to create global tyranny—a UN-dominated new world order."[4]

The Birch Society never believed that it was the thugs from around the world that represented the biggest threat, and they made sure their readers remembered that. "The UN should be viewed as a vehicle through which corrupt, power-seeking elites in this country and elsewhere intend to acquire power over the entire world," wrote Grigg.[5] The Council on Foreign Relations was singled out as "the most visible part of this international Power Elite." This power elite had one goal, "absolute power" resulting in "a reign of terror beyond our imagination."

This attitude was no surprise to faithful JBS readers, and it was no surprise to me. My father had crisscrossed the country selling the same ideas in the 1960s. What I didn't want to do was get into a fuss with Mother about all of this. I thanked her for the magazine and assured her that I'd read it.

"You better listen," she told me. "These are serious times. Come back to the Church and be saved."

"Please, Mother, let's not get into that again. Not now."

"Fine," she said. "How's Kevin? Does he have a girlfriend?"

My mother could always catch me unprepared, tricking me into conversations I never intended to have. On this particular one, however, I'd already made up my mind. I would not and could not discuss Kevin's girlfriend any more than I could discuss Brian's. A woman who just announced that 9/11 was a punishment for homosexuality would not be pleased to hear that two of her grandsons had boyfriends.

My youngest son had come out over a year before. His announcement was, to say the least, a complete shock. I'd never, ever picked up a hint that Kevin was also "in the family," as Brian liked to say. I was so sure that Kevin didn't know what he was talking about that I suggested, not very diplomatically, that he get into counseling and rid himself of this ridiculous notion.

In one of my most embarrassing—and unkind—moments, I told him, "I gave one son to the cause. I'm not giving another."

An hour later, I found my youngest child curled on his bed crying. I stretched out next to him and sobbed with him. "I'm so sorry," I said. "Can you ever forgive me?"

My son reached his arms out to me. "I love you," he said. "Always."

The next morning, I realized that I had a lot more to learn about being gay. I called a counselor—not for Kevin—but for me.

———

My boys decided—and my husband and I agreed—that coming out to their grandmother was inviting trouble. "She'll blame you for sure," Kevin said.

"She'll blame you twice," Brian pointed out.

As the aftermath of 9/11 continued, I was grateful that we'd made that decision. Mother continued her diatribes against the sexual sinners who'd brought God's vengeance on the rest of us, and before long she'd added another bogeyman to the mix: the Russians.

This struck me as odd and irrational given the demise of the USSR more than ten years earlier, and I dismissed it as more proof that she was losing her grip on reality. It wasn't until recently that I realized why she thought the way she did. I discovered a short video from 2011, *Exposing Terrorism: Inside the Terror Triangle*, with Arthur R. Thompson, CEO of the JBS. (John McManus remains with the society as its president.) In his nineteen-minute speech, Thompson argues that 9/11 may have been authorized and directed by former KGB agents. Since the collapse of Communism, he argued, the KGB has spread out into terrorist activities around the world, and "Islamic terror is in reality the old Communist terror dressed up to look Muslim."[6] Thompson then weaves this thinking into the old idea about our country merging into a New World Order. This new international government would establish peace in the "name of ending the War on Terror."

Not knowing about this video at the time, I lumped Mother's chatter about the Russians with a whole lot of things Mother said that seemed irrational, much more irrational that her usual radical right-wing rhetoric. She determined that bears were crossing the state lines in Yellowstone Park and that no one was doing anything about it. She insisted that Christ was coming and that he'd appear in the Vatican with the Pope at his side. She claimed that pollution helped her flowers grow and that the government was secretly watching everything she did.

The staff at her assisted-living apartment became alarmed. Then, after she trapped herself in the bathroom, unable to figure out how to push the alarm button she wore on a chain around her neck, we increased her level of care. One day, she could not find her apartment and wandered up and down the halls of the building for several hours. Another day she called me, frantic about the bugs in her apartment. When I arrived to help, she looked at me and said, "What are you doing here? Go away. I don't want you."

The administrator of the facility thought Mother needed round-the-clock care, which they couldn't give. With great reluctance, all the professionals finally said the D word: dementia. My sister Mary found a small center just outside Marshfield that specialized in care for patients with advanced Alzheimer's.

To my surprise, once Mother settled in her new home, she became less and less combative. The staff called her "our sweet Laurene" and lavished attention, care, and kisses on her. Though they couldn't stop the progression of her illness, the women never failed to keep Mother as comfortable and as happy as possible.

One morning in the early spring of 2005, I pulled my car into the parking lot at Mother's home. In the front hall, I peeled off my wet raincoat and dropped it onto the bench. Most of the residents were settled in front of the television in time for one of their favorite shows. As I walked into the main room, I could hear the announcer saying, "Come on down. You're the next contestant on *The Price Is Right*."

In the dining room, my mother was alone, perched in her wheelchair. As usual, she was staring at the newspaper in her lap—she couldn't see to read anything, but holding the paper gave her comfort. I sat down next to her, took her hand, and reminded her who I was. I'd hoped, just like always, for just a hint of recognition, but she stared at me like she'd never seen me before. "Fifteen minutes," I told myself.

I was so intent on escaping that I almost missed Mother's words. "I remember a story," she whispered. "I'll tell you."

I leaned in closer. Her voice was so tiny and scratchy; I knew she didn't talk often. I reached for a small cup of water on the table and held it for her while she took a few sips.

"Listen to me," she began. "Spain was my favorite place. I went with my husband a long time ago. Everyone was Catholic and I was so happy."

The minute she said "Spain," I knew the story. I'd heard it dozens of times since that first time, the night she and Dad returned from a long European vacation. As my old mother talked, I pondered the irony that the one memory that had survived Mother's dementia-plagued brain was about civil war, Communists, and a young boy shot in the head.

My ninety-two-year-old mother, who barely knew her name and seldom recognized her children, recalled perfectly the strange, dark tale. "That's real devotion, real patriotism," Mother said as she finished. Her eyes filled with tears for that boy, dead sixty years or more, a boy she'd never met, whose name she did not know.

Mother looked at me. "How very sad," I said.

"It's not sad at all, young lady," she sniped. "It's a marvelous story. The father had such principles, such integrity." Her anger took me by surprise. The feeble old lady had disappeared; in her place was the powerful, fiery, resolute Laurene.

But in a blink, my old mother was back, drooling and yawning.

One of the staff came over, released the brakes on the chair, and backed Mother away from the table.

"I love you," I said.

My mother turned her head away.

Our visit was definitely over.

After that, Mother ate less and slept more. She began to repeat words, over and over. Her doctor described the condition as "echolalia," a parrot-like repetition of words that indicated the terminal stages of dementia. The staff thought she was a 33 rpm record caught in a groove.

Mother settled on one phrase and repeated it for hours on end. "Over the river, over the river, over the river, over the river." When I heard her, I remembered the song she sang to my children when they were little, "Over the river and through the woods to Grandmother's house we go. The horse knows the way to carry the sleigh over the white and drifted snow."

She'd exhaust herself with the talking and then she'd cry. Several times, the staff thought she must have been in pain, but no one could find anything wrong with her. She didn't have cancer or heart disease or diabetes, but she was dying. She was ninety-three then; she wouldn't reach ninety-four.

———

Late in June of 2007, my daughter drove three hours from her home in Wauwatosa, Wisconsin, to Marshfield to see her grandmother. I knew Sarah had been planning to go, and I hugged her so close to my heart for making this decision.

My sweet daughter, bone of my bone and heart of my heart, had walked a bumpy road with her grandmother. It would have been easy for her—and in every way understandable—if she'd skipped this final visit, but Sarah had never been one to take the easy way.

I could still see my daughter, age six, standing over a neighbor girl she'd punched. I dashed out the door and pulled Sarah into the house. "What are you doing?!" I screamed as I shook her. "No fighting."

"She called Brian names and made him cry," Sarah said. "I was protecting my brother."

I sent her to her room even though I admired her grit. That was how she approached everything—head-on.

Thirty-one years later, my all-grown-up Sarah called me from my mother's bedroom. "Grandmother is having a really good day and she wants to talk to you now." Sarah pressed the phone to my mother's ear.

"This is Claire," I said. "I'm so glad you called. I love you, Mom."

Silence.

"Don't you want to say something to your daughter?" Sarah suggested to her grandmother.

"What should I say?" Mother said.

"Tell her you love her," Sarah suggested.

There was a long pause. I waited. My daughter waited.

Finally, Mother answered, "I can't say that," she blurted out. "I'm not sure I do."

Those were the last words I ever heard from my mother.

———

Both of my parents are dead. They lie next to each other in the Gate of Heaven Cemetery in Marshfield, Wisconsin. There is an empty plot next to my dad's, a plot for one of the children, just in case. I doubt it will ever be needed. All the Conner kids have moved away now, gone from Marshfield to new lives in other towns.

For the years between my father's death and my mother's, I was the grave tender. Early in the spring, I pulled the crab grass crawling up the memorial stone and yanked out the weeds around his bronze veteran's plaque. On Father's Day, I brought flowers. In July, I marked the anniversary of his death. In September, it was his birthday.

Every visit gave me time to think—think about my father, my mother, and me.

The day after my mother's funeral, I made my final trip up St. Joseph Avenue to the cemetery. I turned off the main road onto a narrow gravel path and parked. I picked my way between the headstones until I stood over my parents.

Familiar Wisconsin surrounded me: ripe manure wafting up from Weber's farm, muddy earth dampened by the night shower, the perfume of climbing roses drifting from a garden on Broadway. A little flock of sparrows hopped from the metal fence to a nearby bush and back again, chirping and pecking. Somewhere, a dog barked and a horn honked.

Funeral flowers were strewn over Mother's grave. My father's plot was bare. I picked a lily from one arrangement and placed it at Dad's head along with a crumpled photograph. The fading black-and-white was a fifty-nine-year-old picture of me, sitting on my daddy's lap. I was a funny thing with my thick glasses, wild hair slipping out of barrettes, and toddler-chubby legs. Dad's arm circled my waist, holding me steady. While I looked at the camera, my father looked at me. Both of us were smiling.

For years, I'd clung to that picture as proof—proof that my dad had loved me. And by extension, proof that my mother had loved me, too. She may not have been in the photo, but I'd decided that she had to have been the photographer, the loving Mom who captured her husband and her baby girl in one perfect moment.

I sat on my father's grave and remembered my conspiracy-fighting parents who never slowed down or backed down. When their battles cost them their friendships and financial security, they fought the fight. When their dark vision of Communism didn't happen, they found new enemies. When the John Birch Society was pushed to the fringe of the fringe, they held the fort. Even when their radical politics and their uncompromising positions tore them from their children, they pressed on.

I thought about my parents' bodies locked in the coffins beneath me and their souls soaring in the vast eternity of an endless July day. I cried because I knew they were not coming back and I'd never know if they had even the slightest regret.

Since my parents died, I understand more about my father and his evolution into a Communist-fighting, traitor-naming right-winger. I have some idea now how revealing the Conspiracy and stopping the Communists before they took over the United States became his focus, his purpose, his everything. My mother was his rock-solid, totally committed partner.

When I left Marshfield that day, I said farewell to my parents and to the ideas that had consumed them. I had no idea that the radical right wing was about to emerge from hibernation and stage one of the most dramatic political resurrections ever. All it took was a financial crisis that paralleled the Great Depression, an African American Democrat in the White House, and huge doses of fear and fanaticism.

The slumbering John Birch Society was about to be born again, wrapped in the flag.

Acknowledgments

I awoke this morning with devout thanksgiving for my friends, the old and the new.
— RALPH WALDO EMERSON

Heartfelt thanks and gratitude to my sister Janet, who reminded me to keep writing. "Only you can tell this story," she told me. One day, when I imagined that my manuscript was finished, I asked her how to find an agent. And she told me.

Janet led me to Jo Ann Deck, an incredible woman who became my literary agent and trusted friend. I'm eternally grateful for Jo Ann's enthusiasm for *Wrapped in the Flag* and her support during the long, arduous process of getting the manuscript buffed and polished. Thank you, Jo Ann, for asking that "one little question" of yours and for believing in me, even when I wasn't sure I believed in myself.

Special thanks to Alison Strickland and Judy Huge, who read every word I wrote and offered excellent suggestions for improvements. A big shout out to Ted Strickland for pitching *Wrapped in the Flag* to anyone who'd listen and to Art Huge for attending my talks and offering smart suggestions. I'm also grateful to Karen Casey, Julie Miller, Karen Pell, Frank and Kathy Mann, Ed and Pat Besse, and Nancy Wysocki for loving my early stories. All of you helped me press on as my first two years of writing grew into three and then four and then five. Thanks to Kathy Hepinstall, author of *Blue Asylum*, who reminded me to make my father and my mother come alive.

I'm grateful for the help of tech-savvy friends John Thomas, savior of my computer, and Yvonne and Hank Charneskey, wizards of photography and video. My website—claireconner.com—is the creation of Ja-lene Clark of Gather Insight, who helped me visualize a message in this Internet world.

I owe a huge debt to Ernie Lazar, John Birch Society researcher, who could find everything I couldn't. Because of Ernie's extensive FOIA requests, FBI reports of Birch Society activities, including the reports of my father's efforts, are part of this book.

My friend Caroline Fenderson took up the cause for this book early on, reading my stories, offering great suggestions and introducing me to Abhi Jannamanchi, the pastor of the local Unitarian Universalist congregation, where I have been warmly welcomed. Caroline also said, from the first, that Beacon Press was the perfect home for my book.

Indeed, Caroline was right. At Beacon I have found a team of dedicated professionals who believe in *Wrapped in the Flag* and in me. Helene Atwan, extraordinary editor, asked such insightful questions during the first edits that I ended up rewriting much of the book. I'm grateful to Helene for the faith she placed in me and for her enthusiastic support for this project. Thanks also to Crystal Paul for helping me get the hang of the editing process and for keeping communication flowing smoothly between my office in Florida and Beacon's offices in Boston.

The Beacon staff—from the copy editors and designers to the marketing team—has exceeded my expectations. You are the best team a writer could have.

Special thanks to my children: Brian, for reminding me to take out "the textbooky parts"; Kevin, for listening to me while I sorted out ideas; Sarah and Sean, for offering a welcoming home away from home; Andrew and Lisa, for understanding that Mom hasn't vanished; Sophia and Veronica, for pulling me out of my world with wonderful stories about theirs.

Thanks to my brother Larry, who walked so much of this journey with me, and to my sister Mary and my brother Jay R., who were there during the toughest of the John Birch days. Special appreciation to Bill, who offered help in more ways than I can count. Finally, my husband, Bob, has been my rock. Without him, this book would never have been written. You are my darling.

Notes

Introduction: November 1963

1. Kent Biffle, "Incident-Free Day Urged for JFK Visit," *Dallas Morning News*, Sunday, November 17, 1963, in *The Assassination Story: Newspaper Clippings from the Two Dallas Dailies* (Dallas: American Eagle Publishing, 1964), 6. Television appeal of Jesse Curry, Dallas police chief: Gerald Blaine, *The Kennedy Detail: JFK's Secret Service Agents Break Their Silence* (New York: Simon & Schuster, 2010), 155–56.
2. "Newly Discovered Footage of JFK's Final Moments," YouTube.com.
3. The Sixth Floor Museum at Dealey Plaza collections, object #1999.023.0017, http://www.jfk.org.
4. "Suspected Killer Defected to Russia in '59," *Dallas Morning News*, November 23, 1963, in *The Assassination Story*, 5.
5. Original broadcast, KRLD-TV, November 24, 1963, YouTube.com.
6. Procession of John Kennedy's casket to the Capitol, funeral procession, and burial at Arlington National Cemetery, November 24 and 25, 1963, YouTube.com.

Chapter One: Rally Cry

1. Joseph McCarthy, "Enemies from Within," speech, Wheeling, West Virginia, February 9, 1950, *History Matters*, http://www.historymatters.gmu.edu.
2. Speech on the Illuminati and founding principles of the conspiracy: Robert Welch, "More Stately Mansions," in Robert Welch, *The New Americanism and Other Speeches and Essays* (Boston: Western Islands Publishers, 1967), 125–38.
3. India photos: Bengal Famine of 1943, parts 1–4, http://www.oldindianphotos.in.
4. Discussion of the Korean War: David Halberstam, *The Fifties* (New York: Random House, 1993), 62–86.
5. General Douglas MacArthur, "Farewell Address to Congress," April 19, 1951, *The Annals of America: Volume 17, Cold War in the Nuclear Age* (Chicago: Encyclopedia Britannica, 1968), 79–84.
6. Halberstam, *The Fifties*, 49–59; Robert Griffith, *The Politics of Fear: Joseph McCarthy and the Senate* (Amherst: University of Massachusetts Press, 1987), 214–16.
7. Lee A. Daniels, "Ralph W. Zwicker, 88, General And Figure in McCarthy Censure," obituary, *New York Times*, August 12, 1991.
8. Arthur Herman, *Joseph McCarthy: Reexamining the Life and Legacy of America's Most Hated Senator* (New York: Free Press, 1999), 247–53.
9. Thomas C. Reeves, *The Life and Times of Joseph McCarthy* (New York: Stern and Day, 1999), 672.

Chapter Two: The Captain's Law

1. Richard Hofstadter, *The Paranoid Style in American Politics and Other Essays* (New York: Vintage Books, 2008), 3.
2. The director of *Black Beauty* was Max Nosseck, a German-born director who left his coun-

try when the Nazis came to power. *Black Beauty* (1946) was his biggest commercial hit, but he never considered the film representative of his style. He left the United States in the 1950s and returned to Germany, where he resumed his career. http://www.allmovie.com.

3. Griffin Fariello, *Red Scare: Memories of the American Inquisition* (New York: Avon Books, 1995), 315–20.

4. David Halberstam, *The Fifties* (New York: Random House, 1993), 9.

5. Robert Welch, *The Politician* (Belmont, MA: Belmont Publishing, 1963). After my father's death, in 1992, my mother explained that Dad had been given a copy of the manuscript in 1956 during their first visit to Welch's home in Belmont.

Chapter Three: Sacrifices

1. Helene Zuber, "Can Spain Overcome Franco: Poking into the Hot Ashes of History," *Spiegel Online International*, December 31, 2004, http://www.spiegel.de. Retrieved April 18, 2012.

2. In-depth discussion of the Roman Catholic Church's teachings on chastity, birth control, and sex: Peter De Rosa, *Vicars of Christ: The Dark Side of the Papacy* (New York: Crown Publishers, 1988), 318–65.

3. "The Catholic Encyclopedia: Occasions of Sin," *New Advent*, 2009, http://www.newadvent .org.

4. In 1917, three children in Fatima, Portugal, claimed to have seen six apparitions of Mary. As young children in Catholic school, we heard frequent remarks about the promises of Our Lady of Fatima to the children, and we waited for the Pope to reveal the details of those promises. He never did. See more at the Fatima Network, http://www.fatima .org.

5. Hugh Thomas, *The Spanish Civil War* (New York: Modern Library, 2001).

6. Mother's story was not totally accurate; here's another version: Antony Beevor, *The Spanish Civil War* (New York: Penguin, 1982), 103.

7. Antonio Cazorla Sanchez, *Fear and Progress: Ordinary Lives in Franco's Spain 1939–1975* (Malden, MA: John Wiley & Sons, 2010), 17–56.

Chapter Four: Textbook Wars

1. Frederik Nebeker, *Dawn of the Electronic Age: Electrical Technologies in the Shaping of the Modern World, 1914 to 1945* (Hoboken, NJ: John Wiley & Sons, 2009), 118.

2. Cardinal Stritch refusing ecumenical discussion: "Religion: Catholics Barred," *Time*, July 19, 1954.

3. Mother and Dad reported some of these details to me after the meeting. We also discussed the Regina situation in a number of conversations over the years in which they filled in even more details about the evening.

4. Conflict over U.S. textbooks: "E Pluribus Confusion," *Time*, September 10, 1979, and "Mississippi Mud," *Time*, May 16, 1960.

5. G. Edward Griffin, *The Life and Words of Robert Welch: Founder of The John Birch Society* (Thousand Oaks, CA: American Media, 1975), 112.

6. Ibid., 140.

7. Gail Collins, *As Texas Goes . . . How The Lone Star State Hijacked the American Agenda* (New York: W. W. Norton, 2012), 98.

8. More about Mel and Norma Gabler: Educational Research Analysts, http://www.text bookreviews.org. Collins discusses Texas's power over textbooks in "The Textbook Wars," in Collins, *As Texas Goes*, 98–106.

9. The Gablers' views were outlined in their newsletters. Readers can see newsletters from 1997 to 2011 at Educational Research Analysts, http://www.textbookreviews.org.
10. "Education: Was Robin Just a Hood?," *Time*, December 31, 1979.
11. History of McGuffey Readers: McGuffey Readers World, http://www.mcguffeyreaders.com.
12. Donald T. Critchlow, *Phyllis Schlafly and Grassroots Conservatism: A Woman's Crusade* (Princeton, NJ: Princeton University Press, 2005), 98. Robert Welch described Phyllis Schlafly as a Birch member: Robert Welch, *John Birch Society Bulletin*, March 1960, in *The White Book of the John Birch Society for 1960* (Belmont, MA: John Birch Society, 1960), 13.
13. Critchlow, *Phyllis Schlafly*, 338n37.
14. Changes in the Texas curriculum detailed: Jeff Schweltzer, "Descending Again into Darkness: An Extraordinary Revolution of Willful Ignorance," *Huffington Post*, January 27, 2010. More about Texas: Tim Walker, "Don't Know Much About History," National Education Association, June 2010, http://www.nea.org.

Chapter Five: Hard Right

1. Donald T. Critchlow, *The Conservative Ascendancy: How the GOP Right Made Political History* (Cambridge, MA: Harvard University Press, 2007), 56.
2. History and analysis of Robert Welch and the John Birch Society: Jonathan M. Schoenwald, *A Time for Choosing: The Rise of Modern American Conservatism* (New York: Oxford University Press, 2001), 62–99. Among his conclusions: "By 1962, it [the John Birch Society] had become by default the most quoted (and perhaps respected) of all the so-called extremist groups," 91.
3. Robert Welch, *The Blue Book of the John Birch Society* (Belmont, MA: John Birch Society, 1961), 179.
4. Schoenwald, *A Time for Choosing*, 70.
5. Description of the founding meeting of the John Birch Society: G. Edward Griffin, *The Life and Words of Robert Welch: Founder of the John Birch Society* (Thousand Oaks, CA: American Media, 1975), 257–74.
6. Welch, *The Blue Book*, 72.
7. Ibid., 73.
8. Robert Welch, *The Life of John Birch* (Boston: Western Islands Publishers, 1961, repr. of Henry Regnery ed., 1954).
9. William T. Miller, "How the Chinese Killed John Birch," *Life*, May 12, 1961.
10. Welch, *The Life of John Birch*.
11. The Order of the Illuminati: Manly P. Hall, *Secret Teachings of All Ages* (New York: Penguin, 2003), 566–78.
12. Robert Welch discussed the Illuminati at length in "More Stately Mansions," in Robert Welch, *The New Americanism and Other Speeches and Essays* (Boston: Western Islands Publishers, 1966), 125–37.
13. The Illuminati and the New World Order: Robert Welch, "What Conspiracy?," in *The Historical Significance of Robert Welch* (Appleton, WI: John Birch Society, 1993), 29–38.
14. Dollar bill: Terry Melanson, "The All-Seeing Eye, The President, The Secretary and The Guru," Illuminati Conspiracy Archive, July 2001, http://www.conspiracyarchive.com.
15. Great Seal: Manly P. Hall, *The Secret Destiny of America* (Los Angeles: Philosophical Research Society, 1944, rep. 1972), 173.
16. John Robinson, *Proofs of a Conspiracy* (Boston: Western Islands Publishers, 1967, orig. 1798).
17. Gary Allen, *None Dare Call It Conspiracy* (San Pedro, CA: GSG & Associates, 1972), 18.

18. Ibid., 85.

19. John F. McManus, *The Insiders: Architects of the New World Order* (Appleton, WI: John Birch Society, 2004).

20. Contemporary John Birch Society and conspiracies: Dan Barry, "Holding Firm Against Plots by Evildoers," *New York Times*, June 6, 2009.

Chapter Six: Twisted

1. Leonard Zeskind, *Blood and Politics: The History of the White Nationalist Movement from the Margins to the Mainstream* (New York: Farrar, Straus and Giroux, 2009), 482.

2. Robert Welch, *The Blue Book of the John Birch Society* (Belmont, MA: John Birch Society, 1961), 181.

3. See autobiographical note in Revilo Pendleton Oliver, *The Jewish Strategy: How the Jews Have Survived Thousands of Years of Persecution and Why We of the West May Not Survive This Century* (Earlysville, VA: Kevin Alfred Strom, 2001), http://www.heretical .com.

4. Oliver's typewriters: Carl T. Bogus, *Buckley: William F. Buckley Jr. and the Rise of American Conservatism* (New York: Bloomsbury Press, 2011), 181.

5. John B. Judis, *William F. Buckley, Jr.: Patron Saint of the Conservatives* (New York: Simon and Schuster, 1988), 137.

6. Revilo P. Oliver, "History and Biology," *American Opinion*, December 1963 (available as an e-book download).

7. Comments on World War II and imposing Communism: "Americans would soon know how the Japanese had been maneuvered and tricked into destroying our fleet and killing so many of our men . . . we had fought for the sole purpose of imposing the beasts of Bolshevism on a devastated land," Revilo P. Oliver, "What We Owe Our Parasites," 1968, on *Revilo P. Oliver*, http://www.revilo-oliver.com.

8. Revilo Oliver, "Revised Historiography," *Liberty Bell*, May 1980, on *Revilo P. Oliver*.

9. Revilo P. Oliver, "The 'Holohoax,'" November 1984, "Biography of Revilo P. Oliver," *The Academic JFK Assassination Site*, http://karws.gso.uri.edu/JFK/JFK.html.

10. "From '76 to 1966: The Spirit of Independence Calls You Back," program of New England Rally for God, Family, and Country, Boston, July 2–4, 1966. Oliver's comments at the rally: William W. Turner, *Power on the Right* (Berkeley, CA: Ramparts Press, 1971), 26; Revilo P. Oliver, "Conspiracy or Degeneracy?," July 2, 1966, in five parts, YouTube.com.

11. Oliver forced to resign from John Birch Society: "John Birch Society," Political Research Associates website, http://www.publiceye.org.

12. Arthur Goldwag, *The New Hate: A History of Fear and Loathing on the Populist Right* (New York: Pantheon Books, 2012), 288.

13. Zeskind, *Blood and Politics*, 393.

14. My parents were correct about Mao; he was responsible for the deaths of 40–70 million people, making him a greater mass killer than Hitler or Stalin. See Jonathan Fenby, *Modern China: The Fall and Rise of a Great Power, 1850 to the Present* (New York: Ecco, 2008), 351. Another source: Daniel Jonah Goldhagen, *Worse Than War: Genocide, Eliminationism, and the Ongoing Assault on Humanity* (New York: Public Affairs, 2009), 53.

Chapter Seven: Moving Up

1. Richard Hofstadter, *The Paranoid Style in American Politics and Other Essays* (New York: Vintage Books, 2008), 29–30.

2. David Halberstam, *The Fifties* (New York: Random House, 1993), 707–8.

3. CASE ad: Robert Welch, *The Blue Book of the John Birch Society* (Belmont, MA: John Birch Society, 1961), insert.

4. Robert Welch, *John Birch Society Monthly Bulletin*, January 1960, in *The White Book of the John Birch Society for 1960* (Belmont, MA: John Birch Society, 1960), 11.

5. Robert Welch, *John Birch Society Monthly Bulletin*, February 1960, in *The White Book of the John Birch Society for 1960*, 20.

6. Robert Welch, *John Birch Society Monthly Bulletin*, May 1960, in *The White Book of the John Birch Society for 1960*, 22.

7. Ibid., 24.

8. Robert Welch, *John Birch Society Monthly Bulletin*, June 1960, in *The White Book of the John Birch Society for 1960*, 2.

9. UN insignias: Robert Welch, *John Birch Society Monthly Bulletin*, October 1959, 2.

10. War on Christmas in the 1950s and today: Michelle Goldberg, "How the Secular Humanist Grinch Didn't Steal Christmas," Salon.com, November 21, 2005.

11. "Birch Group Lists Units in 34 States," *New York Times*, April 12, 1961.

12. The structure of the society: Welch, *The Blue Book*, 86 (front groups), 159 (authoritarian control), 161 (removing members).

13. Jonathan M. Schoenwald, *A Time for Choosing: The Rise of Modern American Conservatism* (New York: Oxford University Press, 2001), 86.

14. "The Americanists," *Time*, March 10, 1961.

15. G. Edward Griffin, *The Life and Words of Robert Welch: Founder of the John Birch Society* (Thousand Oaks, CA: American Media, 1975), 227.

16. Welch, *The Blue Book*, 180–81.

17. Schoenwald, *A Time for Choosing*, 78.

18. Council members listed in Welch, *The Blue Book*, 180–81.

19. Welch explains the Draskovich situation: Robert Welch, "False Leadership," in *The Historical Significance of Robert Welch* (Appleton, WI: John Birch Society, 1993), 197–201.

20. Welch, *The Blue Book*, 180.

21. Jane Mayer, "Covert Operations: The Billionaire Brothers Who Are Waging a War against Obama," *New Yorker*, August 30, 2010.

22. Fred C. Koch, "Koch Answers Drew Pearson 'Smear Job,'" *Palm Beach Post*, February 15, 1964, http://www.scribd.com.

23. Fred Koch, *A Business Man Looks at Communism* (Farmville, VA: Farmville Herald, 1960), University of Southern Mississippi Digital Collections, http://www.digilib.usm.edu, 14.

24. Ibid., 16.

25. Ibid., 28.

26. Koch brothers' lawsuits: Brian O'Reilly and Patty De Llosa, "The Curse on the Koch Brothers: One of the Biggest Family Feuds in Business History May Soon Come to a Climax," *Fortune*, February 17, 1997.

27. "The Forbes 400," http://www.forbes.com/forbes-400/list.

28. David Weigel, "Tea Party Patrons Point New Recruits Toward 2010," *Washington Independent*, March 15, 2010, http://www.washingtonindependent.com.

29. Donald L. Barlett and James B. Steele, *The Betrayal of the American Dream* (New York: Public Affairs, 2012), 33.

30. John Birch Society Council Meeting minutes, papers of Thomas Anderson, FBI Files, and Documents Pertaining to Extreme Right Individuals, Groups, and Their Assertions, http://sites.google.com.

Chapter Eight: The Black Book

1. Robert Alan Goldberg, *Barry Goldwater* (New Haven, CT: Yale University Press, 1995), 137.
2. Father John Dussman, *The Clarion*, April 28, 1963.
3. Events described in Chicago newspaper: Jack Mabley, "Strange Threat to Democracy," *Chicago Daily News*, July 26, 1960.
4. Robert Welch, *The Politician* (Belmont, MA: Belmont Publishing, 1963), 278.
5. G. Edward Griffin, *The Life and Words of Robert Welch: Founder of the John Birch Society* (Thousand Oaks, CA: American Media, 1975), 240.
6. "Confidential Classified Report of the District Intelligence Office, Ninth Naval District, September 16, 1960," released under FOIA, unclassified March 4, 1984.
7. Patrick T. Reardon and Ed Baumann, "J. Mabley, Longtime Chicago Columnist," obituary, *Chicago Tribune*, January 9, 2006.
8. Jack Mabley, "Bares Secrets of Red-Haters," *Chicago Daily News*, July 25, 1960.
9. Quotes in Mabley's articles: Welch, *The Politician*, 278; Griffin, *The Life and Words of Robert Welch*, 240.
10. Mabley, "Strange Threat to Democracy."
11. Welch outlines attacks: Welch, *The Politician*, ix–xi.
12. Laurene Conner, "How the Conners Became Involved in the John Birch Society," remarks to the Council Meeting of the John Birch Society, Appleton, WI, October 14, 1995.
13. "Stillwell Connor [our name was often misspelled as 'Connor'] Discusses the John Birch Society," April 3, 1961, NBC Universal Archives, clip 5112482696-s01, http://www.nbc universalarchives.com.
14. "The Birch-Barkers," *Time*, April 14, 1961; "Thunder Against the Right," *Time*, November 24, 1961.
15. "Confidential Classified Report of the District Intelligence Office."
16. Robert Welch, "False Leadership: William F. Buckley and the New World Order," in *The Historical Significance of Robert Welch* (Appleton, WI: John Birch Society, 1993), 147–48.
17. John Birch Society, *Responsible Leadership through the John Birch Society* (Belmont, MA: John Birch Society, c. 1965), 17.

Chapter Nine: Stirring the Pot

1. Robert Welch, *John Birch Society Bulletin*, September 1960, in *The White Book of the John Birch Society for 1960* (Belmont, MA: John Birch Society, 1961), 2.
2. G. Edward Griffin, *The Life and Words of Robert Welch: Founder of the John Birch Society* (Thousand Oaks, CA: American Media, 1975), 27–46.
3. Robert Welch, *The Blue Book of the John Birch Society* (Belmont, MA: John Birch Society, 1961), 110.
4. Barry Goldwater, *The Conscience of a Conservative* (LaVergne, TN: Bottom of the Hill Publishing, 2010, orig. 1960).
5. Welch, *The Blue Book*, 119–20.
6. Welch, *John Birch Society Bulletin*, September 1960, in *The White Book of the John Birch Society for 1960*, 7.
7. Rick Perlstein, *Before the Storm: Barry Goldwater and the Unmaking of the American Consensus* (New York: Nation Books, 2001), 82–95.
8. Ibid., 94–95.
9. Welch, *John Birch Society Bulletin*, September 1960, 7.
10. Ibid., 9.

11. Ibid., 13.
12. 1960 election results: *AnythingPolitics*, http://www.uselections.org.
13. David Greenberg, "Was Nixon Robbed? The Legend of the Stolen 1960 Presidential Election," Slate.com, October 16, 2000.
14. Perlstein, *Before the Storm*, 140.
15. Jonathan M. Schoenwald, *A Time for Choosing: The Rise of Modern American Conservatism* (New York: Oxford University Press, 2001), 62.
16. Robert Welch, *John Birch Society Bulletin*, February 1961, in *The White Book of the John Birch Society for 1961* (Belmont, MA: John Birch Society, 1962), 12.
17. Robert Welch, *John Birch Society Bulletin*, March 1961, in *The White Book of the John Birch Society for 1961*, 21.
18. Robert Welch, *The Politician* (Belmont, MA: Belmont Publishing, 1963), x–xi.
19. Ibid., xi.
20. "The John Birch Society: Patriotic or Irresponsible, It Is Subject of Controversy," *Life*, May 12, 1961.
21. Ibid.
22. "The Americanists," *Time*, March 10, 1961.
23. "Beware the Comsymps," *Time*, April 21, 1961.
24. "Charges Reds Began Attack on Birch Group," *Chicago Tribune*, April 2, 1961.
25. "Birch Society Leaders Propose 3d Party Here," *Chicago Tribune*, April 14, 1962.
26. John D. Morris, "Birch Unit Pushes Drive on Warren," *New York Times*, April 1, 1961, front page.
27. "John Birch Fantasies," editorial, *New York Times*, April 22, 1961.
28. "The Harmless Ones," *Time*, August 11, 1961.
29. Robert Welch, *John Birch Society Bulletin*, April 1961, in *The White Book of the John Birch Society for 1961*, 12–13.
30. Perlstein, *Before the Storm*, 110.
31. Robert Welch on *Meet the Press*, transcript, May 21, 1961, http://www.scribd.com.
32. Robert Welch, *John Birch Society Bulletin*, February 1962, in *The White Book of the John Birch Society for 1962* (Belmont, MA: John Birch Society, 1963), 5–10.
33. Ibid., 6–7.
34. Ibid., 7.
35. Ibid., 10.
36. Griffin, *The Life and Words of Robert Welch*, 307.
37. Ibid., 306.
38. "Unitarian Church Sets Talk by Birch Leader," *Chicago Tribune*, February 25, 1962.
39. Frank Hughes, "2,000 Attend Birch Society Seminar Here," *Chicago Tribune*, July 1, 1962.

Chapter Ten: The Uncivil War

1. "The Unhelpful Fringes: The Present-Day Radicals, Left or Right, Bring Us Neither Hope Nor Realism," *Life*, May 12, 1961.
2. Philip Dodd, "Hint Pentagon to Reprimand Gen. Walker," *Chicago Tribune*, June 10, 1961.
3. Jonathan M. Schoenwald, *A Time for Choosing: The Rise of Modern American Conservatism* (New York: Oxford University Press, 2001), 105.
4. Philip Dodd, "U.S. General Suspended in Birch Furor," *Chicago Tribune*, April 18, 1961, front page.
5. Schoenwald, *A Time for Choosing*, 106.
6. Ibid., 101.

7. William F. Buckley Jr., *Cruising Speed: A Documentary* (New York: G.P. Putnam's Sons, 1971), 112.
8. John Howard Griffin, *Black Like Me* (San Antonio, TX: Wings Press, 2004, orig. 1961), 14.
9. Ibid., 123.
10. Ibid., 131.
11. "Black Like Me," *Time*, March 28, 1961.
12. Robert Welch, *The Blue Book of the John Birch Society* (Belmont, MA: John Birch Society, 1961), 29.
13. "Civil Rights: The Little Rock School Integration Crisis," Dwight D. Eisenhower Presidential Library and Museum, http://www.eisenhower.archives.gov.
14. Schoenwald, *A Time for Choosing*, 105.
15. Robert Welch, *The Politician* (Belmont, MA: Belmont Publishing, 1963), 267.
16. Robert Welch, *John Birch Society Bulletin*, January 1961, in *The White Book of the John Birch Society for 1961* (Belmont, MA: John Birch Society, 1962), 16.
17. Ibid., 12–13.
18. Gregory L. Schneider, *The Conservative Century: From Reaction to Revolution* (Lanham, MD: Rowman & Littlefield, 2009), 85.
19. Robert Welch, *John Birch Society Bulletin*, June 1961, in *The White Book of the John Birch Society for 1961*, 5.
20. John Wicklein, "Birch Society Will Offer $2,300 For Impeach-Warren Essays," *New York Times*, August 5, 1961, front page.
21. Ibid., 39.
22. Welch, *John Birch Society Bulletin*, June 1961, 3–5.
23. Welch, *The Blue Book* , 97, 98.
24. Robert Welch, *John Birch Society Bulletin*, August 1961, in *The White Book of the John Birch Society for 1961*, 18.

Chapter Eleven: Here We Go Again and Again and Again

1. "Keep Politics Out of Aid, Pope Pleads," *Chicago Tribune*, July 15, 1961.
2. "Food for Peace," *Chicago Tribune*, January 26, 1961.
3. Robert Welch, *The Blue Book of the John Birch Society* (Belmont, MA: John Birch Society, 1961), 31.
4. David A. Bosnich, "The Principle of Subsidiarity," *Religion & Liberty* 6, no. 4, Acton Institute for the Study of Religion and Liberty, http://www.acton.org.
5. Robert Welch, *John Birch Society Bulletin*, January 1962, in *The White Book of the John Birch Society for 1962* (Belmont, MA: John Birch Society, 1963), 16.
6. Stillwell John Conner, "The UN: A Study in Deception," *American Opinion*, 1963, in Box 19, Folder 12, Norman Allderdice Collection, Hoover Institution Archives, 3.
7. Ibid., 4–5.
8. Ibid., 14.
9. Ibid., 16.
10. "Red China Loses," *Chicago Tribune*, December 19, 1961.
11. Conner, "The UN," 10.
12. Welch, *John Birch Society Bulletin*, January 1962, 17–18.
13. Vincent Butler, "Rally Demands U.N. Assembly Shut Its Doors on Red China," *Chicago Tribune*, September 22, 1961.
14. Robert Welch, *John Birch Society Bulletin*, June 1962, in *The White Book of the John Birch Society for 1962*, 1.

15. Ibid., 1–8.

16. Ronald Reagan, "Ronald Reagan Speaks Out Against Socialized Medicine," 1961, You Tube.com.

17. Lack of care for indigent and elderly before Medicare: Rosemary Stevens, PhD, "Health Care in the Early 1960s," *Health Care Financing Review* 18, no. 2 (Winter 1996).

18. Reagan on Kennedy: Quintard Taylor Jr., "The Rise and Fall of Liberalism," History 101: Survey of the History of the United States, http://faculty.washington.edu.

19. October 28, 1980, Carter-Reagan debate, Commission on Presidential Debates, http://www.debates.org.

20. "1962: Reagan Warns that Medicare Will Lead to Socialism, Destruction of American Democracy," *History Commons*, http://www.historycommons.org.

Chapter Twelve: The End of the World

1. Sheldon Harnick, "The Merry Minuet," 1958, YouTube.com.

2. "Russia Warns U.S. Against Cuba Attack," *Chicago Tribune*, September 12, 1962.

3. Robert Welch, *The Blue Book of the John Birch Society* (Belmont, MA: John Birch Society, 1961), 32, 33.

4. Ibid., 32.

5. John Hersey, *Hiroshima* (New York: Alfred A. Knopf, 1946).

6. "Cold War: A Brief History," Atomic Archive, http://www.atomicarchive.com.

7. *Duck and Cover*, Archer Productions, 1951, http://www.archive.org.

8. John F. Kennedy, "A Message to You from the President," *Life*, September 15, 1961.

9. "Shelter Skelter," *Time*, September 1, 1961.

10. "What You Should Know about the National Plan for Civil and Defense Mobilization," Executive Office of the President, Office of Civil and Defense Mobilization, December 1958, 29; *A Secret Landscape: America's Cold War Infrastructure*, http://www.coldwar-c4i.net.

11. "Timeline," *The Cuban Missile Crisis*, 1997, http://library.thinkquest.org.

12. Bay of Pigs: Arthur M. Schlesinger Jr., *A Thousand Days: John F. Kennedy in the White House* (New York: Houghton Mifflin, 1965), 250–97.

13. John F. Kennedy, "Radio and Television Report to the American People on the Soviet Arms Buildup in Cuba," October 22, 1962, John F. Kennedy Presidential Library and Museum, http://www.jfklibrary.org.

14. Jack Raymond, "Big Force Masses to Blockage Cuba," *New York Times*, October 23, 1962, front page.

15. Michael Dobbs, *One Minute to Midnight: Kennedy, Khrushchev and Castro on the Brink of Nuclear War* (New York: Knopf, 2008), 280.

16. Schlesinger, *A Thousand Days*, 829–30.

17. Barry Goldwater, *The Conscience of a Conservative* (LaVergne, TN: Bottom of the Hill Publishing, 2010, orig. 1960), 74.

18. Ibid., 81.

19. Welch, *The Blue Book*, 109–10.

20. Ibid., 109.

21. Ibid., 110.

22. Goldwater, *The Conscience of a Conservative*, 80

23. Ibid., 80–81.

24. Ibid., 81.

25. Ibid., 82.

26. Ibid., 81.

27. Constance Hayes, "Robert J. Morris Is Dead at 82; Crusader Against Communists," *New York Times*, January 2, 1997.

28. Robert Welch, *John Birch Society Bulletin*, February 1961, in *The White Book of the John Birch Society for 1961* (Belmont, MA: John Birch Society, 1962), 12.

29. "4,000 High School Seniors Win Illinois Scholarships," *Chicago Tribune*, April 18, 1963.

30. "Kerner Says Birch Society Dangerous," *Chicago Tribune*, February 6, 1962.

Chapter Thirteen: Civil Rights Marching

1. Studs Terkel, foreword, John Howard Griffin, *Black Like Me* (San Antonio, TX: Wings Press, 2004), 12.

2. "Daley Assails Plan to Move Negroes Here," *Chicago Tribune*, May 3, 1962.

3. Robert Welch, *Two Revolutions at Once* (Belmont, MA: John Birch Society, c. 1960), 19.

4. Robert Welch, *John Birch Society Bulletin*, September 1963, in *The White Book of the John Birch Society for 1963* (Belmont, MA: John Birch Society, 1964), 79.

5. Roy Reed, "Birch Society Is Growing in the South," *New York Times*, November 8, 1965, front page.

6. "Who Was James Meredith?," John F. Kennedy Presidential Library and Museum, http://www.jfklibrary.org.

7. "Though the Heavens Fall," *Time*, October 12, 1962.

8. John W. Finney, "Walker Challenges Rusk and Rostow on Loyalty," *New York Times*, April 6, 1962, front page.

9. Ibid.

10. Jonathan M. Schoenwald, *A Time for Choosing: The Rise of Modern American Conservatism* (New York: Oxford University Press, 2001), 117.

11. "Though the Heavens Fall," *Time*, October 12, 1962.

12. Robert Welch, *John Birch Society Bulletin*, December 1962, in *The White Book of the John Birch Society for 1962* (Belmont, MA: John Birch Society, 1963), 26.

13. "New Note in Dixie," *Time*, January 25, 1963.

14. "They Fight a Fire That Won't Go Out," *Life*, May 17, 1963. Photos by Charles Moore.

15. Arthur M. Schlesinger Jr., *A Thousand Days: John F. Kennedy in the White House* (New York: Houghton Mifflin, 2002), 963–68.

16. Robert Welch, *John Birch Society Bulletin*, June 1963, in *The White Book of the John Birch Society for 1963*, 14–15.

17. Ibid., 16.

18. 1963 March on Washington, National Archives, http://www.usnational archives.org.

19. Martin Luther King Jr., "I Have a Dream," August 28, 1963, YouTube.com.

Chapter Fourteen: A Big Texas Howdy

1. Lawrence Wright, *In the New World: Growing Up with America from the Sixties to the Eighties* (New York: Vintage Books, 1989), 16.

2. Robert Welch, *Interim Bulletin*, August 30, 1963, Section D. Civil Rights, in *The White Book of the John Birch Society for 1963* (Belmont, MA: John Birch Society, 1964), 3.

3. Despite what I thought, the thirteenth century has been described as the high point of the Middle Ages by a number of scholars. One major work on the subject is James Joseph Walsh, *The Thirteenth, Greatest of Centuries* (Charleston, SC: Nabu Press, 2011, orig. 1907).

4. Robert Welch, *John Birch Society Bulletin*, September 1963, in *The White Book of the John Birch Society for 1963*, 1, 9–10.

5. Ibid., 12.

6. Ibid., 45.

7. Ibid., 61.

8. Ibid., 60.

9. Ibid., 82.

10. Ibid., 78.

11. The Highlander Center, http://highlandercenter.org.

12. Welch, *John Birch Society Bulletin*, September 1963, 86–87.

13. Ibid., 23.

14. "2000 Hail Welch as 'Great Patriot,'" *Los Angeles Herald-Examiner*, September 24, 1963.

15. Donald A. Cowan, "Letter to the President," November 15, 1963, *University of Dallas Crusader* 2 (1964): 44.

16. Arthur M. Schlesinger Jr., *A Thousand Days: John F. Kennedy in the White House* (Boston: Houghton Mifflin, 1965), 1023–25.

17. Gerald Blain, *The Kennedy Detail: JFK's Secret Service Agents Break Their Silence* (New York: Gallery Books, 2010), 156.

18. Kent Biffle, "Incident-Free Day Urged for JFK Visit," *Dallas Morning News*, November 17, 1963.

19. "Testimony of Mrs. John Bowden Connally, Jr.," Warren Commission Hearings, vol. IV, p. 147, Assassination Archives and Research Center, http://www.aarclibrary.org.

20. KLIF (Dallas), November 22, 1963, *The JFK Assassination: As It Happened*, http://www.jfk-assassination-as-it-happened.blogspot.com. ·

21. William Manchester, *The Death of a President: November 1963* (New York: Harper & Row, 1967), 48–49.

22. Ibid., 48.

23. Schlesinger, *A Thousand Days*, 753.

24. Wright, *In the New World*, 29–48.

25. Bernard Weissman, chair, American Fact-Finding Committee, "Welcome Mr. Kennedy to Dallas," *Dallas Morning News*, November 22, 1963.

26. Larry Grove, "Why Did It Happen Here? Residents of Dallas Ask" and "City Still Stunned After JFK's Death," *Dallas Morning News*, November 24, 1963, in *The Assassination Story: Newspaper Clippings from Two Dallas Dailies* (Dallas: American Eagle Publishers, 1964), 9.

27. "Suspected Killer Defected to Russia in '59," *Dallas Morning News*, November 23, 1963, in *The Assassination Story*, 5.

28. "Decker Says: Police Did Everything Possible," *Dallas Morning News*, November 25, 1963.

29. Robert Welch, *John Birch Society Bulletin*, December 1963, in *The White Book of the John Birch Society for 1963*, 8.

30. Facts about the Warren Commission: *History Matters*, http://www.history-matters.com.

31. "Wanted for Treason Handbill," in *The Warren Commission Report: Report of the President's Commission on the Assassination of President John F. Kennedy* (New York: St. Martin's Griffin, 1992), 298.

32. Ibid., 296–97, 345, 369.

Chapter Fifteen: Crossfire

1. In James Reston, "Republicans Seek to Divorce Welch," *Boston Herald*, February 7, 1962.

2. Ibid.

3. In William F. Buckley Jr., "Goldwater, the John Birch Society, and Me," *Commentary*, March 2008.

4. Lyndon B. Johnson, "Let Us Continue," November 27, 1963, at Voices of Democracy: The U.S. Oratory Project, (text) www.umd.edu or (audio) www.americanrhetoric.com.

5. *The Confederacy* and *The Union* were two popular record albums from Time/Life.

6. John B. Judis, *William F. Buckley, Jr.: Patron Saint of the Conservatives* (New York: Simon & Schuster, 1988), 138–39.

7. Barry Goldwater, *The Conscience of a Conservative* (LaVergne, TN: Bottom of Hill Publishing, 2010), 26–27.

8. For background on these organizations, see Arnold Forster and Benjamin R. Epstein, *Danger on the Right: The Attitudes, Personnel and Influence of the Radical Right and Extreme Conservatives* (New York: Random House, 1964), 115–64.

9. On the Christian Crusade: Ibid., 68–86.

10. Pamela Ebert Flattau et al., *The National Defense Act of 1958: Selected Outcomes* (Washington, DC: Science and Technology Policy Institute, March 2006), Institute for Defense Analyses, http://www.ida.org.

11. William F. Buckley Jr., *God and Man at Yale: The Superstitions of "Academic Freedom"* (Chicago: Regnery Press, 1951).

12. Judis, *William F. Buckley, Jr.*, 59–62, 212fn (baptismal sponsor).

13. William F. Buckley Jr., *Cruising Speed: A Documentary* (New York: G. P. Putnam's Sons, 1971), 73–74.

14. Carl T. Bogus, *Buckley: William F. Buckley Jr. and the Rise of American Conservatism* (New York: Bloomsbury Press, 2011), 181.

15. Ibid., 183.

16. Robert Welch, *The Historical Significance of Robert Welch* (Appleton, WI: John Birch Society, 1993), 146.

17. Judis, *William F. Buckley, Jr.*, 194.

18. Welch, *The Historical Significance of Robert Welch*, 151.

19. Forster and Epstein, *Danger on the Right*, 151–61.

20. Ibid., 152.

21. States' Rights Party: Donald T. Critchlow, *The Conservative Ascendancy: How the GOP Made Political History* (Cambridge, MA: Harvard University Press, 2007), 47.

22. Forster and Epstein, *Danger on the Right*, 248–49.

23. Judis, *William F. Buckley, Jr.*, 195–96.

24. Ibid., 196.

25. Buckley in *National Review*, April 22, 1961, quoted in ibid., 196–97.

26. Ibid., 197.

27. Bogus, *Buckley*, 189.

28. Ibid., 191–193.

29. Welch, *The Historical Significance of Robert Welch*, 191.

30. Bogus, *Buckley*, 192.

31. Skull and Bones: Judis, *William F. Buckley, Jr.*, 76, 368, 414.

32. Enrico Peppe, "IC's Top 25 Philosophical & Ideological Conservative Books: #18, *The Conservative Affirmation* by Willmoore Kendall," *Intellectual Conservative*, March 17, 2004, http://www.intellectualconservative.com.

33. George H. Nash, "Willmoore Kendall: Conservative Iconoclast (II)," *Modern Age* (Summer 1975): 236–48, Intercollegiate Studies Institute, http://www.mmisis.org.

34. Willmoore Kendall and George W. Cary, *The Basic Symbols of the American Political Tradition* (Washington, DC: Catholic University of America Press, 1970), 94.

35. Alexander Keyssar, *The Right to Vote: The Contested History of Democracy in the United States* (New York: Basic Books, 2000), 4–7.

36. 1790 census, http://www.census.gov.

37. Kendall and Cary, *The Basic Symbols of the American Political Tradition*, 9–12.

38. Willmoore Kendall, "The Civil Rights Movement and the Coming Constitutional Crisis," paper presented at Southern Political Science Association meeting, November 14, 1964, http://www.mmisi.org.

39. Leo Paul S. deAlvarez, "The Missing Passage of the Vanderbilt Lectures," *Willmoore Kendall: Maverick of American Conservatives* (Lanham, MD: Rowman & Littlefield, 2001), 145.

40. Forster and Epstein, *Danger on the Right*, 254.

41. "Welch Would Curb U.S. Voting Rights," *Boston Herald*, July 28, 1965.

42. My parents' ideas were not original. See Keyssar, *The Right to Vote*, for a long list of reasons commonly given to limit suffrage.

43. Ari Berman, "The GOP War on Voting: In a Campaign Supported by the Koch Brothers, Republicans Are Working to Prevent Millions of Democrats from Voting Next Year," *Rolling Stone*, September 15, 2011.

44. Ibid.

45. Ibid.

Chapter Sixteen: Carrying the Cross

1. Robert Welch, *The Blue Book of the John Birch Society* (Belmont, MA: John Birch Society, 1961), 58.

2. "Fr. Thomas Matthias Cain, O.P.," Find A Grave, http://www.findagrave.com.

3. Thomas Aquinas: New Advent, http://www.newadvent.org.

4. Catholic Answers, http://www.catholic.com.

5. Laurene K. Conner, *No Man's Voice Should Sound an Uncertain Note: A Focus on Latin America* (Inglewood, CA: Catholic Fact Research Association, 1964), reviewed in *Wanderer*, January 30, 1964.

6. Stillwell John Conner, "The Catholic Church and the John Birch Society," *Ramparts* (Spring 1964): 16–25.

7. The Modernist heresy: Peter De Rosa, *Vicars of Christ: The Dark Side of the Papacy* (New York: Crown Publishers, 1988), 261–69.

8. Welch, *The Blue Book*, 59.

9. Laurene K. Conner, *The New Age Movement: A Dark and Hostile Agent—A Terrible Reality* (Hudson, WI: Wanderer Forum Foundation, 1991); Laurene K. Conner, *Pax Christi: The Spider's Web* (Marshfield, WI: Wanderer Forum Foundation, 1988).

10. Conner, *No Man's Voice Should Sound an Uncertain Note*.

11. History of the Wanderer Forum Foundation: http://www.wandererforum.org/history.

12. Laurene K. Conner, *A Crumbling Edifice: Consciousness-Raising and the Erosion of Religious Life* (Hudson, WI: Wanderer Forum Foundation, 1989), 1. Other works by Laurene K. Conner: *Networking for Radical Social Change*, 1988; *His Vision and His Hope for the Faithful in the United States*, 1989; *An Unholy Alliance: Catholic Educators and Marxist Revolution*, 1990; *Turbulent Waves of Error*, 1992; and *The Popes of Conciliar Renewal*, 2003.

13. Karen Armstrong, *The Battle For God: A History of Fundamentalism* (New York: Ballantine, 2000), 311–13.

14. Ibid., 312.

15. Max Blumenthal, *Republican Gomorrah: Inside the Movement That Shattered the Party* (New York: Nation Books, 2010), 19.

16. Walter Olson, "Invitation to a Stoning: Getting Cozy with Theocrats," *Reason*, November 1998, http://www.reason.com/archives. Also, Jeff Sharlet, *The Family: The Secret Fundamentalism at the Heart of American Power* (New York: Harper Perennial, 2009), 347–51.

17. Olson, "Invitation to a Stoning."
18. Blumenthal, *Republican Gomorrah*, 19.
19. Ibid., 26–27.
20. Frank Schaeffer, *Crazy for God: How I Grew Up as One of the Elect, Helped Found the Religious Right, and Lived to Take All (Or Almost All) of It Back* (Cambridge, MA: Da Capo Press, 2007), 300.

Chapter Seventeen: AuH₂O

1. Glenn Garvin, "He Was Right," *Reason*, March 2002, http://www.reason.com.
2. Barry Goldwater announcing his candidacy, January 3, 1964: 4President.org.
3. Ayn Rand interview, "Gallery of Colorful People," 1959, You Tube.com.
4. Gregory L. Schneider, *The Conservative Century: From Reaction to Revolution* (Lanham, MD: Rowman & Littlefield, 2009), 110–11.
5. Ibid., 111.
6. Ayn Rand, *Atlas Shrugged* (New York: Penguin Books, 1996), 1069.
7. "William Buckley on Ayn Rand & *Atlas Shrugged*," *Charlie Rose*, from March 24, 2006, YouTube.com.
8. Robert Welch, *The Blue Book of the John Birch Society* (Belmont, MA: John Birch Society, 1961), 119–20.
9. William F. Buckley Jr., "Goldwater, the John Birch Society, and Me," *Commentary*, March 2008, http://www.commentarymagazine.com.
10. G. Edward Griffin, *The Life and Words of Robert Welch: Founder of the John Birch Society* (Thousand Oaks, CA: American Media, 1975), 307.
11. Robert Alan Goldberg, *Barry Goldwater* (New Haven, CT: Yale University Press, 1995), 138.
12. Rick Perlstein, *Before the Storm: Barry Goldwater and the Unmaking of the American Consensus* (New York: Nation Books, 2009), 62–63.
13. Ibid., 63.
14. Ibid., 64.
15. Goldberg, *Barry Goldwater*, 139.
16. Perlstein, *Before the Storm*, 266–67.
17. Goldberg, *Barry Goldwater*, 184.
18. "The News from New Hampshire," *Time*, March 20, 1964.
19. John B. Judis, *William F. Buckley, Jr.: Patron Saint of the Conservatives* (New York: Simon and Schuster, 1999), 226–27.
20. F. Clifton White with William J. Gill, *Suite 3505: The Story of the Draft Goldwater Movement* (New Rochelle, NY: Arlington House Publishers, 1967), 89, 209, 257–60.
21. Theodore H. White, *The Making of the President 1964* (New York: Harper, 2010), 144–45; Robert D. Novak, *The Prince of Darkness: 50 Years Reporting in Washington* (New York: Three Rivers Press, 2008), 107–8.
22. "Thurmond to Bolt Democrats Today," *New York Times*, September 16, 1964.
23. Jeffrey Gettleman, "Final Word: My Father's Name was James Strom Thurmond," *New York Times*, December 19, 2003.
24. "Amid the Disarray, a Phenomenon," *Time*, April 24, 1964.
25. "Deep in the Heart of It," *Time*, May 15, 1964.
26. "The Man on the Bandwagon," *Time*, January 12, 1964.
27. Perlstein, *Before the Storm*, 387–93.
28. "Goldwater's 1964 Acceptance Speech," WashingtonPost.com.

29.   "Presidential Campaign Slogans," *Presidents of the United States*, http://www.presidents usa.net.

30.   "Presidential Commercials, 1964 Johnson vs. Goldwater," Museum of the Moving Image: The Living Room Candidate, http://www.livingroomcandidate.org.

31.   Goldberg, *Barry Goldwater*, 226.

32.   Ibid., 220.

33.   Larry Harnisch, "Ronald Reagan and 'A Time for Choosing,'" *Daily Mirror* (UK), February 10, 2011, http://latimesblogs.latimes.com.

34.   Ronald Reagan, "A Time for Choosing," October 27, 1964, National Center for Public Policy Research, http://www.nationalcenter.org.

35.   Goldberg, *Barry Goldwater*, 237.

36.   "1964 Presidential General Election Results," *Dave Leip's Atlas of U.S. Presidential Elections*, http://www.uselectionatlas.org.

37.   James Reston, "What Goldwater Lost," *New York Times*, November 4, 1964.

38.   "Democrats Rout GOP," *Dallas Morning News*, November 4, 1964; Theodore H. White, "Memo to a Future Historian," *Life*, November 13, 1964.

39.   "Republicans: The Party Future," *Time*, November 4, 1964.

40.   Geoffrey Kabaservice, *Rule and Ruin: The Downfall of Moderation and the Destruction of the Republican Party, from Eisenhower to the Tea Party* (New York: Oxford University Press, 2012), 98–118.

41.   In Perlstein, *Before the Storm*, 514–15.

42.   "Never Again," *Time*, January 29, 1965.

43.   Goldberg, *Barry Goldwater*, 237.

44.   Robert Welch, "Reflections on the Elections," supplement to *John Birch Society Bulletin*, December 1964, in *The White Book of the John Birch Society for 1964* (Belmont, MA: John Birch Society, 1965), 7.

45.   Ibid., 1.

46.   Ibid., 2.

47.   Ibid., 4.

48.   Ibid., 6.

49.   Robert Welch, "False Leadership: William F. Buckley and the New World Order," in *The Historical Significance of Robert Welch* (Appleton, WI: John Birch Society, 1993), 171.

Chapter Eighteen: Something's Happening Here

1.   This quote has been attributed to Grace Slick, Robin Williams, and others.

2.   Lou Cannon, *President Reagan: The Role of a Lifetime* (New York: Public Affairs, 2000), 163.

3.   Terry H. Anderson, *The Movement and the Sixties: Protest in America from Greensboro to Wounded Knee* (New York: Oxford University Press, 1995), 144.

4.   Harry Maurer, *Strange Ground: An Oral History of Americans in Vietnam 1945–1975* (New York: DaCapo Press, 1998), 133-135.

5.   Ibid.

6.   The "Great Society" was the collective term for Lyndon Johnson's social agenda: Medicare, food stamps, Head Start, public broadcasting, environmental programs, and civil rights and fair housing legislation. See Joseph A. Califano Jr., "What Was Really Great about the Great Society," *Washington Monthly*, October 1999, http://www.washingtonmonthly.com.

7.   Anderson, *The Movement and the Sixties*, 183–86.

8.   "President Lyndon B. Johnson's Address to the Nation Announcing Steps To Limit the War in Vietnam and Reporting His Decision Not To Seek Reelection, March 31, 1968," LBJ Presidential Library, http://lbjlibrary.org.

9. "Russia Hails Re-election of Johnson," *Chicago Tribune*, November 5, 1964.
10. "Reflections," *Chicago Tribune*, November 5, 1964.
11. Walter Trohan, "Johnson Gets 61.4 Pct. of U.S. Popular Vote," *Chicago Tribune*, November 5, 1964, front page.
12. "The John Birch Society: A Report," *Chicago Tribune*, November 15, 1964.
13. Ben H. Bagdikian, "In the Hearts of the Right, Goldwater Lives!," *New York Times*, July 18, 1965.
14. Donald Janson, "Birchers to Seek Offices 'On Own,'" *New York Times*, March 27, 1966.
15. Donald T. Critchlow, *The Conservative Ascendancy: How the GOP Right Made Political History* (Cambridge, MA: Harvard University Press, 2007), 78–79.
16. "The John Birch Society and the Conservative Movement—Part 1," editorial, *National Review*, October 19, 1965.
17. Ibid.
18. "The John Birch Society and the Conservative Movement—Part 2," editorial, *National Review*, October 19, 1965.
19. Lisa McGirr, *Suburban Warriors: The Origins of the New American Right* (Princeton, NJ: Princeton University Press, 2001), 219.
20. Ibid.
21. "The Wallace Dilemma," *Time*, August 2, 1968.
22. Susanna McBee, "The Spoiler from the South," *Life*, August 2, 1968.
23. "Lake County, Indiana: 'Microcosm of the Politics of Fear,'" *Life*, September 20, 1968.
24. "Support from the Guts," *Time*, March 1, 1968.
25. Anderson, *The Movement and the Sixties*, 212.
26. Ibid.
27. Robert Welch, *John Birch Society Bulletin*, November 1968 (Belmont, MA: John Birch Society), 11.
28. Ibid., 12.
29. Dan T. Carter, *The Politics of Rage: George Wallace, the Origins of the New Conservatism, and the Transformation of American Politics* (Baton Rouge: Louisiana State University Press, 1996), 343.

Chapter Nineteen: A Good Man Is Hard to Find

1. Stephan Lesher, "John Schmitz Is No George Wallace . . . but the American Party Loves Him Anyway," *New York Times*, November 5, 1972.
2. Robert Welch, *John Birch Society Bulletin*, January 1969 (Belmont, MA: John Birch Society), 3–4.
3. Ibid., 6.
4. Ibid., 12.
5. Ibid., 16.
6. Ibid., 18–19.
7. Statistics on the Vietnam War: 15th Field Artillery website, http://www.landscaper.net.
8. "The My Lai Massacre," *Time*, November 28, 1969.
9. Joseph Eszterhas, "The Massacre at Mylai," *Life*, December 5, 1969.
10. Barry Sadler, "The Ballad of the Green Berets," top-40 hit in 1966, played extensively during the war in Vietnam.
11. Terry H. Anderson, *The Movement and the Sixties: Protest in America from Greensboro to Wounded Knee* (New York: Oxford University Press, 1996), 397.
12. Ibid., 402.

13. Donald T. Critchlow, *The Conservative Ascendancy: How the GOP Right Made Political History* (Cambridge, MA: Harvard University Press, 2007), 105–7.

14. Anderson, *The Movement and the Sixties*, 400.

15. Robert Welch, *Bulletin of the John Birch Society*, March 1969 (Belmont, MA: John Birch Society), 9.

16. John Fund, "Out of Gear: Remembering John Schmitz, a Cheerful Extremist," January 12, 2001, John G. Schmitz website, http://www.johngschmitz.com/; "John George Schmitz, Colonel, United States Marine Corps, Member of Congress," Biographical Information, Arlington National Cemetery, http://www.arlington cemetery.net.

17. John G. Schmitz, *Stranger in the Arena: The Anatomy of an Amoral Decade, 1964–1974* (Santa Ana, CA: Rayline Printing, 1974), 11.

18. Schmitz children: Gregg Olsen, *If Loving You Is Wrong: The Shocking True Story of Mary Kay Letourneau* (New York: St. Martin's Press, 1999), 25–29.

19. Ronald Yates, "Senate Hopeful Far Right, Far Out, Far Behind," *Chicago Tribune*, February 28, 1982.

20. Robert Welch, "A Letter of Encouragement," *The Historical Significance of Robert Welch* (Appleton, WI: John Birch Society, 1993), 109.

21. Ibid., 110.

22. Ibid., 125.

23. Ibid., 109.

24. "The Headless Horseman," *Time*, August 14, 1972.

25. Dan T. Carter, *The Politics of Rage: George Wallace, the Origins of the New Conservatism, and the Transformation of American Politics* (Baton Rouge: Louisiana State University Press, 1996), 417–18.

26. Ibid., 424.

27. Maggie Riechers, "Racism to Redemption: The Path of George Wallace," *Humanities* 21, no. 2 (March/April 2000), http://www.neh.gov.

28. "The Headless Horseman."

29. Marjorie Hunter, "G.O.P. Conservative Seeks Third Party's Nomination," *New York Times*, August 3, 1972.

30. "The Hard-Luck Crusade," *Time*, November 6, 1972.

31. Yates, "Senate Hopeful Far Right."

32. "Wood County, WI Vote Totals 1972 Election," *Marshfield (WI) News Herald*, November 8, 1972.

33. James Ridgeway, *Blood in the Face: The Ku Klux Klan, Aryan Nations, Nazi Skinheads, and the Rise of a New White Culture* (New York: Thunder's Mouth Press, 1995), 130–31.

34. Daniel Levitas, *The Terrorist Next Door: The Militia Movement and the Radical Right* (New York: St. Martin's Griffin, 2002), 122–23.

35. "Conservative Group Gives Prizes to Senator Byrd and William Loeb," *New York Times*, May 11, 1972; "John G. Schmitz, Biodata," John G. Schmitz website, http://www.johng schmitz.com.

36. Olsen, *If Loving You Is Wrong*, 20–24.

37. Schmitz, *Stranger in the Arena*.

38. John B. Judis, *William F. Buckley, Jr.: Patron Saint of the Conservatives* (New York: Simon & Schuster, 1988), 317–20.

39. L. Brent Bozell, foreword, in Schmitz, *Stranger in the Arena*, v–vi.

40. Matt Coker, "John G. Schmitz, In His Own Words," January 18, 2001, *OC (CA) Weekly*, http://www.ocweekly.com.

41. Anastasia Toufexis and Joseph J. Kane, "Color Gloria Allred All Rebel," *Time*, December 3, 1984.

42. Richard Bergholz, "Birch Council Drops Schmitz: Furor Over Remarks Leads to His Removal," *Los Angeles Times*, February 24, 1982.

43. "Fouling Up," *Time*, August 2, 1982.

44. Olsen, *If Loving You Is Wrong*, 43–54.

45. Ibid., 55.

46. John Cloud et al., "A Matter of Hearts," *Time*, May 4, 1998.

47. Mark Weber, "John Schmitz, RIP," *Journal of Historical Review*.

48. John Schmitz: John G. Schmitz website, www.johngschmitz.com.

49. Schmitz, *Stranger in the Arena*, 314.

Chapter Twenty: One Woman's Heart

1. In Gloria Feldt, *The War on Choice: The Right-Wing Attack on Women's Rights and How to Fight Back* (New York: Random House, 2004), 20.

2. Alan F. Guttmacher and Anthony Ravielli, *Pregnancy and Birth: A Book for Expectant Parents* (New York: New American Library, 1959 and 1964).

3. Laurence H. Tribe, *Abortion: The Clash of Absolutes* (New York: W.W. Norton, 1992), 146.

4. Ibid., 139.

5. Lennart Nilsson, *A Child Is Born* (New York: Dell, 1965).

6. Nilsson photos: "The Drama of Life Before Birth," *Life*, April 30, 1965.

7. Sandra Matthews and Laura Wexler, *Pregnant Pictures* (New York: Routledge, 2000), 195–96.

8. Peter De Rosa, *Vicars of Christ: The Dark Side of the Papacy* (New York: Crown Publishers, 1988), 365–67.

9. Ibid., 374.

10. See CatholicReference.net.

11. De Rosa, *Vicars of Christ*, 376–77.

12. Ibid.

13. Charles E. Rice, *The Vanishing Right to Life: An Appeal for a Renewed Reverence for Life* (Garden City, NY: Doubleday, 1969).

14. "A Stunning Approval for Abortion," *Time*, February 5, 1973.

15. Max Blumenthal, *Republican Gomorrah: Inside the Movement That Shattered the Party* (New York: Nation Books, 2009), 25.

16. Ibid.

17. Frank Schaeffer, *Crazy for God: How I Grew Up as One of the Elect, Helped Found the Religious Right, and Lived to Take All (Or Almost All) of It Back* (New York: De Capo Press, 2007), 289.

18. Ibid.

19. Ibid., 297–98.

20. Robert Welch, *John Birch Society Bulletin*, July 1976 (Belmont, MA: John Birch Society, 1976), 52.

21. "What Is the Hyde Amendment?," American Civil Liberties Union website, July 21, 2004, http://www.aclu.org.

22. Robert M. Baird and Stuart E. Rosenbaum, eds., *The Ethics of Abortion: Pro-life vs. Pro-choice* (Amherst, NY: Prometheus Books, 2001), 58–59.

23. Rice, *The Vanishing Right to Life*, 38.

24. Dr. and Mrs. J.C. Willke, *Handbook on Abortion* (Cincinnati: Hiltz Publishing, 1971), 35.

25. Dr. and Mrs. J.C. Willke, *Why Can't We Love Them Both: Questions and Answers about Abortion* (Cincinnati: Hayes Publishing, 1997), 234–44.
26. Feldt, *The War on Choice*, 103.
27. Rice, *The Vanishing Right to Life*, 46.

Chapter Twenty-one: Bang the Drum Slowly

1. George J. Church et al., "Reagan Coast-to-Coast," *Time*, November 17, 1980.
2. Sara Diamond, *Roads to Dominion: Right-Wing Movements and Political Power in the United States* (New York: Guilford Press, 1995), 205–11.
3. Gregory L. Schneider, *The Conservative Century: From Reaction to Revolution* (Lanham, MD: Rowman & Littlefield, 2009), 147–48.
4. Ronald Reagan, "First Inaugural Address," January 20, 1981, *American Rhetoric*, http://www.americanrhetoric.com.
5. Diamond, *Roads to Dominion*, 172–77.
6. Ed Magnuson et al., "The Conservatives Are Coming," *Time*, November 24, 1980.
7. Reagan on the homeless: *Good Morning America*, January 31, 1984.
8. Steven V. Roberts, "Reagan on Homelessness: Many Choose to Live in the Streets," *New York Times*, December 23, 1988.
9. William Kleinknecht, *The Man Who Sold the World: Ronald Reagan and the Betrayal of Main Street America* (New York: Nation Books, 2009), 188.
10. Ibid.
11. Ibid., 196.
12. P.J. O'Rourke quotes: *Good Reads*, http://www.goodreads.com.
13. "I've Had a Bum Rap," *Time*, May 17, 1976.
14. Quoted in Will Bunch, *Tear Down This Myth: How the Reagan Legacy Has Distorted Our Politics and Haunts Our Future* (New York: Simon & Schuster, 2009), 52.
15. Robert Welch, *John Birch Society Bulletin*, January 1981 (Belmont, MA: John Birch Society, 1981), 1–2.
16. William B. Guidry, "Pending Legislation," in ibid., 25.
17. Robert Welch, *John Birch Society Bulletin*, July 1981 (Belmont, MA: John Birch Society, 1981), 4.
18. Thomas N. Hill, "The Making of Tragedies," *John Birch Society Bulletin*, March 1982 (Belmont, MA: John Birch Society), 2–3.
19. Ibid.
20. Herb Joiner, "Aid and Trade—STOP Financing Communism," *John Birch Society Bulletin*, October 1987 (Belmont, MA: John Birch Society, 1987), 12.
21. William E. Dunham, "Birch Tax Reform Movement," *John Birch Society Bulletin*, August 1982 (Belmont, MA: John Birch Society, 1982), 5–6.
22. Diamond, *Roads to Dominion*, 212–14.
23. Robert Welch, supplement to *John Birch Society Bulletin*, April 1982 (Belmont, MA: John Birch Society, 1982), 1.
24. Robert Welch, *John Birch Society Bulletin*, December 1982 (Belmont, MA: John Birch Society, 1982), 2, 11–12.
25. Rep. Lawrence P. McDonald (1935–1983) biographical information: Congress.gov.
26. Strobe Talbott et al., "Atrocity in the Skies: KAL Flight 007 Shot Down by the Soviets," *Time*, September 12, 1983.
27. Ibid.
28. Thomas Frank, *The Wrecking Crew: How Conservatives Ruined Government, Enriched Themselves, and Beggared the Nation* (New York: Henry Holt, 2008), 232–33.

29. Alan Stang, "Congressman Larry McDonald: Prisoner of War," Rense.com, August 29, 2003.
30. Christian Gomez, "Larry McDonald—An American Hero Remembered," John Birch Society website, September 1, 2010, http://www.jbs.org.
31. "Cash Crunch, Feuding Plague John Birchers," *Chicago Tribune*, August 28, 1986.
32. Ibid.
33. Suzanne Spring, "John Birch Society Still Fighting Communism," *Observer-Reporter* (Washington, PA), March 7, 1985.
34. Benjamin Wilson, "The Rise and Fall of Laetrile," February 17, 2004, *Quackwatch: Your Guide to Quackery, Health Fraud and Intelligent Decisions*, http://www.quackwatch.org.
35. Stephen Barrett, MD, "A Close Look at Robert W. Bradford and His Committee for Freedom of Choice in Medicine," March 20, 2012, ibid.
36. Ibid.
37. A.J. Matt Jr., "Stillwell Jay Conner: 1910–1992," *Wanderer*, July 23, 1992.
38. "In Memoriam—Stillwell J. Conner," *John Birch Society Bulletin*, August 1992 (Appleton, WI: John Birch Society), 30.

Chapter Twenty-two: Attention Must Be Paid

1. Leonard Zeskind, *Blood and Politics: The History of the White Nationalist Movement from the Margins to the Mainstream* (New York: Farrar, Straus and Giroux, 2009), 490.
2. Michael Riley, "White & Wrong," *Time*, July 6, 1992.
3. Ibid.
4. Arthur R. Goldwag, *The New Hate: A History of Fear and Loathing on the Populist Right* (New York: Pantheon Books, 2012), 285.
5. William F. Jasper, "To Free Education," *John Birch Society Bulletin*, August 1988 (Belmont, MA: John Birch Society, 1988), 9.
6. John F. McManus, "Merger Mania," ibid., 3, 5.
7. John F. McManus, *The Insiders: Architects of the New World Order*, 5th ed. (Appleton, WI: John Birch Society, 2004), 53–54.
8. George H. W. Bush, "Address Before a Joint Session of the Congress on the Persian Gulf Crisis and the Federal Budget Deficit," September 11, 1990, George Bush Presidential Library and Museum, Public Papers, 1990–September, http://www.bushlibrary.tamu.edu.
9. McManus, *The Insiders*, 77.
10. Ibid., 79.
11. William Jefferson Clinton, "First Inaugural Address," YouTube.com.
12. Short biography of John F. McManus: John Birch Society website, http://www.jbs.org.
13. John F. McManus, "It All Fits!," *John Birch Society Bulletin*, November 1993 (Appleton, WI: John Birch Society, 1993), 3–10.
14. Ibid., 10.
15. "Brady Background Checks in the Brady Law," Brady Campaign to Prevent Gun Violence, http://www.bradycampaign.org.
16. Daniel Levitas, *The Terrorist Next Door: The Militia Movement and the Radical Right* (New York: St. Martin's Griffin, 2002), 301–16.
17. Ibid., 290.
18. Andrew Macdonald, *The Turner Diaries* (Fort Lee, NJ: Barricade Books, 1978).
19. Zeskind, *Blood and Politics*, 482.
20. Macdonald, *The Turner Diaries*, 36–39.
21. Ibid., 41.

22. Ibid., 158–59.

23. *Timothy McVeigh Trial: Documents Relating to McVeigh's Arrest and the Searching of His Vehicle,* University of Missouri-Kansas City Law School website, "Famous Trials: Oklahoma City Bombing Trial," http://law2.umkc.edu.

24. Bill Hewett, "April Mourning," *People,* May 15, 1995; photo of Chris Fields holding Baylee Almon: "Oklahoma City Bombing, 1995," World's Famous Photos, http://www.worlds famousphotos.com.

25. Penny Bender Fuchs, "Jumping to Conclusions in Oklahoma City?," *AJR: American Journalism Review* (June 1995), http://www.ajr.org.

26. Steven Emerson, *American Jihad: The Terrorists Living Among Us* (New York: Free Press, 2002), 17–18.

27. Ibid., 48–49.

28. "Terror Hits Home: The Oklahoma City Bombing," Federal Bureau of Investigation, http://www.fbi.gov.

29. "Sketch and Photo of Timothy McVeigh," ibid.

30. David Johnston, "Terror in Oklahoma; Just Before He Was to Be Freed, Prime Bombing Suspect Is Identified in Jail," *New York Times,* April 22, 1995.

31. Ibid.

32. Mike German, "Behind the Lone Terrorist, a Pack Mentality," *Washington Post,* June 5, 2005.

33. Levitas, *The Terrorist Next Door,* 114.

34. Ibid., 111.

35. James Ridgeway, *Blood in the Face: The Ku Klux Klan, Aryan Nations, Nazi Skinheads, and the Rise of a New White Culture* (New York: Thunder's Mouth Press, 1990, 1995), 132.

36. Ibid.

37. Levitas, *The Terrorist Next Door,* 127.

38. Ibid., 301–12.

39. Mark England and Darlene McCormick, "The Sinful Messiah," *Waco Tribune-Herald* series, *Fort Worth Star Telegram,* March 3, 1993.

40. Justin Sturken and Mary Dore, "Remembering the Waco Siege," ABC News, February 28, 2007.

Chapter Twenty-three: Hell in a Handbasket

1. "His Holiness John Paul II, Short Biography," Holy See Press Office, March 6, 2005, http://www.vatican.va.

2. John Paul II, "Letter to Families," February 2, 1994, http://www.vatican.va.

3. Mary M'Cord Brown, "Garb for Defense a Wardrobe Must" and "War-Time Easter Parade," *Rocky Mountain News* (CO), Sunday April 5, 1942.

4. Richard L. Franklin, "101 Peculiarities Surrounding the Death of Vincent Foster," *Progressive Review,* http://www.prorev.com/foster.htm. "Hillarycare" was the nickname given to the Clinton health-care plan, introduced in 1993. Information about the plan and its defeat: Paul Starr, "The Hillarycare Mythology," *American Prospect,* September 13, 2007, http:// prospect.org.

5. Edward Klein, *The Truth about Hillary* (New York: Penguin, 2005), 51–65.

6. Catechism of the Catholic Church, part 3, section 2, chapter 2, article 6, St. Charles Borromeo Catholic Church website, http://www.scborromeo.org.

7. Gregory M. Herek, "Facts About Homosexuality and Mental Health," http://psychology .ucdavis.edu.

8. Howard Chua-Eoan et al., "That's Not a Scarecrow," *Time*, October 19, 1998.

9. Tom Morton, "Matthew Shepard Funeral Put Westboro Baptist Church on the Map," *Billings (MT) Gazette*, March 2, 2011, http://www.billingsgazette.com.

10. Michelle Goldberg, *Kingdom Coming: The Rise of Christian Nationalism* (New York: W.W. Norton, 2006), 50–60.

11. Ibid., 54.

12. John F. McManus, "Homosexuals in the Military?," *Birch Log*, December 10, 1992, http://www.scribd.com.

13. Michael Sean Winters, *God's Right Hand: How Jerry Falwell Made God a Republican and Baptized the American Right* (New York: Harper One, 2012), 322.

14. Jean Hardisty, *Mobilizing Resentment: Conservative Resurgence from the John Birch Society to the Promise Keepers* (Boston: Beacon Press, 1989), 103.

15. See Fred Clarkson, "Impeachment Rally in Georgia," Political Research Associates, 2010, http://www.publiceye.org.

16. "John Birch Society Seeks Clinton Impeachment," *Reading (PA) Eagle*, November 16, 1977, http://readingeagle.com.

17. Clarkson, "Impeachment Rally in Georgia."

18. Ibid.

19. Ibid.

20. Ibid.; Melinda Henneberger, "The Georgia Republican Who Uses the I-Word," *New York Times*, May 5, 1998.

21. John McManus, "The JBS: Alive, Well, and Growing," *New American*, September 23, 2002, http://www.scribd.com.

22. Roy Rivenburg, "Conservative Camp Roasts More Than Just Weenies: Birch Society Summer Target Liberals, Plots," *Los Angeles Times*, July 1996.

23. Ibid.

24. Ibid.

25. "Articles of Impeachment and Judiciary Committee Roll Call Votes," *Washington Post*, December 19, 1998.

26. Thomas B. Edsall, "From the Fringe to the Center of the Debate," *Washington Post*, December 15, 1998.

27. Thomas A. Burzynski, "David Shippers Goes Public," *American Opinion*, 1999, retrieved from *Studies in Reformed Theology*, http://www.reformed-theology.org.

28. Ibid.

29. Clifford Orwin, "Compassionate Conservatism: A Primer," *Defining Ideas: A Hoover Institution Journal* (March 1, 2011), http://www.hoover.org.

30. "Election 2000 Florida, Florida, Florida," from NBC-TV's coverage of Election Night 2000, YouTube.com.

31. Jeffrey Toobin, "Precedent and Prologue," *New Yorker*, December 6, 2000.

32. "2000 Presidential General Election Results," *Dave Leip's Atlas of U.S. Presidential Elections*, http://www.uselectionatlas.org.

33. George W. Bush, "Inaugural Address," January 20, 2001, American Presidency Project, http://www.presidency.ucsb.edu.

34. "Protesters Line Inaugural Parade Route," *CNN Reports*, January 20, 2001, http://www.cnn.com.

35. John F. McManus, *The Insiders: Architects of the New World Order* (Appleton, WI: John Birch Society, 2004), 110.

36. Ibid., 10.

37. Ibid., 121.
38. David Armstrong, "Dick Cheney's Song of America: Drafting a Plan for Global Dominance," *Harper's*, October 2002, http://harpers.org.
39. McManus, *The Insiders*, 125.
40. "Iraq's Goals Are Not Our Goals," *New American*, December 12, 2005, http://www.scribd.com.
41. See Washington National Cathedral website, http://www.nationalcathedral.org.
42. Tyler Drumheller, *On the Brink: An Insider's Account of How the White House Compromised American Intelligence* (New York: Carroll & Graf, 2006), 35–40.
43. Thomas E. Ricks, *Fiasco: The American Military Adventure in Iraq* (New York: Penguin, 2006), 377–78.
44. Paul Steinhauser, "More Disapprove of Bush Than Any Other President," *CNN Politics*, May 1, 2008, http://www.cnn.com.

Chapter Twenty-four: Bedtime Story

1. Michael Sean Winters, *God's Right Hand: How Jerry Falwell Made God a Republican and Baptized the American Right* (New York: Harper One, 2012), 342.
2. Pat Robertson, "Robertson's Statement Regarding Terrorist Attack on America," press release, Official Site of Pat Robertson, http://www.patrobertson.com.
3. "The United Nations: The Growing Threat, A Special Report," *New American*, October 22, 2001.
4. William Norman Grigg, "The UN Is NOT Your Friend," in ibid.
5. Ibid.
6. Arthur R. Thompson, "Exposing Terrorism: Inside the Terror Triangle," 2009, YouTube.com.

Index